TEXTUALIZING
THE FEMININE

Oklahoma Project for
Discourse and Theory

OKLAHOMA PROJECT FOR DISCOURSE AND THEORY

SERIES EDITORS

Robert Con Davis, University of Oklahoma
Ronald Schleifer, University of Oklahoma

ADVISORY BOARD

TEXTUALIZING THE FEMININE

On the Limits of Genre

By Shari Benstock

University of Oklahoma Press
Norman and London

By Shari Benstock

(with Bernard Benstock) *Who's He When He's at Home: A James Joyce Directory* (Champaign, 1980)

Women of the Left Bank: Paris, 1900–1940 (Austin, 1986; London, 1987)

(ed.) *Feminist Issues in Literary Scholarship* (Bloomington, 1987)

Femmes de la rive gauche: Paris 1900–1940 (Paris, 1987)

(ed., with Morris Beja) *Coping with Joyce: Essays from the Copenhagen Symposium* (Columbus, 1988)

(ed.) *The Private Self: Theory and Practice in Women's Autobiographical Writings* (Chapel Hill, 1988; London, 1988)

Textualizing the Feminine: On the Limits of Genre (Norman, 1991)

Library of Congress Cataloging-in-Publication Data

Benstock, Shari, 1944–
    Textualizing the feminine : on the limits of genre / by Shari Benstock.
        p.   cm. — (Oklahoma project for discourse and theory; v. 7)
    Includes bibliographical references and index.
    ISBN 0-8061-2358-3 (alk. paper)
    1. Literature, Modern—20th century—History and criticism—Theory, etc.   2. Femininity (Psychology) in literature.   3. Psyanalysis and literature.   4. Authorship—Sex differences.
5. Feminism and literature.   6. Literary form.   I. Title.
II. Series.
PN771.B38   1991
801'.959'0904—dc20   91-2516
                                                                    CIP

The paper in this book meets the guidelines for permanence and durability of the Committee on Production Guidelines for Book Longevity of the Council on Library Resources, Inc. ∞

Textualizing the Feminine: On the Limits of Genre is Volume 7 of the Oklahoma Project for Discourse and Theory.

This book is for Isabelle and Suzanne

Contents

Series Editors' Foreword   ix
Acknowledgments   xiii
Introduction: Writing and Subjectivity   xv

Part I. Textualizing the Feminine: From the Place of
    Oversight
Chapter 1. The Law of the Phallus (as) The Law of Genre   3
Chapter 2. Signifying the Body Feminine   23

Part II. Piece Work: Textual Body Parts
Chapter 3. Apostrophizing *Finnegans Wake*   49
Chapter 4. Letters: *The Post Card* in the Epistolary Genre   86
Chapter 5. Ellipses: Figuring Feminisms in *Three Guineas*   123
Chapter 6. Unveiling the Textual Subject: *Helen in Egypt*
    and *Ulysses*   163
Epilogue   190
Notes   197
Selected Bibliography   231
Index   243

Series Editors' Foreword

Shari Benstock's *Textualizing the Feminine: Essays on the Limits of Genre* is an important contribution to The Oklahoma Project for Discourse & Theory as it significantly extends the exploration of the cultural import of contemporary work on discourse theory that is our best hope for the series. *Textualizing the Feminine* pursues the interdisciplinary work of the series by offering a remarkable analysis of the nature of gender and genre and the limits of genre as a frame from which to explore literary practices. Positioned within and between feminist, literary, and textual theory, this volume approaches "theory" with a canny skepticism about its potential androcentrism; it grasps with great insight the vulnerability of critique that shares and deploys androcentric suppositions. Benstock is fully cognizant, in other words, of the male subject implicitly directing the byways of Joyce's, Freud's, and Lacan's texts. *Finnegans Wake,* she admits in chapter 3, presents "an unusual entry point for a work of feminist criticism"— unusual enough that for some readers it will "block the entrance" to feminist discourse "not only because it is an esoteric, almost occult text, but because Joyce personifies for feminism the Male Modernist Master whose versions of the feminine (Molly Bloom and ALP, for instance) often are seen to rewrite patriarchy and reinscribe the feminine within the terms of the masculine."

But if the texts of Freud, Lacan, Joyce, and even Derrida are androcentric in the most macrological view of Western culture— *by* male theorists who posit the transcendental phallus of signification which *belongs* to those same men—they are also by now key Western "sexual-textual cultural constructions" and as such are potentially "crucial" to a "rethinking of feminist assumptions" concerning the cultural matrices that underlie Western gender distinctions to begin with. Such monumental texts help Benstock map the limits of gender and sexuality in texts by Gertrude Stein, H.D., Freud, Joyce, and so on insofar as they mark, or are congruent with, the limits of textuality. Implicit here, as in much cultural theory since Emile Durkheim, is the assumption of conflicting cultural discourses inscribed in the cultural texts of actual social spheres. "To lose one's genre," or one's gender-marked place in such cultural discourses, Benstock posits, entails losing "one's ability to signify" in any cultural text or venue. For Benstock, the working assumption of the double-voiced dialogue of gender and genre creates a measure of theoretical turning room in which to explore the economies of gender in actual texts, even in the "high" modernism of a Male Master such as Joyce. This tactical interfacing of gender and genre allows Benstock to avoid putting dominant Western texts, texts by men, off limits to feminist critique—texts that otherwise would be taken as continuous and always hegemonic representations of monolithic and reified patriarchy.

In Benstock's work, in other words, we see a book that goes well beyond conventional feminist critiques of modernism by examining "the laws of sexuality and categories of representation that support cultural constructions of the feminine." Patent here is her distinction between what she calls "woman-in-the-feminine," the cultural space of the feminine, and the "feminine" per se which, for her, signifies "all that is lost, overlooked, or denied in culture." This distinction enables Benstock to address questions which have hitherto been given short shrift or have been summarily dismissed by feminist critics and others primarily because they are such difficult questions. Her focus on language and subjectivity, and on the intersections of feminism, psychoanalysis, and grammatology (interests that align her with feminist theorists like Julia Kristeva, Teresa de Lauretis, and Alice Jardine), constitutes a critique of more conventional feminist theories. Especially, her emphasis on our "cultural investment in notions of cohesive, predictable, integrated selfhood and the power of authorial consciousness and control" enables her to critique American feminists' investments in gynocritics—the recovery of the female text signed and authorized by the female subject.

Thus, the brilliance of Benstock's reading of individual texts—*Antigone, Finnegans Wake, La Carte Postale: de Socrate à Freud et audelà, Three Guineas, Helen in Egypt,* and *Ulysses* among them—owes ultimately to her reading of cultural discourses from quite different vantages, centrally "feminism" but also "modernism," "post-modernism," "deconstruction," and "psychoanalysis." She reads through these positions with ease and does so without either opposing them irrecoverably or (the greater danger) losing the sense of their differences. Like the best feminist criticism and the best theoretical analyses, her discourse and her sense of discourse are heuristic rather than definitive, exploratory rather than argumentative. For all of Benstock's incisiveness, that is, she is not trying simply to persuade, to answer questions, to apply theory to interpret texts, but actually to pose questions that will spark further theoretical speculation by feminists and nonfeminists alike. In meeting these goals, *Textualizing the Feminine* will undoubtedly fuel ongoing debates about the place of post-structuralist theories within feminism and cultural critique. Moreover, it will contribute to those debates a compelling argument for feminist consideration of post-structuralist discourse that many have rejected too soon.

Finally, we believe that *Textualizing the Feminine* marks a decisive direction for cultural criticism by defining a mode of post-semiotic, post-structuralist critique, that is, cultural critique at the intersection of gender, aesthetic, and ideological concerns—particular intersections of knowledge and power. Like the other volumes of The Oklahoma Project for Discourse & Theory—by J. Fisher Solomon, Jonathan Culler, Jon Stratton, Marjorie Perloff, Thomas A. Sebeok, and Christopher Norris—Benstock's advances our understanding of the possible tactics of cultural critique not through mere speculation but through the test and text of actual practice.

ROBERT CON DAVIS
RONALD SCHLEIFER

Norman, Oklahoma

Acknowledgments

If this book can be said to have had a beginning, it took place on a stiflingly hot Midwest afternoon in August 1981. Preparing to leave the University of Illinois for a year's work in France on *Women of the Left Bank* and surrounded by packing boxes and overflowing suitcases, I wrote the opening paragraphs of "On the Margin of Discourse: Footnotes in the Fictional Text." First appearing in *PMLA* 98 (Spring 1983), a portion of this essay, now substantially changed, is included in chapter 3. Two other previously published (and now significantly revised) essays appear in chapters 3 and 4: "The Letter of the Law: *La Carte Postale* in *Finnegans Wake*," *Philological Quarterly* 63 (Spring 1984), and "From Letters to Literature: *La Carte Postale* in the Epistolary Genre," *Genre* 18 (Fall 1985). A portion of chapter 3 appeared as "Apostrophizing the Feminine in *Finnegans Wake*," *Modern Fiction Studies* 35 (1989).

Because my professional life in the past decade has been unusually peripatetic and also laden with administrative and editorial responsibilities, work on this project has been subject to frequent interruption and delays. It has also been enriched by colleagues and students at the institutions where I worked in these years, the universities of Illinois, Tulsa, and Miami, and by my experiences as editor of *Tulsa Studies in Women's Literature* and coeditor, with Celeste Schenck, of "Reading Women Writing" at Cornell University Press.

My thanks to everyone who responded to versions of this book: Jacques Aubert, Bernard Benstock, Christine van Boheemen, Robert Con Davis, Barbara Harlow, Regina Haslinger, Claude Jacquet and members of the Paris-based Groupe Recherche de

Acknowledgments

James Joyce, Anne Larsen, Karen Lawrence, Jane Marcus, Pat McGee, Laurent Milesi, Jean-Michel Rabaté, Ronald Schleifer, Lindsey Tucker, and James G. Watson. My thanks also to Janet E. Dunleavy and Kimberly Devlin, who invited me to speak at two conferences in spring 1987 at the University of Wisconsin, Milwaukee, and the University of California, Riverside, and to Augustine Martin and Terence Dolan of University College Dublin, who asked me to address the James Joyce Summer School in 1989. At the kind invitation of Claude Jacquet and under the auspices of the Groupe Recherche de James Joyce, I delivered a paper on translation in Joyce and H.D. (now part of chapter 6) on 6 May 1988. I am particularly grateful to Marlena Corcoran's generous response to this paper.

No one provided more astute commentary on my work or more encouraging words during my days (and nights) of fatigue than Suzanne Ferriss. I am grateful to her and to Isabelle de Courtivron, to whom this book is dedicated, for continuing support and friendship.

Finally, my thanks to the University of Miami for a summer fellowship (1988) to support work on this project. I especially appreciate the work of Diane Edwards and other staff members in Women's Studies at the University of Miami, who assisted this project with good humor and patience. As always, Berni Benstock shared his wit and wisdom.

SHARI BENSTOCK

Miami Beach, Florida

Introduction

Writing and Subjectivity

In this book I consider the textual ordering of sexual difference. My points of departure are constituent textual elements that play presumably tangential roles in representing subjectivity: punctuation (ellipses, dashes, quotation marks, parentheses), "marginalia" (footnotes, prefaces, epilogues), grammatical-rhetorical modes (forms of address, parts of speech), and letters (alphabetic units and genres of writing). Focusing on image and metaphor as primary modes of representation, literary criticism often dismisses as perfunctory the work of grammar or punctuation. We read "beyond" devalued cursory forms or details, interpreting the message emblazoned on the textual facade, often ignoring the bricks and mortar that support its edifice.

Western notions of cognition that equate knowing with seeing support such traditional and dominant ways of reading. For example, the interpretive models that guide our reading practices situate representation within the visual field, emphasizing visual imagery but not always taking into account spatial orderings or discursive practices that construct this focus. We understand little about how other senses—hearing, touch, taste, and smell—contribute to textuality or how they are marshaled within the visual order. Focusing on what gets lost in this process, the following chapters address issues of textual organization within psychosexual structures: how writing restages the drama of subjectivity, and how conscious/unconscious psychic structures stage a scene of writing. Specifically, how do textual forms that escape or confound the privileged visual order of cognition figure in accounts of psychosexual subjectivity?

My shorthand for the reading practice that opens this question is "psychogrammanalysis," which investigates the sexual organization of textuality and the textual structuring of the psyche. The textual functions I isolate for analysis constitute the ground where theories of sexuality and textuality meet and miss each other. Registers of psychically repressed terms over which representation stakes its claims, these discursive practices inhabit textual blind spots. If writing cannot help but inscribe sexual difference, as feminist theory and criticism have demonstrated, then what is the relation of these textual forms to gendered writing and reading practices?

Appropriated as a signifier of difference, the feminine has commonly been understood to mark difference from a masculine universal. A singular mode by which all women must conform to type, the feminine has since time immemorial been fetishized as a wardrobe of stylistic flourishes—decorative, auxiliary, and *inessential*—that express, paradoxically, the "essence of the feminine." [1] I refer to these traditional, culturally coded norms and expectations as "woman-in-the-feminine." Within this structure, "the feminine"—whose singularizing modifier I place tacitly under erasure—signifies all that is lost, overlooked, or denied by the cultural category "woman-in-the-feminine." The feminine is not a category; diverse and disruptive, it subverts (while also shoring up) efforts to categorize. Reverberating within and against cultural codes, it opens "woman-in-the-feminine" to self-difference.

The feminine never achieves full clarity, however, because it cannot be understood apart from the cultural construction whose traces it bears. Consequently, the feminine has been almost lost on the side of feminism. It is too close to "femininity," the measure of our oppression, and too easily interpreted within the old codes. Retextualized as Hélène Cixous's *écriture féminine* or Luce Irigaray's *parler femme*, the feminine threatens to find its place in an idealized, lost presymbolic space ("writing the body") or to topple over into psychotic speechlessness or its opposite, logorrhea. Reactivated as a desiring woman's body, the feminine risks becoming another *masculine* fantasy of sexual difference.

Rather than reinstating the feminine as the textual signature of Woman, I want to discover how psychosexual-textual structures *fail* to represent woman-in-the-feminine and how the feminine works within the cultural construct to support and subvert systems of representation. The writings of Jacques Derrida, Julia Kristeva, and Jacques Lacan provide theoretical support for my investigations, each opening a different facet of the psychosexual-textual structure to analysis.

My argument is not that there is anything inherently "feminine" in the forms of rhetoric, grammar, and punctuation I discuss but rather that apostrophes, ellipses, footnotes, and certain epistolary forms, orthographical conventions, and alphabetic signifiers occupy a textual space of loss or oversight. Apparently escaping the law of representation, they are overlooked by interpretive procedures. Often thought to be matters of style rather than substance, perfunctory rather than performative, these signifiers occupy a textual space that overlaps a cultural space, a margin of difference or a vanishing point of meaning, that is psychosexually coded "feminine."

Part I, "Textualizing the Feminine: From the Place of Oversight," includes two companion chapters that remap the juncture of psychoanalytic and grammatological accounts of sexual-textual difference. Chapter 1, "The Law of the Phallus (as) The Law of Genre," analyzes the institution of identity structures in relation to the symbolic modes of speech and writing. Of particular interest is Lacan's work on infant sensory imprinting ("letters") and his theory of *lalangue*. Lacan's "return to Freud" mapped language onto psychic structures; thus it opened (but for the most part overlooked) possibilities for theorizing the psyche-as-text. Reading psychic structures as a scene of writing, Derrida discovers what psychoanalysis ignores or gives only lip service to within its own practice—the conscious/unconscious theorized as a textual relation. In "Freud and the Scene of Writing" and in the essays collected under the title "To Speculate—on Freud" and "The Purveyor of Truth," Derrida shuttles between Freud and Lacan, weaving together elements of the psyche-as-text.[2]

Elsewhere, Derrida's grammatological writing practices focus attention on textual elements considered to be either perfunctory or marginal, that is, stylistic embellishments ancillary to structures of meaning.[3] These "embellishments" often display a textual feminine defined within a sexually coded critical vocabulary (invagination, hymen). Such terms are stumbling blocks to many feminists for whom they mark a site of colonization over the female body, the construction of a feminine inscribed *au masculin*. But for my analysis, they open an important question: if feminine sexuality is the vanishing point of meaning within psychic structures, as Freudian/Lacanian theory argues, does it also mark textual limits? The immediate problem is how the psyche textualizes the female body as the repressed ground of unconscious representations and how literary texts figure the female body to represent psychosexuality.

Chapter 2, "Signifying the Body Feminine," discusses Kristeva's formulation of the symbolic/semiotic in relation to bodily drives and textual structures. While Lacan revised Freud's drive structures within a three-part schema (Need, Desire, Demand), Kristeva theorized a signifying process that articulates Freud's oral, anal, and scopic drives and linguistic signs. She traces the roots of symbolizing structures in physiological functions, and her theory joins linguistic matter to the materiality of the human body, where representation is already at work within the drives. In this, she follows Freud's obsession to materialize the unconscious.

Analyzing the linguistic effects of psychic structures apparent in "poetic language," Kristeva illustrates her claim that the psyche and body are textually joined. As a linguist and practicing psychoanalyst, she formulates both sides of the psycho-textual question. While this work constitutes her major theoretical contribution, it is widely misunderstood, especially as it touches on psychosexual textuality. On the one hand, her work is often seen as "essentialist," projecting either a fantasy of mother-child bonding located in the Imaginary or relegating women's creativity in a non-symbolic area where the semiotic endlessly pulsates in desire.[4] On the other hand, her textual analysis, which examines the writings of twentieth-century avant-garde European men writers, appears to eclipse the psycho-textual issues of women's writing so important to feminist criticism. In larger measure than either Lacan or Derrida, however, Kristeva focuses on the psychosexual determinants of textual practices. Two aspects of that work are of particular importance to my analysis: first, the relation of the semiotic to the gendered subject; second, the process by which a semiotic "un-signifying" that stands outside representative, cognitive orders challenges cognition and representation in poetic language.

Part II, "Piece Work: Textual Body Parts," includes four essays that reflect the theoretical concerns of Part I. These essays are not meant to be an application, or textual illustration, of the theories outlined in the opening section. Rather, they raise in different terms the questions that trouble psychoanalytic and textual theories of representation. Chapter 3, "Apostrophizing *Finnegans Wake*," reads a doubled apostrophic structure within James Joyce's text: the rhetorical form of apostrophe that invokes the feminine as a call to pure sound ("O tell me all about Anna Livia!") and the effects of the grammatical mark (') missing from the title that undoes the structure of subjectivity ("Finnegans"). Chapter 4, "Letters: *The Post Card* in the Epistolary Genre," situates the "Envois" section of Derrida's text within the generic boundaries of epistolary fiction. Reading the relation between "letters" and "literature" as a reenactment of the Law of Genre and within the terms of Freud's pleasure principle, I suggest that "Envois" turns the law inside out, exposing what is lost when epistolary discourse usurps women's letters and reinscribes them under the signature of a male writer. "Envois" also analyzes the letter as alphabetic unit within a psychosexual alphabet drawn from Freud's *The Pleasure Principle* and Joyce's *Finnegans Wake* and incorporates the dissemination of "letters" within the apostrophic structure of *fort/da*. Chapters 3 and 4 read each other as opposite sides of the letter: genre form and alphabetic signifier.

Chapter 5, "Ellipses: Figuring Feminisms in *Three Guineas*," unsettles this mirroring structure. Organizing her argument around an exchange of letters, Woolf enfolds the letter within the grammatical-geometrical figure of ellipsis that effects textual displacements of narrative alignments and confuses genres. That is, it confounds the linear plot of phallologic and patriarchal oppression. Woolf's ellipses open onto a textual unconscious, creating a permeable textual boundary rather like the traversable inner boundary that separates the semiotic from the symbolic in Kristeva's formulation of the *thetic* or the *hymen* that confuses borderlines between textual interiority and exteriority in Derrida's works.

Chapter 6, "Unveiling the Textual Subject," analyzes H.D.'s

Helen in Egypt and Joyce's *A Portrait of the Artist as a Young Man* and *Ulysses* in terms of translation. My interest is less in the traditional sense of translation as the act of turning one language into another (although this meaning is never entirely lost to the analysis) than in the *action* of translation, especially as it transports meaning from one place to another. This chapter examines the operation of translation, focusing on what is carried over or left behind in the process—that is, what of the textual-sexual body becomes a residue of meaning that resists translation and transportation. Helen figures these questions for H.D.'s text as Stephen Dedalus does for *Portrait* and *Ulysses*. Both protagonists illustrate failed attempts at "translation" as a division and dissemination of the textual body figured as spatial displacement: Helen between Troy and Egypt, Stephen between Dublin and Paris.

The texts I discuss reflect my interests in literary Modernism and post-Modernism. Occupying places on the borderlines of genre, they resist canonical categories and illustrate the very textual concerns they address. Is *Helen in Egypt* a lyric or an epic poem? How does *Ulysses* as epic incorporate *Portrait* as *bildungsroman* or autobiography? These questions are not rhetorical. Until feminist criticism reopened the case for H.D., she remained buried within a pocket of Modernist practice (Imagism), her later, larger-canvas works considered marginal to Modernism. This displacement and devaluation occurred, in part, because H.D. translated epic forms *au féminin*, scripting women's lives within classical narratives.[5]

Is *Three Guineas* a polemic or a political commentary? Is it fiction or essay? More than fifty years after its publication, the textual status of *Three Guineas* is still in doubt. Androcentric criticism dismisses it as an embarrassing aberration in Woolf's *oeuvre*; feminist criticism reads in it evidence of Woolf's socialist-feminist politics. Thus its place on reading lists in literature, history, or political science is more often taken by *A Room of One's Own*, a work that also opens onto the question of genre but whose tone is considered less "strident" and its argument less biting than *Three Guineas*.

Are genres to be distinguished from each other by style and tone, as Derrida suggests: "Apostrophe. . . . A genre and a tone?"[6] If so, how do we categorize *The Post Card*? It announces a divided text, its second half consisting of essays on psycho-analysis that provide carefully nuanced readings of Freud and Lacan. The "postcards" that preface the essays appear to be an amusing joke, an "aside," an address to love that is perhaps a fiction. Acknowledging desires that go beyond philosophy, *The Post Card* throws grammatology onto the axis of desire and the psychoanalytic movement. Neither philosophy nor fiction, it resists classic modes of theoretical discourse. Can we, therefore, take it seriously?

Although *Finnegans Wake* escapes the high seriousness that is a defining feature of Modernism, there has never been any doubt that it was to be taken seriously as Joyce's *chef-d'oeuvre*. It stands in a pivotal place, repeating the Modernist gesture of textual control and investment in the Word, and also opening itself to another scene of writing, following the liminal trace of unconscious orders. The *Wake* in some senses is a "wake" for the High Modernism beatified by literary history and an "awakening" to what we now call, for lack of a better term, post-Modernism. For more than sixty years, the "work in progress" that became *Finnegans Wake* has served as a proving ground for contemporary theories of textuality, literary history, and canonical definitions.[7]

Even so, *Finnegans Wake* is an unusual entry point for a work of feminist criticism. For some readers, this work alone will block the entrance, not only because it is an esoteric, almost occult text, but because Joyce personifies for feminism the Male Modernist Master whose versions of the feminine (Molly Bloom and ALP, for instance) often are seen to rewrite patriarchy and reinscribe the feminine within the terms of the masculine. But Joyce's writings have been crucial to my rethinking of feminist assumptions about sexual-textual cultural constructions. Feminist criticism pauses before an important critical and theoretical question: to what extent are social-cultural notions of femininity and masculinity related to, even dependent on, the materiality of the body? That is, what is the relation of feminine/masculine gender constructions to our biological genre?

The subtitle of *Textualizing the Feminine* invokes this necessary and ethereal relation: it is written "on the limits of genre." By this I mean genre in all its possible forms. My study participates in a growing field of work on the status of the *signature* in writing. Does the biological genre of a writer determine textual uses (and abuses) of the "feminine" or "masculine?" Can a man write as a woman? Can he allow the (the) feminine that traverses his subjectivity to emerge without creating a fiction of it? That is, can he write at the limits of his own genre? I have no theoretical or practical solution to these questions, which await us at every turn in literary studies and which, by their very natures, cannot be directly addressed.

My approach to the question of gender/genre is from within dialectical, either/or structures: from within the slash (/) or the apostrophic mark of inclusion-exclusion (') that transforms itself into an elliptical curve (. . .) as it deconstructs the literary genre of "letters" or the letter's status as alphabetic symbol and turns translation back on the residue of meaning that escapes or resists its efforts. This work takes place not in the laboratory but in the labyrinth. I follow intricate structures that lead, inevitably and simultaneously, along the two pathways of psychoanalysis and grammatology. They create a double band, a belt or *enceinte*, of writing that is also the double bind of feminist analysis.

EN(S)CRYPTING THE SUBJECT:
MODERNISM AND TEXTUAL PRACTICES

A is an article met is a verb well is a noun.

Gertrude Stein, How to Write

Stein constructs with prepositions, pronouns and conjunctions as much as with nouns and verbs. There is no hierarchy of words or of usage. In 1927 she wrote a piece entitled "Patriarchal Poetry," which implied that patriarchal poetry, along with other hierarchical systems, was dead and needed to be laid to rest.

Ulla Dydo, "Gertrude Stein: Composition as Meditation"[8]

To suggest the implications and complications of my project, I want to comment on Gertrude Stein's writing subjectivity within the literary context of Modernism and the psychosexual context of lesbianism.

Modernist writing focused on the "agency of language" as a vehicle of meaning. To whatever degree other defining characteristics of Modernism operated in juxtaposition, contradiction, or uneasy alignment with each other, the determined emphasis on the Word or Logos overshadowed all other divergences among Modernist writers.[9] The one sacred, common belief seemed to be the indestructibility of the bond between the word and its meanings, between symbol and substance, between signifier and signified. Multiple linguistic experiments that juxtaposed unlike words, altered typography and spelling, translated language into dreams or the discourse of the mad only reinforced meaning. Distorted or disjunctive writing (e.g., Surrealist or stream-of-conscious texts) was thought to mime psychic reality, shoring up meaning rather than undoing it. The Word was sacred: it survived wars and resisted the prerogatives of materialist culture. It masked despair and exposed cultural hypocrisy. The Word held within it the power to restructure and rewrite the world; the writer would succeed where God had failed. Indeed, as Susan Friedman has written, "the artist as seer would attempt to create what the culture could no longer produce: symbol and meaning in the dimension of art, brought into being through the agency of language." [10]

This was the founding premise of Imagism, where form and substance were intimately and irrevocably joined through the image. Various poetic experiments from Vorticism through Surrealism confirmed the transformative powers of language. They revealed surprising new ways that language could "mean," investing an otherwise bankrupt modern society with sense. Writing *Finnegans Wake*, Joyce discovered he could do anything he wanted with language. [11] He had learned its principles, broken its code, mastered its secret, harnessed its energy for his own creative vision. He apparently had realized his early dream of becoming an Author, a "God of creation," the absent center of a linguistic universe.

When Joyce's project is put against Gertrude Stein's, however, one feels that he overstates claims to authorial consciousness and control. Despite the dizzying linguistic brilliance of *Finnegans Wake*, his seems the less daring, more conservative enterprise. While Joyce claimed power over the Word, Stein gave herself up to words. She began by careful observations of linguistic nuance, meticulously noted in thousands of manuscript pages. She submitted to the rhythms and sounds of language, listening carefully to the speech around her. Later, she theorized the relation of grammar and punctuation to rhetoric, drawing attention to the patriarchal, hierarchical structuring of one of our most pervasive symbolic systems.

Stein did what few other writers have had the courage to do: she relinquished her right as a writer to make language submit to her will. Instead, she submitted to linguistic power/play. She discovered through more than fifty years of determined experiment that language, given its free play, tends toward apparently arbitrary alignments of signifer and signified, alignments that are often comic. Moreover, it always "means," even when the contextual moorings of punctuation and grammar are let slip. As language slips and slides away from "intended" meanings to arrive at completely unexpected destinations, context becomes relative rather than overdetermined.

Stein's project appears to be radically self-destructive. Putting into question the determinacy of meaning, her writing plays with the idea that if meaning is not determinant then its opposite might be true. Her detractors have been quick to declare her writing nonsense or gibberish, self-indulgent child's play, or linguistic perversion.[12] She disabused herself of the responsibility to "make sense" in traditional ways. Indeed, her work appears (but only appears) to deny social reality that grounds literary effort in the representational.

Against these claims some feminist critics have lodged a counterclaim: Stein's language renders meaning if one is familiar with its special code: for "textuality" read (lesbian) "sexuality."[13] According to this argument, Stein resists the dominant social code of heterosexist culture by inventing an "antilanguage" that the patriarchy can read only as nonsense. That is, Stein may not have been doing something radically different from her Modernist contemporaries. Hers was *lesbian* Modernism, which inverted traditional meaning structures (thereby maintaining them) and celebrated the Word by substituting its own private word store. Behind this theory of textuality is the belief that Stein's language participates in a governing meaning structure of psychosexual identity: "lesbian."[14]

From the viewpoint of feminism concerned with what Alice Jardine describes as the "sex of the author, narrative destinies, images of women, and gender stereotypes," the theory of Stein's lesbian antilanguage celebrates her as a *woman writer*.[15] It sees her subject matter and literary methods as directly tied to the womanhood she so often tried to deny. Indeed, the peculiar antilogic of her writing seems inextricable from the tensions inherent in her self-image and the desire to be a great writer. Accordingly, the contradictory logic of Stein's writing reflects perfectly internalized contortions and contradictions resulting from her place in culture. Everything about her psychology, her situation as a woman in twentieth-century society, her familial relationships and educational experiences, conspires to make her "readable" as a woman. She can be reclaimed: her experimental writing practices join forces with a pragmatic American feminism.

Surely this is a too fortunate marriage of theory and practice. It demonstrates, however, the potential of Elaine Showalter's socially grounded feminist theory. She writes: "gynocritics begins at the point when we free ourselves from the linear absolutes of male literary history, stop trying to fit women between the lines of male tradition, and focus instead on the newly visible world of female culture." [16] Promising a productive rereading of Stein's biography, this critical method situates her not on the outside of a male literary enterprise but at the center of a female culture to which she could not admit her own membership. Denying her gender in an effort not only to participate in but outdo the male Modernists whom she considered her only worthy opponents, Stein ended up creating a womanly environment for herself, one that allowed her creative tendencies to find expression. If we take off the male Modernist blinders that for so long have restricted our view of Stein's work and put on the gynocritic's glasses, we might discover in Stein's comic verse and engaging wordplay a culturally repressed feminine that is woman-loving, self-loving. In short, all that the patriarchy hates, fears, and denies.

But is this what we discover? Isn't there a *structural* relation between woman-in-the-feminine, which the patriarchy constructs to mirror its fantasies and ease its fears, and a textual feminine put under erasure? To "decode" the literary effects of Stein's writing solely in terms of traditional meaning structures is to deny the richness of that writing, especially as it complicates the binary oppositions it cannot entirely escape or dismiss. For Stein's project to be radical in the ways she declared it to be, she had to do more than substitute lexical codes. She had to uncover, examine, and unsettle the structures that support those codes. This was her life's work. Stein not only resisted confining social-cultural roles but wrestled with the linguistic categories that represent those structures. We are only beginning to learn how she went about a project that questioned the founding categories of thought and language.[17]

Feminist readings of Stein's work, no less than others, cannot avoid these fundamental issues of language and subjectivity. We cannot deny or sidestep Modernist foregrounding of language, with its focus on symbolic systems of representation. If we do so, we bump our noses against the gynocritical reading method that sees language as a tool, a window onto reality, transparent in itself but framing a scene that gives itself to representation. But Djuna Barnes, H.D., Virginia Woolf, and Gertrude Stein did not see *through* a window to an external reality but rather saw *in* language a palpable subject, the "subject" of the literary undertaking. For them, language was not transparent; it structures and mediates "reality." (One thinks of Mrs. Ramsay, seated before the drawing room window in Woolf's *To the Lighthouse*.) These women focused on the relation of language to subjectivity; they knew that language *constructs* external reality rather than describes or mirrors a separate, immutable, constant external. They recognized too that the woman writer participates in sociosymbolic constructions not entirely of her own making, so that her relations with language differ (but how? and to what degrees?) from her male counterparts. The terms of these differences, and the psychic underpinnings of their structures, were of primary interest to these four women writers.[18]

If language cannot be disengaged from its social constructions and historical contexts, it also cannot be separated from psychosexual orders. Language mediates biological categories by representing gender. Employing the terms of recent French critical theory, Alice Jardine writes:

the notion of "Self"—so intrinsic to Anglo-American thought—becomes absurd. It is not something called the "Self" which speaks, but language, the unconscious, the textuality of the text. . . . The assurance of an author's sex within the whirlpool of decentering is problematized beyond recognition. The "policing of sexual identity" is henceforth seen as being complicitous with the appropriations of representation; gender (masculine, feminine) is separate from identity (female, male). The question of whether a "man" or a "woman" wrote a text (a game feminists know well at the level of literary history) is nonsensical. . . . The feminist's initial incredulity faced with this complex "beyonding" of sexual identity is largely based on *common sense* (after all *someone* wrote it??). But is it not that very *sense* ("common to all," i.e., humanism) that the feminist is attempting to undermine? On the other hand, when you problematize "Man" (as being at the foundation of Western notions of the Self) to the extent that French thought has, you're bound to find "Woman"—no matter who's speaking—and *that* most definitely concerns feminist criticism.[19]

Stein tried to trace language to its outermost margins, the limits of its "genre," if you will: a zero-degree, where it split from external "reality"; a moment at which language constituted itself beyond representation and stumbled up against the Lacanian Real—what is behind and anterior to the Imaginary or Symbolic orders. As a result, her narratives have been, to use Jardine's term, "delegitimized" precisely because they relinquished the tenacious grip of mastery over the Word.

An important issue for me is how Stein's discovery was related to her biologically determined womanhood and her problematic social definition as a woman who wanted to be a man (I recognize that Stein in no small measure constructed this definition of herself). Anglo-American feminist critics might respond that Stein's language discoveries were linked to her womanhood *because* her biological sex was so problematic to her. French theorists would perhaps agree, but for different reasons. By its formal characteristics of openness and irrationality, so disparaged by her detractors, Stein's writing might serve as an example of Cixous's *écriture féminine*. Kristeva might recognize "poetic language" in its pulsating rhythms of the semiotic that ruptures the symbolic order. Monique Wittig would no doubt comment that Stein celebrates the female body in ways significantly different from the fetishistic attachment displayed by the patriarchy. Exploring the objectification of the body within her philosophic project, Stein refused to accord the female body a metaphorical status assured by phallic laws. She rewrote the relation of the gendered body to language through "body language." Burying common notions of sense, she discovered non-sense, an Other logic inherent in the language of the body. In so doing, Stein risked burying herself.[20]

Proclaimed the doyenne of the expatriate literary community, Stein was walled up by Modernism. Like many cultural and social movements before it, Modernism found it necessary to hide everything that was antithetical to its undertaking, all that was marginal in the culture it examined. Modernism tried to bury the "feminine," repressing it often and brutally, both in life and literature. It buried women, or excluded them, which amounts to the same thing: Djuna Barnes, Nancy Cunard, Caresse Crosby, H.D., Winifred Ellerman, Mina Loy, Anaïs Nin, Jean Rhys, Edith Sitwell, and Gertrude Stein, among others. In an effort to celebrate and control the Word, its aesthetic denied the conscious/unconscious structuring of language. Finally, Modernism averted its eyes from the female body except to memorialize, fetishize, or aestheticize it. Certainly the Steinian body was of no use to Modernism. Word worship replaced traditional forms of adoration for the female body whose dismembered parts (lips, eyes, hair, breasts) imaged the poet's desire. Instead, Modernism took the Word as a communion wafer on its tongue, turning it into the body and blood of literature.

Gertrude Stein refused to worship before the altar of the Modernist Word. She was little interested in the Latin roots or Greek variants of the ordinary, common words that so charmed her. Intrigued by the principles that guide language construction, she often took words at "face" value ("Foliage is in the trees") or examined them within grammatical and definitional categories ("A sentence has a noun a noun is not only a name it is a manner, and reply").[21] Relentlessly and restlessly she questioned the arrangements of language, the familiar patterns of its organization, its logic. In this literal-minded, "scientific" way, Stein discovered the fragile boundary of categories, rules, and linguistic orders that keep nonsense at bay. She persisted in smudging the borders between sense and nonsense in order to learn how each conditioned the other. She confused the borders between textual body parts: "A noun is hour by hour." The word "hour" is a noun, but the phrase "hour by hour" suggests temporal movements or spatial arrangements (hour / by / hour) that modify the definition. This example is followed by another: "A verb is ever as wherever."[22] These quite typical Stein sentences rely on the verb "to be" (subject-copula-predicate) to explain grammatical functions: "A verb" = "ever as wherever." The word that fills the blank space of the grammatical formula, however, is not a verb: "ever" and "wherever" are adverbs; "acceptable" is an adjective. Although the formula is technically correct (the "linking" verb "to be" must be followed either by a noun or a modifier), the definition is not. Avoiding punctuation that might clarify the arrangement of its internal parts, Stein works the boundaries of meaning: "This is not a sentence this is a reflection." [23]

Turning away from the altar of the Word and turning toward the writing subject, Stein de-composed the terms of representation. She practiced her own form of "de-composition," a precursor of grammatology. Trained both in philosophy and medical science, Stein investigated systems and skeletons, and organized the linguistic breakdown of Modernist formalism. Thus her writing, often referred to as "post-Modernist," as though to suggest its existence both inside and outside the historical boundaries of Modernism, unsettled the founding assumptions of literary practice: the sanctity of authorial control over the text, generic definitions and limits, the security of textual boundaries, and the relation of sensory-cognitive orders.

Although Stein was not a student of psychoanalysis and never used its terminology to describe her discoveries about language, in fact her project opened writing onto the unconscious. She allowed herself to be "operated" by the unconscious, recording its pressures and movements. For instance, her early experiments in "automatic writing," which culminated in *The Making of Americans*, traced the repetition compulsion within syntactic structures and narrative form. [24] The early word portraits and *Tender Buttons* recognize synesthesia as a condition of perception. When duplicated through writing, this other order of meaning (whose cognitive elements continually collapse into each other, despite efforts to categorize and separate them) opens onto psychic well-being. According to Stein, this effect is "well": "Writing may be made between the ear and the eye and the ear and the eye the eye will be well and the ear will be well." [25] Her language vibrates between ear and eye, between verb and noun, as it textualizes the psychic-sensory apparatus. Stein's starting point, however, is language, not the physiological apparatus of seeing-hearing of the psyche that interests Derrida, Kristeva, and Lacan. Her work implies a founding question for my own study in relation to the work of these later theorists: what are the psychosexual structures of textual bodies? I begin with this question, which I locate as a place of oversight within Western theories of cognition.

Before taking up the question, I want to comment on the critical assumption that only experimental writing displays "the feminine" as I describe it. Because Hélène Cixous, Luce Irigaray,

Introduction

Julia Kristeva, and Monique Wittig emphasize the subversive, rupturing, disjuncturing work of the feminine, often supporting their arguments by reference to twentieth-century avant-garde texts or through their own transgressive writing forms, we sometimes assume that feminine = subversive and avant-garde = revolutionary. Neither of these assumptions is true in any categorical sense. The feminine both supports and subverts cultural-social structures. As Kristeva's work on Céline, Jarry, and Artaud demonstrates, subversive—even revolutionary—poetic practices can participate in and arise from elitist and totalitarian impulses.[26] Indeed, this accusation is often brought against Modernism and post-Modernism.

I do not believe that a subversive "feminine" is to be found only in avant-garde writings or that conventional discourse can valorize only woman-in-the-feminine. Nor do I believe that women's desire for a separate discursive space can be found outside the phallic-patriarchal order or that the "feminine" is its signifier. Rather, I have chosen to illustrate my concerns through works that skate on the edge of genre/gender boundaries and trace the seam of unconscious/conscious structures. These "experimental" texts reveal more easily than presumably conventional writings the principles at work in *all* language. Constructed as the Other within systems of representation, the feminine is the vanishing point of representation (as it is of theories of sexuality) that any system must posit *and* exclude in order to achieve a fiction of self-consistency. This is true of all representative orders, and it is why in the chapters that follow I place such emphasis on the cultural investment in notions of cohesive, predictable, integrated selfhood and the power of authorial consciousness and control.

PART I

Textualizing the Feminine From the Place of Oversight

CHAPTER I

The Law of the Phallus (as) The Law of Genre

It is often forgotten that psychoanalysis describes the psychic law to which we are subject, but only in terms of its failing. *This is important for a feminist (or any radical) practice which has often felt it necessary to claim for itself a wholly other psychic and representational domain. Therefore, if the visual image in its aesthetically acclaimed form serves to maintain a particular and oppressive mode of sexual recognition, it does so only partially and at a cost.*

Jacqueline Rose, Sexuality in the Field of Vision[1]

Feminist criticism has long been interested in textual representations of women, how women are imaged in advertising, film, literature, painting, and sculpture. Indeed, the focus on woman *as* image has been so central to feminist writing in the twentieth century that it is often difficult to think beyond its frame of reference. The necessary activity of thinking "beyond" this restrictive frame requires, first, that we analyze its psychosexual-textual structuring devices and, next, consider what is lost to or escapes its constructions. Offering women a prescription for passivity and subjection, cultural images figure sexual difference in the "feminine."[2] That is, masculine fantasies and fears support the spectacle of woman as guarantor of both the image and the systems that create it. This chapter and the following one examine the laws of sexuality and categories of representation that support cultural constructions of woman-in-the-feminine.

Theorists in various fields have analyzed how the literary formula, the cinematic apparatus, and the psychoanalytic machine construct their terms of symbolic figuration within the visual. Working within and across these fields of study, feminist criti-

3

cism has demonstrated that sexual difference cannot be reduced to *visible* difference: something of woman always escapes, is suppressed, or is lost in the process. This "loss" is necessary to the structural operations of the symbolic process, which function by repressing the knowledge of forfeiture and failing. Therefore, what is unavailable to representation, the je ne sais quoi of woman that drives the desire to fully possess her, is easily overlooked—even by feminist criticism. What yet calls out for analysis is not the partiality of these oppressive modes of sexual recognition, which feminist criticism has meticulously documented, but rather what escapes representation's totalizing effort.

I want to shift attention from representations of women to the *failure* of representing woman-in-the-feminine. As it is generally understood, the feminine participates in what Jacqueline Rose calls "the fantasy of absolute sexual difference," a fantasy psychically produced and culturally upheld by a certain visual perspective that "operate[s] like a law which always produces the terms of its own violation." [3] The Law of the Phallus and the Law of Genre, whose ordering principles I discuss below, operate in just this way. The terms of violation are not only, or merely, a reaction *against* the law but are productive of it, generating effects through the categories whose controlling forms and norms they also displace. To understand how the laws of sexual difference produce woman-in-the-feminine and are violated by it, we must see that in our culture the recognition and representation of sexual difference depend almost entirely on the visual order.

Woman-in-the-feminine is first and foremost an image. Produced within a scopic, phallic economy, this fantasy figure marks (out) a horizon of figurability that is also the vanishing point of representation. The image hides its work as representation, however, and denies its status as a signifier within a relational, symbolic system by freezing the representational process as spectacle. In this way, it both announces and obscures its status as construct, focusing attention on content (icon or effigy) rather than on its compositional, mediating process. The image thus blocks out all that is potentially lost to it: for example, what of sexual difference cannot be made visible or how masculine fantasies construct images of the feminine *as* loss by fetishizing the female body. One can discover how laws of visual representation violate their own terms by positing their limit of figurability.

4

From this conjectural perspective, woman-in-the-feminine is seen to be the blind spot not only of the phallic order that defines sexual difference but also of the symbolic order that represents it. The feminine is figured as the representational system's necessary blindness to its own operations and the limit of representation within the field of vision.

Western notions of cognition privilege the visual as the primary means of knowing. The senses are hierarchically ordered within two categories that include the "objective" senses (sight and hearing), which discriminate phenomena by "objectifying" them, and the "mechanical" sense of touch; taste and smell constitute the "subjective" or chemical senses. Reproducing this hierarchy, modes of representation operate primarily within the visual field, incorporating or translating other sense perceptions under the terms of imagery.[4] But the subordinate mechanical and chemical senses are not easily articulated through visual content, nor do they give themselves to "framing" within the image. Rather, they produce effects that challenge the structuring principles of the visual produced across a space in which subject and object are distinguished from each other (in film, between camera and subject, spectator and screen; in literature, between reader and text, and by textual spacing). This space also provides the ground—the conceptual premise and spatial field—for separating the object of speculation from its surroundings. When the secondary and tertiary sensory orders are engaged in textual processes, their properties disarrange the spatial field of pleasure demanded by sight and override any strict separation of the senses. This process provides a clue to the failure of adequately representing woman-in-the-feminine as image. What escapes is all that cannot be objectivized to the eye (what is interior to woman and what the image itself blocks out to vision) and anything that is not immediately available to sight (i.e., hearing, touch, taste, and smell).

What is the relation of these other sensory orders to the categories of grammar, rhetoric, syntax, and genre that reproduce its representational ordering? Psychoanalysis and grammatology claim a relation that, although it cannot be plotted, is spelled out through certain forms of textualization (dreams and the poetic language of avant-garde writings). Lacan theorized the relation of the Imaginary and Symbolic orders by discovering how sense perceptions are imprinted on infants as letters to form a "language" of the unconscious. Derrida deconstructs the hierarchical structure of the senses through grammatological writing practices that bring the theoretical (cognitive) senses of sight and sound under the nontheoretical (chemical) senses to dissolve or "decompose" their orders.

What is at stake for the feminine in these discourses is not immediately evident, except that both psychoanalysis and grammatology acknowledge phallogocentrism (phallus + word) as the primary signifying structure of Western culture. Within this mode of signification, which privileges the visual and the phallic, a supposedly rational/masculine logic constructs its "sense" against irrational/feminine "nonsense." Founded on sexual difference that fears phallic loss (that is, fears the powerlessness of feminization), the signifying system sets itself up as a "universal," masculine order that denies (but also represents) sexual difference. The feminine provides the repressed ground of the system, which elaborates its logic of denied loss *through* the feminine. (Nonsense must be "lost" so that sense can properly function.) The feminine is therefore the site of disorder that the system must posit and repudiate in order to achieve its (illusion of) coherence. Threatening to disrupt the system's fictive coherence, the feminine also represents what the system must repress and invoke in order to stabilize its functions.[5]

Sexual difference signified as *difference from the phallic* is not merely an observable condition represented by human forms; it is a structure that Lacanian and Derridean analyses examine by way of two laws. Lacan articulates the Law of the Phallus, the principle of psychic division and sexual difference; Derrida demonstrates how the Law of Genre that defines textual categories encompasses, but also denies, gender differences. While Lacan's law posits the psychosocial production of sexual difference, Derrida's law defines its inevitable violation: the law that declares gender/genre difference cannot help but trespass its own limits. These laws have much to say to feminism that takes sexual difference as its primary signifier. In a gesture toward feminist critics who have, in general, adopted wary stances toward Lacanian-Derridean discourses, Alice Jardine writes: "To the extent that feminism is primarily a battle against what are perceived as 'false images' of women, it is necessarily bound to some of the most complex epistemological and religious contradictions of contemporary Western culture. That is, the feminist gesture is as much a derivative of the law it is fighting as are its Others—and what is at stake at all of our intersections is, precisely, not to lose sight of that fact." [6] But the Law itself marks the primary impasse at the intersections of feminism, psychoanalysis, and grammatology.

Feminism reads Lacanian analysis not as an effort to unveil the fraudulent nature of the phallic signifier in its structuring of conscious/unconscious discourses according to a law of failure, but rather as a reinscription of phallocentrism. The Law declares that, as a speaking subject, woman must submit to the phallic order, fraudulent though it may be; she therefore speaks (from) subjection. To do otherwise would be to risk exclusion from language in psychosis. It is not surprising, then, that feminists seek "a wholly other discursive and, by implication, political space" beyond the psychoanalytic law. [7]

In a critique of binary, hierarchical polarities within Western metaphysics, Derridean analysis exposes the attempt by psychoanalysis to situate its "truth" beyond metaphysics, in a transcendental phallic signifier that has no signified and orders its truth behind the veil of its own fraudulence. As an institution, psychoanalysis seems to posit for itself a "wholly other discursive . . . and political space," a position that transcends (or even redefines) metaphysics. Showing that psychoanalysis is trapped within Western structures, Derrida questions the notion of a psychic-discursive space "beyond" the metaphysical. [8] His analysis attempts to unsettle, if only temporarily, reigning phallocentric orders through a two-stage process of deconstruction. It first overturns hierarchical relations of sexual difference (masculine/feminine), then displaces the opposition along a relay so that the hierarchy cannot easily reestablish itself. Some feminist theorists argue, however, that deconstruction overturns the masculine/feminine hierarchy only to usurp woman's position of "otherness" for the masculine. Feminist psychoanalytic critics claim that the "relay effect" does not have validity within psychosexual terms. [9]

As feminist discourse circulates around questions of sexual difference, two key insights of psychoanalysis and grammatology are sometimes lost. One is recognition of what Barbara Johnson has called "the difference within," the impossibility of unitary, coextensive subjectivity; the second is the work of the unconscious, especially the operations of desire within psychic structures.[10] Neither psychoanalysis nor grammatology claims a Platonic complementarity of the sexes; hence, these disciplines undo any notion of sexual difference based solely on biological sex differences. Juliet Mitchell comments that if it were possible for "pre-given male or female entities [to] complete and satisfy each other," then desire—the motivational force for all human action—could not exist.[11] According to Lacan, sexual difference is the effect of the psychic Law of the Phallus enjoined on the subject (whether female or male) to take up a social-cultural position as a woman or man. This position may not coincide with biological sexual characteristics; nor is it permanently established.[12] It is constantly renegotiated within the psyche and is subject to change. No "subject position," however, can exist outside or beyond the two sexes.

Grammatology also acknowledges that sexual difference is arbitrary and contingent. Notions of an absolute, consistent, balanced alterity between sets of binary oppositions (male/female) are deconstructed to demonstrate that the law of genre/gender violates and transgresses its own founding principle: "Genres are not to be mixed."[13] The term *différance* exemplifies the effects of the law. Often explained as differing and deferring, *différance* signals sexual-textual difference by exchanging the "e" of "difference" for an "a," whose alteration cannot be heard: difference is visible only to the eye, the "I" of Western cognition. Writing from the position of psychoanalysis, Rose comments that grammatology begs an important question central to its own project: "Behind the Western logos of presence, Derrida locates an architrace or *différance* which that logos would ideally forget, but this then requires a *psychic account* of how/why that forgetting takes place."[14] Drawing attention to what psychoanalysis has overlooked in its own field of inquiry, Derrida might ask: how/why is it that psychoanalysis has forgotten to account for modes of psychosexual *textualization*?[15] Emphasizing the notion of "full" and "empty" speech in the analytic context, Lacan's account of psychic structures fails to provide a textual account of the psyche, that is, to follow Freud's early efforts to theorize the psyche-as-text. At an impasse, psychoanalysis and grammatology each claim that its "law" has been overlooked by the other.

-❉-

FANTASIES OF THE PHALLIC

In Freudian doctrine, the phallus is not a phantasy, if by that we mean an imaginary effect. Nor is it as such an object (part-, internal, good, bad, etc.) in the sense that this term tends to accentuate the reality pertaining in a relation. It is even less the organ, penis or clitoris, that it symbolizes. . . . For the phallus is a signifier . . . intended to designate as a whole the effects of the signified, in that the signifier conditions them by its presence as a signifier.

Lacan, *"The Signification of the Phallus"* [16]

Lacan revised Freud's notions of perceived sexual difference (the phallus as organ) and the theory of "penis envy" by emphasizing the mediating role of symbolic language systems. His Symbolic order is not founded on a principle of anatomical symmetry in which the woman, lacking a penis, is inherently castrated. Creating meaning as symbolization, the Symbolic is an interpretive order, governed by an unconscious structure. It rules through the phallic signifier, which as a signifier holds no inherent meaning. [17] The cultural and social values that are internalized by the infant as the result of the mirror stage process assign the phallus meaning and endow it with power. This "drama" marks the child's entrance into the Symbolic. [18]

From this psychic structuring Lacan drew two conclusions with regard to feminine sexuality: first, because it is founded within a referential structure that takes the male sign (phallus) as its ordering principle, feminine sexuality belongs to a realm of "masquerade"; second, feminine sexuality cannot be separated from cultural representations of the feminine. Lacan states that "images and symbols *for* the woman cannot be isolated from images and symbols *of* the woman. . . . It is the representation of sexuality which conditions how it comes into play." [19] The female body signifies sexual difference as "lack" within *figural* and representational orders (Imaginary/Symbolic); "there is nothing missing in the Real," Lacan reminds us. [20] Note that the assigned meaning (woman = lack) *precedes* any observable, perceptible, anatomical differences between the sexes, e.g., boys have penises, girls do not.

Culture and society assign asymmetrical values to masculine and feminine sexuality within patriarchal systems. Representations of the feminine are "only" representations, but they carry enormous cultural freight. Creating the condition they presumably mirror (feminine sexuality takes on meaning in *response* to cultural images of it), these representations are internalized psychically as the Other, whose first representative is the mother, through whom girls and boys learn to recognize the power of the phallic signifier.

This process of psychic encoding is complicated and often misunderstood. We should not, for example, confuse Lacan's conceptions of sexual difference with existentialist notions of otherness, which presume an externality to difference and a complementarity of the sexes. Simone de Beauvoir writes: "true alterity—otherness—is that of a consciousness separate from mine and substantially identical with mine." [21] For psychoanalysis, true alterity is a fiction inscribed in the unconscious as Desire, a dream of complementarity and self-identity that belongs to the Imaginary register that contains repressed, early infant identifications from which the fantasy that another can fulfill one's desires is constructed. The fantasy of an ideal complementarity is psychically constituted within the unconscious, whose messages—that sexual identity is precarious and constantly renegotiated—cannot consciously be understood.

The psychosexual positioning of subjectivity within the categories "woman"/"man" is inscribed as the place of the Other (i.e., internalized cultural and social values). Lacan distinguishes between the Other, which structures subjectivity from its place in the unconscious, and other (lowercase *o*), which refers to objects and people through whom the subject tries to establish a relation of complementarity as a guarantee of identity. The relation of the subject to an other is an Imaginary one. Beauvoir uses the word "other" in this latter sense, although her comments are grounded in existentialist philosophy, not in psychoanalytic theory. Lacan distinguishes the unconscious relation of the subject to the Other from the mirroring oppositions of "object relations" theory by means of a four-sided figure that plots the Other/other and Subject/ego within Imaginary and unconscious fields. [22]

The unconscious Other is constituted in part around the infant's experience of the mother, or primary caretaker. Ellie Ragland-Sullivan's distinction between (m)Other and Other is particularly helpful, especially to my later discussion of feminine sexuality and the maternal within Kristeva's work:

> The Other(A) [*l'Autre* or big Other], then, is more than the Real other or mother of early infant nurture. In contradistinction to object-relations theory, Lacan's special attention to the relationship between infant and mother during the mirror stages does not mean that the unconscious is created in a static one-to-one equation or with the force of a biological bond. Any constant nurturer could fulfill the function of mother. The formulation (m)Other is meant to express the idea that the human subject first *becomes aware of itself* by identification with a person (object), usually the mother.[23]

The unconscious inscription of (m)Other that the child internalizes is the mother's *relation to the phallus* (usually represented by the father or the "phallic mother"). According to Lacan, this interaction is a determining factor of psychosexuality.[24]

Lacan stresses that there is no true alterity between the sexes ("there is no sexual relation"), which is not to say there is no such thing as sexual difference.[25] Rather, subjectivity (feminine and masculine) is founded on impossible Desire and organized around a primordial lack, a longing for wholeness and completeness that can never be fulfilled. This longing, announced by the baby's first birth cry, initiates language. Lacan explains that "Desire, a function central to all human experience, is the desire for nothing nameable."[26] The human subject searches endlessly, however, for words to name it, confirming another aspect of Lacan's law: "Everything implied by the analytic engagement with human behaviour indicates not that meaning reflects the sexual *but that it makes up for it.*"[27] We can distinguish Desire—which belongs to the Other, is experienced as "alien" and whose "discourse" is the unconscious—from "desire," which belongs to conscious life but cannot perceive its relation to Desire. Blinded to the Other side of Desire, the subject wants to see itself in command of its attachments to objects and people. This second kind of desire participates in transference, seeking an "other" with whom to establish a relationship of complementarity. The transference is doomed to failure (it is known *by* its failure), precisely because no other can assuage Other's Desire.[28]

Reenacted in the psychoanalytic situation, the transfer becomes the mechanism by which the analysand recognizes unnameable, unassuageable Desire. Lacan's point is that "relations between human beings are really established before one gets to the domain of consciousness."[29]

The four-way structuring of Other/other and Desire/desire, set in place by the mirror stage drama, situates the subject within the Symbolic. The mirror stage does not require a looking glass, nor does it reveal castration in the Freudian sense, that is, the presence or absence of a penis. Occurring when the infant is between six and eighteen months of age, it requires that the child have acquired a measure of physiological mastery over the lack of coordination that defined its early months of life. Through a series of identifications with people and objects, the mirror stage reveals a (false) sense of mastery and wholeness, a notion of *the body as a unity*.[30] The sense of mastery and wholeness produced by the "image" or mirrored reflections is belied, however, by the infant's continued physical dependence and lack of coordination. The mirroring effect produced in the infant subverts *and* supports the notion of a self symmetrically "doubled" in a mirror. Infant experiences of the body as part-objects and fragments before the mirror stage provide the principles by which signification (entrance into the Symbolic) can later take place. These experiences are inscribed within the infant as "letters" or signifiers that form the organizing structures of the unconscious.[31] The mirror stage depends, then, on the lettering or imprinting process that takes place in the infant from its first moments of life.

Lacan stressed that human infants are born prematurely in comparison to other animals, thus suffering absolute physical helplessness in the first six months of life, when they experience their bodies as fragmented and disjoined.[32] Uncoordinated, dependent, unable to individuate itself from its surroundings, the baby spends its time looking and listening. The sensory experiences of the outside world form the infant's earliest perceptions, which are lived as identifications that cannot yet be differentiated from each other or from experiences of its own body. These early sensations establish the human capacity for aggressivity and eroticism.[33] The body is eroticized through sensory responses, which sometimes overlap or are not easily distinguished from each other (visual-verbal), and through the primary organs (mouth, anus, urethra) whose functions differentiate them from surrounding body parts. These early experiences of sounds, words, and images form the material of the unconscious, whose modes of signification are associational (combining images, objects, persons), assonantal, and homophonic.[34]

In a radical departure from Freud, Lacan argued that a kind of language, which he described as signifying "letters," mediates these primary body functions and sense experiences. Summarizing Serge Leclaire's work on letters, Ragland-Sullivan explains that Lacan often used the word "letters" to mean "the effect of language, which creates and informs the unconscious: 'letters' defined as localized signifiers. By 'letters' of the body he meant the impact of difference or otherness on being." [35] This difference or "otherness" is not, however, difference from another human being (the mother, for instance, whom the infant cannot yet recognize as separate from itself); certainly it does not refer to sexual difference. Rather, it is an experience of difference within and among body parts, which it begins to differentiate on the basis of their separate functions. The letters that mark these experiences are a mode of signification that will be anchored at the close of the mirror stage when psychic representations of sensory perceptions and experiences of the body undergo primary repression. Partial integration of body parts and motor control allows the infant to assume a false or *mis*recognition (*méconnaissance*) of the body as whole, unitary and coordinated.[36] Ragland-Sullivan comments that the "mirror stage must therefore be understood as a metaphor for the *vision* of harmony of a subject essentially in discord." [37] Lacan calls this the "mirage of maturation" of the infant's power; it belongs to the Imaginary.[38] The false recognition, which forms the basis of the ego or *moi*, is "locked in" by the visual order. The Other constantly challenges this image and the visual ordering that establishes it.

Identity is conferred as an alien Otherness that is both externally mirrored ("other" relations) and internally experienced (the Other). Unable to maintain the sense of coherence or body control, the infant moves in and out of physical and psychic dependence for some time before it fully enters the Symbolic order. The Symbolic functions in structural relation with the unconscious, which is "created" by primary repression of fragmented body experience and synesthetic sensory confusions. The unconscious becomes, in Ragland-Sullivan's words, "a place of loss and disappearance." Two kinds of loss inhabit this realm. Each affects subjectivity: the early sense of unmediated access to the mother, whose loss underwrites Desire for wholeness, and the flickering disappearance-reappearance of the false imago of the mirror stage, which registers grammatical effects within pronomial shifts (I/you, me/she).[39]

If subjectivity is always divided, constructed within unconscious/conscious structures, it is also always gendered. The mirror stage enacts the drama of sexual choice: it enacts a Law of Genre that is not necessarily coextensive with biological sex.[40] Since gender can be articulated only by reference to the phallic signifier, there are particular consequences for those who pass into subjectivity under the sign "Woman." Summarizing the effects of this law, Jacqueline Rose comments that "there is no place prior to the law which is available and can be retrieved [no "pre-discursive reality"]. And there is no feminine outside language . . . because the 'feminine' is constituted as a division in language, a division which produces the feminine as its negative term."[41] "Woman" is not merely a social role imposed by the larger culture, "she" is constructed as a (non)-category in language that signifies the fantasy of wholeness and guarantees (but also resists) the phallic order. Lacanian theory rests on this two-part assertion: (1) the infant, although born with recognizable biological sex characteristics, becomes a gendered subject only when it takes its place within language as a "she" or a "he"; (2) the only signifier for sexuality is the phallus. Feminist criticism's resistance to Lacanian theory often begins here.

-*-

THE SEXUAL FIX, THE GENRE MIX, THE JOUIS-SENS

As soon as the word "genre" is sounded, as soon as it is heard, as soon as one attempts to conceive it, a limit is drawn. And when a limit is established, norms and interdictions are not far behind: "Do," "Do not" say "genre," the word "genre," the figure, the voice, or the law of genre. And this can be said of genre in all genres, be it a question of a generic or a general determination of what one calls "nature" or physis (for example, a biological genre in the sense of gender, or the human genre, a genre of all that is in general), or be it a question of a typology designated as non-natural and depending on laws or orders which were once held to be opposed to physis

The Law of the Phallus (as) The Law of Genre

according to those values associated with techne, thesis, nomos *(for example, an artistic, poetic or literary genre).*

Jacques Derrida, *"The Law of Genre"* [42]

For Lacan, the "truth" of sexual difference is a "phallacy" because it is produced with reference to a signifier that is accorded an insupportable social and cultural value. The phallus is a fiction and a failure. This truth calls to analysis within individual lives, where specificities of the phallacy are played out. Derrida's discursive fantasies of sexual difference, the "sexualized" discourse that makes some feminists uncomfortable, analyzes this phallacy in recognition of the *limits of analysis* as a law of psychoanalysis itself. [43]

Declaring that "genres [genders] are not to be mixed," the Law of Genre inscribes an inevitable "mixing" of genres. The law operates according to "a principle of contamination, a law of impurity, a parasitical economy"; it figures "a sort of participation without belonging—a taking part without being part of or having membership in a set." [44] Establishing a limit between genres, the law opens the possibility that limits can be exceeded, that the boundary can "form, by invagination, an internal pocket larger than the whole." That is, the boundary produced by divisions and limits gives way to an "abounding that remains as singular as it is limitless." [45]

Derrida's comments here do not directly address the psychic fixing of sexual boundaries, but we can see that the Law of Genre operates psychically in the very creation of the order, "Genre." The law that declares the purity of biological genres (male/female) also requires individuals to take up a psychic position within one gender or the other. The result is that the psyche and soma become "mixed up" with each other. Sexual difference, then, is not merely (or only) a difference *between* sexes, it is a difference *within* genders, each contaminated by the "other" genre. [46] Lacan argues that the phallic signifier structures the psyche according to gender oppositions (Phallus/Castration) that the soma must "figure" or represent. [47] Subjectivity is not easily maintained; it is renegotiated daily in human lives, always carrying with it, for both women and men, a tension between psychic identifications and representations, or images, of the body.

This is particularly true for feminine sexuality, which figures the Law of the Phallus as an inevitable transgression of its order, its excesses pointing to an-Other order. What carries over to the feminine, in Jacqueline Rose's words, is "the difficulty inherent in sexuality itself." [48]

From Freud to Lacan, feminine sexuality has marked the failure of psychoanalysis to account fully for the general truth of the phallic law. This strange "truth" posits feminine sexuality both within the phallic (where it represents otherness and lack) and supplementary to it, an excessive "more than" that produces a remainder. Lacan acknowledges this double structure when he says that there is both a phallic *jouissance* and a "*jouissance* of the woman," that is "something more" than the phallic: it exceeds the phallic order and tries to make up for its lack. [49] The word *jouissance*, which cannot be fully translated into another language, exceeds the limits of any definition: it goes beyond sexual pleasure, beyond pleasure itself, and can tip over into pain and psychic dissolution. It marks the place where the phallic signifying system exceeds its own terms, the place where "truth falters" and where the system threatens to collapse (*JL*, p. 151). [50] This is *O*, the slipping point of the Other, where the Phallacy/Phantasy of the law fails to uphold the order it posits. The *O* signifies what "woman necessarily relates to": not to the Phallic but to the site of its potential failure (*JL*, p. 151). [51]

Recognizing feminine *jouissance*, Lacan at once went beyond Freud and reauthorized Freud's claim that all libido is masculine. No signifier for *woman* exists within the Symbolic order ("The woman" does not exist), which accounts for the substitutionary logic around women and the feminine. Jacques-Alain Miller writes: "This is what Freud recognized: just one symbol for the libido, and this symbol is masculine; the symbol for the female is lost. Lacan is thus entirely Freudian in stating that *woman* as a category does not exist." [52]

The absence of the signifier for woman creates a slippage in language categories, which Lacan dramatizes when he strikes through the definite article, "T̶h̶e̶ woman": "*The* woman can only be written with *The* crossed through. There is no such thing as *The* woman, where the definite article stands for the universal" (*JL*, p. 144). This pronouncement divided members of the *école freudienne* in 1973–74 and continues to trouble feminist theorists today. I enter the debate with a question about the structures that support language as a symbolic form: what is the relation of language laws to the psychosocial symbolic construction of gender? This question recognizes that language forms (grammar, rhetoric) play a crucial role in the psychic/generic construction of identity. Language is not merely a social-cultural medium of communication (a tool) but the very fabric of subjectivity. As such, it displays a palpable materiality that provides clues to the gaps, overlaps, and oppositions of its structuring principles. Knots or holes in language signal the Lacanian Real, what cannot be symbolized or imagined; they are evidence of Kristeva's "un-signifying," residues of the "pre-subject," and appear in Derrida's psychoanalytic graphology as spatial and rhythmic "traces." The radical Otherness of the Real, which exists behind and beyond the Other, is signaled as disjunctions in language. Lacan suggests its concreteness by assigning it a linguistic form that collapses the space between signifiers: *la langue* (language, tongue) becomes *lalangue* or *la dite maternelle* (the maternal word, what the mother tongue says that cannot be translated into the grammar of a national language).

In French, Lacan's mother tongue, the definite article cannot be separated from its noun object: article and noun are one, illustrated by the formulation *lalangue* (the "mothertongue"). Moreover, the gender of a word, signaled by the definite article, constitutes its meaning: to change gender is to change meaning. (See chapter 4 for my discussion of Derrida's plays on the different meanings of *le poste* and *la poste* in *The Post Card*.) Striking through the definite article (T̶h̶e̶) denies *femme*/woman a categorical or universal status (*JL*, p. 150).[53] Translated into the Law of Genre, this means that to lose one's genre is to lose one's ability to signify. But the grammatical category that *should* be there to complement and balance the category, The man, beckons to man's Desire for an-other. The phallic order, therefore, creates a fantasy of The woman (woman-in-the-feminine), an other confused as an Other, representative of an absolute order of truth, a holy (m)Other of God, a place of ultimate mystification. Man takes woman for his soul, confusing her with God, the cultural sign for absolute Otherness (*JL*, p. 155). Taken for the Other, the seat of the Symbolic, woman-in-the-feminine is constituted as an absent placeholder that guarantees man's place in the phallic order. Lacan charts the fantasy roots of this impossible task in the "letters" or *percepta* of the infant's first experiences that, repressed as the (m)Other, form the signifying system of unconscious Desire.

Lacan observes that Desire—which by definition can never be fulfilled—constitutes all subjects, whether male or female. Formed in the infant's relation to the mother as primary nurturer, Desire's demand always exceeds the terms of satisfaction. That is, Desire is at once something left over (still desiring) and a lack (yet to be satisfied). The primordial subject desires to know the Real, which, since it cannot be signified as such, can only be guessed at because the Real constantly eludes us. Thus the subject turns the Real, which it cannot know directly, into Imaginary objects of Desire.[54] Lacan writes: "The real is beyond the *automaton*, the return, the coming-back, the insistence of the sign, by which we see ourselves governed by the pleasure principle."[55] Against the Real's solid resistance to symbolization, the signifier repeats itself, knocking against the door of the Real, producing excess "noise" to cover over its lack of knowledge. The production of signifying excess in an effort to make "sense" is pleasurable. At one level, it does make sense, a *jouis-sens*, that signals a Real (e.g., feminine *jouissance*) that the masculine Imaginary or the Phallic Symbolic cannot encompass.[56] *Jouis-sens*, the language of unconscious Desire, is produced by *lalangue*, about which Lacan writes: "The unconscious is a knowledge, a know-how of lalangue. And what one knows how to do with lalangue surpasses by far what one is capable of accounting for in terms of language."[57]

What would *jouis-sens* look like if it were written? From what materials would it be constituted? We might try to constitute a graphic relation of Desire and *jouissance* by grafting Lacan's *lalangue* onto Derrida's grammatology. That is, rather than confining *lalangue* to *parlêtre* (a speaking being [*l'être*] as *lettre* [letter]) as Lacan does, we might try to graph it, spell it out, and punctuate it. The texts I discuss in the second half of this book illustrate what we would see: "de-compositions" of common sense and sensory orders. Words break up into their constituent letters; letters dissolve into shapes; genres reveal their genders; quotation marks leave bite "imprints" on the page; the text takes on a material weight and density, giving itself to the textile;

the simultaneity of perception is now deferred-displayed on a temporal-spatial grid, a plane surface; the textual body is fragmented, partitioned, and segmented down to the last phoneme, grapheme, and diacritical marker of the resistant residue of subjectivity and sexuality. Derrida's own writing provides many examples of *jouis-sens*; and, using Freud's idea of the mystic writing pad as a metaphor for imprinting percepta on the psyche, he reintroduces the materiality of language as graphic element. He takes literally the notion of textualizing the sexual (and sexualizing the textual) as a reminder that subjectivity goes beyond *parlêtre*.

One of the places Derrida appears to part company with Lacan's speculations on subjectivity and sexuality is precisely on the Lacanian divide of genre/gender, that is, the psychosocial construction of subjectivity. Lacan writes that all speaking beings must line up on one side or the other of this divide ("woman," "man") in order to speak or write from a gendered position.[58] But Derrida's writings resist this formula by writing in a remainder, a residue (*ce qui reste*)—often apparent in a sliding or overlapping of sense perceptions—to demonstrate the failure of every human effort to line up on, or speak from, one side of the genre/gender divide. Derrida puts the visual metaphors of perceived sexual difference into question by referring to knots or skeins of sexualized voices and writing subjectivities that cannot easily be unwound and categorized, straightened out, and made to line up in order according to a law of sexed discourse. Thus, his writing works not only the margins of discourse (where sense falls into "nonsense") but it also circles within and around the interstices of a textual-sexual weave to suggest the irreducible filaments, grains, liquids, ashes, tastes and smells of multiple genres that are never fully repressed or unexpressed. One could say that his writing brings to consciousness the "letters" of the unconscious, extending and celebrating the very notion of "letters."

While Lacanians may acknowledge that Derrida replicates the constant renegotiation of the sexual divide on which subjectivity is premised, marking and remarking the places where the Law of the Phallus succeeds by failing, the moments of slippage (*jouissance* and *significance*), they would no doubt argue that this psychographology cannot really challenge or displace the Law itself. From this perspective, Derrida can play the game only because the Law remains in place and urges the questions: "Who speaks? To whom? Who replies? To whom?"[59] He can play the game at all only because he speaks/writes from one side or the other of a gendered division. It is his constant crossing and recrossing of the divide that makes feminists, for instance, so uneasy: is he trying to co-opt the feminine gender/genre for himself? This question interests Lacanians not at all.

Arguing that "there is no domain of the psychic without text," Derrida returns to Freud's early efforts to theorize the psyche by means of a "structural model of writing" that is nonphonetic, not dependent on speech (*SW*, p. 199). Although he was never able entirely to get beyond the mnemonics of writing, Freud discovered—undoubtedly without full knowledge of that discovery—that "psychic *content* will be *represented* by a text whose essence is irreducibly graphic" (*SW*, p. 199). Freud's model, a child's toy magic writing slate, provides the means to account for the graphic aspects of psychic structuring, composed as a "metaphorics of the written trace" (*SW*, p. 200), which Derrida defines here and elsewhere as a breaching or engraved furrowing of difference.[60] The machine creates a double-sided writing whose traces can never be completely erased. With certain (significant) limitations, this metaphor for psychic inscription works well: it acknowledges that percepta cannot be directly imprinted on the psyche but must undergo repression in order to function psychically.

Freud's machine images this operation as a simultaneous process of "manuscription" and erasure that takes place across a trilayered surface (celluloid covering sheet, to which a sheet of waxed paper is attached, and a wax slab). He writes in the "Note": "If we imagine one hand writing upon the surface of the Mystic Writing-Pad while another periodically raises its covering sheet from the wax slab, we shall have a concrete representation of the way in which I tried to picture the functioning of the perceptual apparatus of our mind."[61] This two-handed operation involves *at once* inscription and erasure, memory and repression. The writing pad preserves, as indentation in the wax and as "writing" on the bottom layer of a waxed sheet, a trace of what it has inscribed. This trace registers an inscription that can be read only when the sheet is pulled up, that is, when it is "erased." The paper exposes a double inscription: on one side it preserves the indentations of the writing instrument and on the other a bas-relief of the ridges made on the wax slab appears. Moreover, the writing on the underside is a negative of the top writing: it can be read only "backward."

Conceived in this way, psychic lettering is not just a reservoir of effects, a kind of affectional dictionary whose meanings can be determined, but a textual space in which the materiality of "letters" form part of their "meaning." Without losing sight of Freud's important discovery of a scriptural metaphor for simultaneous memory and repression of percepta, we must not take the mystic writing pad too literally as a model of psychic structures. The slate writing, for example, does not adequately inscribe the relation of unconscious/conscious language orders, which do not condition each other in a one-to-one way. Certainly, they do not function as reversed images of each other. Although their laws are similar, as Lacan has demonstrated, each order is a closed system with its own logic.[62]

Freud's model is significant, however, as a metaphor not only of psychic textuality but of psychic *textures*. It models a materiality to psychic life not fully accounted for by Lacan's theories. Derrida returns to Freud's "scene of writing" to discover the production of psychic material. Materiality does not suggest identity-as-essence or matter, however: the trace is graphic but not graphite. It opens a relational system of impression and erasure, points of contact and interruption through which the subject both perceives and loses itself that is both spatial and temporal. Within the hieroglyphic structure of this grammatological practice, writing traces the outer/inner limits of subjectivity, its vanishing point marked by a trace—what is "recorded" when speech fails, for example. This trace (knot, pathway, temporal break, spatial elision, or layering) is the mark of a structure that does not discount its own material representation. Thus Derrida dreams of a psychoanalytic graphology that would analyze "the forms of signs, even within phonetic writing, the cathexes of gestures, and of movements, of letters, lines, points, the elements of the writing apparatus (instrument, surface substances, etc.)" (*SW*, pp. 230–31). The texts I examine incorporate these textual elements, which mark what of subjectivity is lost to representation: the pathways of Lacan's "letters," the collapsed structure of *la-langue*, or the categorical destruction of "The woman" cannot be accounted for by the image. Indeed, they are precisely what escapes it.

Writing provides a time and space for the unrepresentable within the psychic account, and thereby stages Desire and *jouissance*. Lacan describes Desire as the "remainder" of the subject, constituted as an unmet satisfaction which has no content. In mathematical terms, Desire is the zero, a place that is both constitutive of the numerical chain and empty.[63] If Desire is "empty," graphically portrayed as a space of writing, woman's supplementary *jouissance* produces an excessive unsignifying. The force of its production (*jouissance* is violent) cannot, however, be hermeneutically accounted for within the terms of the phallic signifying system.[64] Rather like a tourist in an unfamiliar country, Lacan was left to point to an image of *jouissance* in the ecstacy of St. Teresa as sculpted by Bernini.[65] But what escapes this image of feminine sexuality as sainthood, *lalangue* as swooning excess? Jacqueline Rose remarks that the supplementary "beyond" of feminine sexuality or mystic sainthood refers at once to [woman's] most total mystification as absolute Other (and, hence, nothing other than other), and to a *question*, the question of her own *jouissance*, of her greater or lesser access to the *residue of the dialectic* [emphasis added] to which she is constantly subjected."[66] How might we trace this *jouis-sens*, the pathway of orgasmic, ecstatic "sense" that is the residue of *jouissance*? How do we account for the "residue," remainder (*ce qui reste*) of subjectivity without constructing it as *imago*, icon, or statue, or thinking of it as an essence, an elixir of "truth"? Kristeva tries to come to terms with similar questions when she examines the reactivation of semiotic residues within textuality—positing the body as a site of signification. How the body comes to signify is the subject of the next chapter.

CHAPTER 2

Signifying the Body Feminine

*In "woman" I see something that cannot be represented, something that is
not said, something above and beyond nomenclatures and ideologies.*
                    Julia Kristeva, *"Woman Can Never Be Defined"*

*The opposition between feminine and masculine does not exist in pre-
Oedipality. And Kristeva knows this as well as anybody. Any strengthening
of the semiotic, which knows no sexual difference, must therefore lead to a
weakening of traditional gender divisions, and not at all to a reinforcement
of traditional notions of "femininity."*
                    Toril Moi, Sexual/Textual Politics[1]

On the conflicted ground of representation, "woman-in-the-
feminine" stands at the crossroads of the psychic and the textual,
its "-feminine" a silent reminder of what remains to be analyzed.
Julia Kristeva's work prepares the ground for such analysis by
theorizing signifying processes that take into account both the
speaking subject (the subject of psychoanalysis) and aesthetic,
textual productions (text-as-practice). The construction of the
body within signifying processes is a central focus of this text/
analysis. But it is the role played by the gendered body within
Kristeva's theory of signification that most troubles feminist criticism. I want to examine some confusions surrounding these issues, focusing on her formulation of the semiotic/symbolic processes as textual and material relations for which metaphors of
the female body are both instructive and cautionary. As in the
previous chapter, I stress the process of (en)gendering subjectivity because this represents, practically speaking, the site of
greatest blindness to psychosexual-textual theories.

Kristeva comments that "the symbolic order is assured as soon
as there are images which secure unfailing belief, for belief is

in itself the image: both arise out of the same procedures and through the same terms: *memory, sight and love.*"[2] That is, the symbolic secures the image as fantasy. One such fantasy, a powerful version of woman-in-the-feminine, is the phallic mother; another is the mute feminine deity. Kristeva has squarely faced these disturbing fantasies of woman in her recent work. In Jacqueline Rose's words, she has come "face to face with . . . the most grotesque and fully cultural stereotypes of femininity."[3] My interest is in what these fantasies exclude or attempt to hide, and here Kristeva's earlier work on semiotic and symbolic structures is particularly helpful. It examines the contradictory positioning of the subject between the Law of the Phallus/Law of Genre, which institutes subjectivity, and the heterogeneous, subversive semiotic forces that try to overturn the law by tearing at its material fabric—the body, site of signification. Kristeva returns to Freudian drive theory to discover how/why biological drives turn against symbolic signifying structures, upsetting their ordering principles and mutilating their material fabrications. The question of initial importance to her work, the role of semiotic processes in the creation of "poetic language" or text-as-practice, can be reframed from the perspective of her later work on destructive fantasies of the feminine linked to the pre-Oedipal mother: what role does the psychosexual construction of gender play in poetic language? That is, is gender at work in the text-as-practice? This question requires a reexamination of Kristeva's theory of subjectivity, with particular attention to its own textual structure. She explains that fantasies, which are grounded in sight and images, articulate the autoerotic body of infanthood to the specularized narcissistic order of the symbolic, initiated at the mirror stage when the child's body is revealed not only as an object of its own speculation but also as a viewing subject that can return (to itself) the gaze.[4] The semiotic unsettles—and in psychosis actually dismantles—the privileged order of symbolic signification, the domain of propositions, positions, and judgment. It challenges the *Aufhebung*, or sublation, that installs the phallic signifier. The semiotic represents all that the symbolic cannot order according to its terms, what is excluded (and therefore necessary) to its founding principles. The semiotic is not, however, a separate discursive place in which an alternative symbolic order (feminine, rather than masculine, for instance) might establish itself. It cannot signify *as such* but operates within and through the symbolic, from which it cannot be disengaged. Neither is the semiotic an Imaginary space; indeed, it localizes drive energies that challenge the governing *imago* of the symbolic. The semiotic is destructive of the symbolic, surging against the bond between language and the *imago* that was forged during the mirror stage. Kristeva writes: "In 'artistic' practices the semiotic—the precondition of the symbolic—is revealed as that which also destroys the symbolic, and this revelation allows us to presume something about its functioning" (*R*, p. 50). This "functioning" offers itself to analysis in the psychoanalytic setting and to "practice" or "work" in the text.

The relation of the semiotic to the symbolic is one of the most difficult and least understood areas of Kristeva's work, particularly within the terms of her revision of (but also dependence on) Lacan's categories: Real, Symbolic, Imaginary. The relation is neither binary nor hierarchical; neither can the semiotic be termed "feminine" and the symbolic "masculine," although critics often rely on this shorthand (I do so myself from time to time). While her work is strongly influenced by André Green, Kristeva is more strictly Lacanian than she sometimes appears to be. As it operates within the symbolic, the semiotic is something like the "Other within," and its Otherness—following Lacan—is doubled: primary repression (the basis for which the semiotic and symbolic can come into being) creates the (m)Other, whose effects are Lacan's "letters"; the Other, a more diverse and fully social-historical structure, appears with secondary repression (which cannot come into being without primary repression) at the close of the mirror stage.

Because the semiotic exists within the unconscious, the subject cannot have direct access to it. Its work within the symbolic, however, suggests the very failure of the symbolic to order entirely the subject's universe and to assume an omniscient, all-powerful status. The semiotic is a necessary (and unavoidable) remnant of an archaic state prior to gender, anterior to sexual difference and the entrance into subjectivity. While we may describe its effects as "feminine," they appear so only from the perspective of gendered subjectivity as it is socially, culturally, and historically defined—that is, under the terms of patriarchy at any moment in history.

It is when we come to the role of Lacan's Imaginary in the construction of subjectivity and its relation to the semiotic (in Kristeva's terms) or the unconscious (in Freud's terms) that we feel caught in contradictions and confusions. The semiotic is not equivalent to Lacan's Imaginary, nor is the unconscious co-extensive with the Imaginary. The Imaginary, a more fully conscious state working in conjunction with the Symbolic, draws on semiotic material that then attacks the reigning *imago* of the Imaginary, an *imago* that reflects social-cultural values and priorities, including the primacy of vision. Luce Irigaray's critique of the gaze, especially its place in the hierarchical ordering of the senses and its role in reflecting self-sameness and organizing sexual difference, illuminates the presumed power of sight within the psychoanalytic setting. Irigaray's critique of Freud against (but also by way of) Lacan overlooks crucial differences in their descriptions of how vision/image/gaze work in the construction of sexual difference. Like Freud, Irigaray assumes castration to be an effect of sight: the boy sees the absence of a penis on the girl's body; the girl realizes the boy has an anatomical part she is missing.

Lacan's return to Freud, however, constitutes a radical revision of Freud's explanation of how gender identity comes about and— more important for feminist readings of psychosexuality—how it is that female/feminine comes to signify lack and absence, male/ masculine to signify plenitude and power. Lacan argues against the anatomical equivalence between female and feminine, male and masculine; he argues against the idea that subjects can be "gendered" prior to the mirror stage. These two claims constitute areas of greatest resistance to Lacan's work, especially by feminists. Irigaray's critique of the gaze takes perhaps too literally an apparent one-for-one relation of biological sex and social definition of gender; for her the gaze both constructs gender (it registers Real differences between the sexes) and orders social priorities (boys, because they have a visible sex organ have social-sexual power; because girls' sexual organs cannot [yet] be seen, they are presumed to be lacking). The gaze in Lacan's work has a quite different meaning and status than it holds in Irigaray's analysis, and the mirror stage has nothing to do with girls' and boys' recognizing anatomical differences between their bodies. In Irigaray's model, only girls suffer castration (while boys fear it); in Lacan's model, both girls and boys suffer castration as the mark of their accession to subjectivity, the symbolic, and language.[5]

Kristeva's work puts greater emphasis on the relation of body to psyche, body to text, than does Lacan's, but she rarely departs from his assumptions about psychic structures and the process by which infants enter into subjectivity. Her most important contribution to psychoanalytic discourse is her theory of the semiotic and its relation to drives and primary processes; in this she makes her own return to Freud, to an area that Lacan tended to disregard. An organization of primary processes and drive energies within the body, the semiotic encompasses "species memory" and "bio-energetic neuron maps."[6] When these energies are expended textually, they mark poetic language with archaic inscriptions of the body. These traces, which open outward to a radical, primordial otherness that cannot be fully incorporated within the symbolic, signify differences among natal organ systems and body parts. They are traces of the *experience* of differentiation, which is intimately and immediately tactile (the feel of another's skin, temperature changes outside the womb), olfactory (odor of the mother's body, which the infant can correctly identify within seven days of birth), gustatory (saliva, milk), and rhythmic (sucking). These "residues of first symbolization," as Lacan refers to them, attack the signifying forms that would assimilate them (*R*, p. 49). They tear at the image-order of language and try to dismantle the rhetorical-grammatical structures that support it.

Tracing the etymology of "semiotic" to its Greek root, Kristeva focuses on the ability of the semiotic to dispose drive energies by displacement and condensation of the primary processes:

σημεῖον = distinctive mark, trace, index, precursory sign, proof, engraved or written sign, imprint, trace, figuration. This etymological reminder would be a mere archaeological embellishment (and an unconvincing one at that, since the term ultimately encompasses such disparate meanings) were it not for the fact that the preponderant etymological use of the word, the one that implies a *distinctiveness*, allows us to connect it to a precise modality in the signifying process. This modality is the one Freudian psychoanalysis points to in postulating not only the *facilitation* and the structuring *disposition* of drives, but also the so-called *primary processes* which displace and condense both energies and their inscription. Discrete quantities of energy move through the body of the subject who is not yet constituted as such and, in the course of his development, they are arranged according to the various constraints imposed on this body—always already involved in a semiotic process—by family and social structures. [*R,* p. 25; emphasis in original]

Note that the semiotic is already inscribed, organized as "constraints imposed on this body . . . by family and social structures." That is, the semiotic mediates "species memory" and is mediated by the infant's social and historical context.[7] She agrees with Lacan, then, that the structure of representation is already at work in the drive as a distancing and reference to the Other.[8] The semiotic organization does not display, of course, subject-object spatialization; it constitutes instead a psychosomatic modality that organizes relations among body parts and family members (*R,* pp. 28–29). This is not yet topological space; consequently, when the semiotic surges against the symbolic within the artistic text, it reorganizes symbolic spatiality. (The changes it effects are discussed below.)

For Kristeva, language is a defensive construction, and its poetic "distortions" are the effects of attacks by drive residues. To a greater degree than Lacan, she insists on the physiological energy bases of semiotic materials within the historical/social framework of the biological:

As a precondition to the symbolic, semiotic functioning is a fairly rudimentary combinatorial system [Lacan's "letters"], which will become more complex only after the break in the symbolic. It is, however, already put in place by a biological setup and is always already social and therefore historical. This semiotic functioning is discernible before the mirror stage, before the first suggestion of the thetic [the structuring division of semiotic/symbolic]. But the semiotic we find in signifying practices always comes to us *after the symbolic thesis,* after the symbolic break, and can be analyzed in psychoanalytic discourse as well as in so-called "artistic" practice. . . . The thetic gathers up these facilitations and instinctual semiotic stases within the positing of signifiers, then opens them out in the three-part cluster of referent, signified, and signifier, which alone makes the enunciation of a truth possible. In taking the thetic into account, we shall have to represent the semiotic (*which is produced recursively on the basis of that break*) as a "second" return of instinctual functioning within the symbolic, as a negativity introduced into the symbolic order, and as the transgression of that order. [*R,* pp. 68–69; emphasis added]

The "biological setup" to which Kristeva refers includes the oral, anal, scopic, and invocatory drives; the infant experiences the social structure into which it is born by way of the senses, "taking in" an outside world that it initially experiences as part of its own yet-to-be-distinguished "self."

Although it appears that Kristeva theorizes a binary model of the psyche, the symbolic and semiotic are co-dependent, conditioning each other. The predominance of the symbolic over the semiotic is tenuous and constantly renegotiated. Her work repeatedly emphasizes that the symbolic is not monolithic and unitary but rather unstable and shifting, shot through by the effects of the "semiotic." The thetic, a permeable psychic boundary created within and from the symbolic to form an internal border with the semiotic, de-centers the familiar binarism of the Freud-Lacan model. The thetic does not add another "layer" to the psychic construct but rather redefines the relation of the subject to the symbolic order. Acting to sustain subjectivity, and therefore allied to the necessary repressions that create the possibility of subjectivity, the thetic signifies both rupture and boundary. More a filter than a prophylactic barrier, it sustains the symbolic against semiotic drives that would destroy it.

Crucial to the semiotic/symbolic relation, the thetic is one of the least understood aspects of Kristevan theory, perhaps because it gives itself both to temporal and spatial metaphors: it is a phase that occurs toward the end of the mirror stage and involves the splitting or cutting (*coupure*) of the semiotic *chora*, and it is a boundary marker created as an effect of Castration, or secondary repression (*R*, p. 43). Positing the subject as thesis or judgment, the thetic is not guaranteed or established once and for all time but is constantly reproduced within subjectivity. As the place where psychosexuality announces itself according to the Law of Genre, the thetic posits a horizon of sexual identity. The signifying process, therefore, involves a continual crossing/rupturing of this boundary (*R*, p. 79). I want to examine this process in some detail because it bears on the textual work of the semiotic.

The thetic depends on two forms of repression. Primary repression, which takes place at the beginning of the mirror stage, creates the unconscious by repressing *representations* of desire for the mother, fragments and part-objects of the body, sensory impressions of the world recorded as the "letters" already inscribed in the pre-Oedipal period. Kristeva emphasizes the role of primary processes in creating semiotic material that undergoes repression. As we have already seen, the pre-Oedipal, pre-mirror stage infant experiences itself as coextensive with the mother. This state of apparent at-oneness with the mother is thrown into crisis when the child misapprehends itself as separate, whole, complete, and in control of itself. The joy (*jouissance*) in discovering separation and difference is coupled with pain in the loss of an Imaginary identification with the mother. In order to become a subject, however, the child must experience this pain of separation and absence. This is achieved through realization of a spatial ordering that is at the heart of signification.[9]

Secondary repression, which is directly involved in establishing the thetic, has to do with the Desire of the Other operating within the unconscious. It is achieved through Castration, understood not as the feared loss of the penis but the intervention of the phallic signifier (the Name of the Father), which allows the child to posit itself within the symbolic and enter language. Secondary repression sets the conscious-unconscious in place, thereby securing the structural apparatus of the symbolic-semiotic. The second repression hides the first, necessary repression on which it is founded: the world of false, mirror-stage dualities is taken literally by the child, who of course does not realize that the construction of mirroring effects depends on the primary repression of (m)Other representations. Thus the ego or *moi* (signified by the pronomial forms "you" and "me") is constructed as a defense against the alien being reflected back to the child through others.

In order to function fully within language, however, the child must come into a triangular structure ("I, me, she/he/it" pronomials), which the phallic signifier opens up as it traverses the mother-child relation. That is, secondary repression provides for the thetic instance, without being coextensive with it: the thetic secures the relational forms of subjectivity (first-, second-, and third-person pronomials) by separating the subject from images (including the false mirror image) and objects.[10] Kristeva comments that the thetic phase "posits the gap between the signifier and the signified as an opening up toward every desire but also every act, including the very jouissance that exceeds them" (*R*, p. 47). Although Castration "transfers semiotic motility onto the symbolic order" (*R*, p. 47), there are residues of first symbolizations that resist transference because repression can never be complete (if it were, it would fully block the semiotic, and symbolization could not take place). These residues not only announce an Other order but implement it through linguistic effects—phonological patterns, rhythms, pronomial shifts, silences, grammatical gaps, disruptions, and syntactical overlaps, among many other "disruptions." Jacqueline Rose comments that these effects give evidence of "the subject's difficult passage into the proper order of language."[11] But this statement hardly suggests the violence and volatility at work in semiotic irruptions within the symbolic: what is at stake is the "life" of the subject as subject.

Kristeva argues that language both derives from the death drive and is a defense against it, warding off its attacks by situating the signifier in the body (*R*, p. 49).[12] The subject is "subject to" death.[13] The most instinctual of the drives, the death drive threatens thetic foreclosure (psychosis, schizophrenia). Poetic language, however, offers a special textual case in which the attacks do not result in psychosis but lead to what Kristeva calls a "second-degree thetic." The precondition for the thetic, the semiotic "pulverizes" the thetic in poetic language but does not destroy it (*R*, pp. 50, 51). This function does not constitute an intellectual acceptance of necessary repression but is rather an "affective process," an attachment onto the signifier of what remains outside the symbolic order. What remains outside (not subject to) the symbolic are "instinctual, corporeal foundations stemming from the concrete history of the concrete (biological, familial, social) subject" (*R*, p. 162). The death drive withdraws this material from the unconscious and introduces it into the symbolic order as the transgression of the symbolic, where it "*takes up a position as already positivized and erotized in a language* that, through drive investment, is organized into prosody or rhythmic timbres" (*R*, p. 163; emphasis in original).[14] That is, it does not appear as "content" (idea or image) but as movement.

This movement should not be confused with repetition compulsion, a return of the repressed in the psychoanalytic sense (*R*, pp. 159–60).[15] Indeed, it is a return of that which *cannot be* repressed: the semiotic residues have not been sublated into the symbolic. Kristeva emphasizes that any effort to sublate the semiotic onto a pure signifier always leaves a remainder (*R*, p. 51). These repeated returns, in fact, oppose repression, "reintroducing 'free energy' into 'bound energy'" (*R*, p. 161). She argues that the poetic subject, unlike the speaking subject of psychoanalysis, is not a subject of the unconscious (*R*, p. 164). Consequently, the text-as-practice "has no unconscious" (*R*, pp. 160–61). Whereas in psychosis residues of drive energy work on and in the body, in artistic practice they are available as a text that batters and fragments the totality of the object of speculation and representation. This special kind of text constitutes a performance that destroys "narrative and metalanguage, with all their lock-step univocal seriousness" and "tear[s] the veil of representation to find the material signifying process" (*R*, p. 103). As it explodes the symbolic and expulses unbound semiotic energies, it of necessity acts "with reference to a moment of stasis, a boundary, a symbolic barrier" (*R*, p. 102). This stasis/boundary (both temporal and spatial) is the thetic that preserves and (temporarily) undoes the primacy of the symbolic system.[16] Without this boundary, Kristeva explains, "the process would never become a practice and would founder instead in an opaque and unconscious organicity" (*R*, p. 102).

The poetic text-as-practice represents an expenditure of energy charges transferred not as content but as the economy or movement of rejection (negativity, the death drive) that works "on and in the very place of symbolic and social censorship" and is "discernible through the *positions* that absorb and camouflage it" (*R*, p. 164, 123; emphasis in original).[17] We can know of the semiotic only through the symbolic where the movement of nonsymbolized semiotic negativity is felt as pressure or pulsion and registered as rhythm. Note that this force has a tacticity that can be recorded textually, as spacing or the disturbance of syntactic/grammatical forms (I will return to this point in a moment). Note also that semiotic negativity, when transferred to the symbolic, is positivized. To understand how this works, we must return to Lacan's earlier claim that when the death drive withdraws from the unconscious, it "takes up a position as already positivized and erotized in language" (*R*, p. 163). The semiotic negativity that attacks and reorganizes the symbolic is a residue of early corporeal inscriptions of differentiation, the distinction of body parts (prior to and different from the body as image/object in the mirror stage), "scissions" of matter that cannot be brought into the visual order. Moreover, these semiotic processes already participate in oppositional orders (pleasure and pain, positive and negative) that the child experiences synesthetically.

Lacan speculated that adult sexual pleasure is, in Ragland-Sullivan's words, "first inscribed at the instant of lived pleasure, at the edges (*bords*) which originally demarcated each erotogenic zone of 'difference'" within the infant's body.[18] He followed Freud's notion that body orifices, especially the mouth and anus, produce pleasure. Kristeva discusses these sites in relation to the necessary positing of the body as an object, a "detached alterity," that takes place at the mirror stage and sets up the symbolic. She argues that the "loss" or primary repression necessary to establishing the symbolic order is already prefigured as both pain and pleasure in the physiological processes of ingesting and expulsing food through the alimentary system. Thus these body orifices are sites of pleasure and aggressivity, or aggression *as* pleasure, what she calls "the jouissance of destruction" (*R*, p. 150), and the synesthesia of their affects (pleasure experienced as pain, and vice versa) will later operate within the textual semiotic as it attacks, and tries to shatter, the reigning order of *imago*. This activity bears on the thetic as rupture, but the passage of the death drive through the thetic positivizes negativity and also preserves the thetic as an internal horizon of identity.

Claiming that "the literary function subverts the symbolic function," Kristeva stresses that, while psychoanalysis "may speak of fantasies in literature, it never mentions the economy of the subject bound up with those fantasies that dissolves the symbolic and language" (*R*, p. 149). That is, psychoanalysis overlooks the *jouissance* harbored by aggression, a *jouissance* of the death drive, which in pre-Oedipality is apparent in oral, muscular, urethral, and anal aggressivity (*R*, p. 150). Among these drives, anality is the last to be sublimated and is, therefore, the most important precondition for the subject-object relation set up at the mirror stage. Language acquisition depends on the suppression of anality "through the definitive attachment of the rejected object [feces], through its repression under the sign" (*R*, p. 152).

But of all the drives, anality displays the highest degree of aggressivity (the sadism that, according to Freud, derives from the death drive), and returns with greatest force to produce textual effects. It returns as pain positivized as pleasure whose organization is already in place in the pre-mirror stage when

> energy surges and discharges erotize the glottic, urethral and anal sphincters as well as the kinetic system. These drives move through the sphincters and arouse pleasure at the very moment substances belonging to the body are separated and rejected from the body. This acute pleasure therefore coincides with a loss, a separation from the body, and the isolating of objects outside it. Before the body itself is posited as a detached alterity, and hence the real object, this expulsion of objects is the subject's fundamental experience of separation—a separation which is not a lack, but a discharge, and which, although privative, arouses pleasure. [*R*, p. 151]

While the force of expulsion can produce an irreparable violence that prevents formation of the symbolic (child schizophrenia), it can also be a mechanism of reactivation, especially when it is coupled with oralization (*R*, p. 153).

Before exploring the implications of anality-orality for the textual subject, I want to underscore the most important conclusions to be drawn from Kristeva's observations. First, psychoanalytic theory overlooks the challenge that the literary, textual function makes to the symbolic. Second, in theorizing the symbolic function, psychoanalysis represses the pleasure bound up with the aggressivity within expulsion (rejection) and objectification necessary to the symbolic. Because this aggressivity-pleasure (sadistic eroticism) is imprinted on the body, it can never fully be repressed. A residual force, it is by definition excessive, unbound energy that returns to attack the symbolic function that would repress it (and in so doing, it renews itself). It signals a *jouissance* of destruction that is positivized, turned to aesthetic pleasure by way of the thetic that it "pulverizes." There is a crucial (but often overlooked) connection between psychoanalysis' silence on literary subversions of the symbolic and the symbolic repression of pleasure associated with drive aggressivity. The "economy of the subject" bound up with literary fantasies is an economy of the senses that the fantasy-as-image must suppress in order to sustain itself. Specific forms of pleasure are repressed by the symbolic: the tactile, gustatory, and (more ephemerally because it is entirely unbound from muscular constrictions) the olfactory sensory experiences of the oral, anal, muscular, and urethral mechanisms. Inscribed on the infant's body as "letters," these sensory experiences will be marshaled under the visual order of the symbolic—but never completely or successfully, and not without a certain libidinal violence.

How does the poetic text "affirm" the negativity of drive attacks (rejection, destruction) and keep it from being suppressed under "paranoid paternal unity"? Kristeva locates two modalities—oralization and homosexual phratry, the "poetic" and "mastering" aspects of textuality—that carry out this signifying process. She describes oralization as "a reunion with the mother's body, which is no longer viewed as an engendering, hollow, and vaginated, expelling and rejecting body, but rather as a vocalic one—throat, voice, and breasts: music, rhythm, prosody, paragrams, and the matrix of the prophetic parabola," while the second, "always inseparable from the first," is the "reunion with brothers' bodies," a "reconstitution of a *homosexual phratry* that will forever pursue, tirelessly and interminably, the murder of the One, the Father, in order to impose *one* logic, *one* ethics, *one* signified" (*R*, p. 153).[19] Rather than two sides of the textual coin, these modalities are seamed, like the symbolic and semiotic: the " 'mastering' modality is a lining of the first, 'poetic' modality" (*R*, p. 153).

Kristeva argues that oralization is a "mediator" between the "sadism of rejection and its signifying sublimation" and that its pleasure "combats the superego and its linear language" (*R*, pp. 153–54). Registered in the body as gesture (the infant's burrowing movement toward the mother's body or the rotating movement of the baby's head that accepts or rejects the breast), oralization operates in the text as the breakup of subject/predicate sequences, redistribution of the phonematic order, syntactical and morphological changes. Proceeding from an eroticization of the oral cavity, this modality is most easily observed in sounds and rhythms (indeed, this is where Kristeva places the emphasis of her textual analysis). But oralization reorders textual spatiality, subverting the distance and separation between object and subject, word and thing, on which the symbolic is premised.[20]

Concluding that the signifying process "straddl[es] the corporeal and natural on the one hand, the symbolic and social on the other" (*R*, p. 155), Kristeva draws a closer relation between the body and signifying practices than either Freud or Lacan, reading the structure of symbolization in physiological processes. She does not claim, however, that we can have direct access to the body (even our own), unmediated by language and culture; rather, she articulates *how* language and culture mediate the body. Interestingly, the model she sketches for the signifying system is drawn from the body itself, not in a metaphorical sense but in the very operations of its material energies. In the next section of this chapter, I suggest that the maternal might provide a structural dynamic for her theory of psychic processes—the semiotic/symbolic/thetic. Unlike Freud, who was eager to discover an apparatus that could materially convey his theory of how percepta were psychically registered, or Lacan, who has pictured the Imaginary, Symbolic, and Real orders in graphs, sketches, and mathematical formulas, Kristeva has avoided trying to construct a textual model of the psyche. All the more surprising, since textuality provides a primary focus of her analysis. She examines closely, of course, the ideational content of the maternal body as it symbolizes femininity and sexual difference for our culture. But within the context of her own work, the predictable thematic elements of the maternal metaphor are less interesting than its structure, which repeats a corporeal, textual figure. That is, the maternal metaphor can be seen as both a static icon and a dynamic, productive signifying system. The semiotization of the maternal body opens a space between "maternal" and "metaphor." My question is: what occupies this space?

-❧-

THE MOTHER, TOO, IS A METAPHOR.
HÉLÈNE CIXOUS, "THE LAUGH OF THE MEDUSA"

Through a body, destined to insure reproduction of the species, the woman-subject, although under the sway of the paternal function (as symbolizing, speaking subject and like all others), more of a filter *than anyone else—a*

thoroughfare, a threshold where "nature" confronts "culture." To imagine
there is someone in that filter—such is the source of religious mystifications,
the font that nourishes them: the fantasy of the so-called "Phallic" Mother.
Kristeva, Desire in Language [21]

The maternal metaphor within Kristevan theory and the role of the mother-child dynamic within the relation of "maternal" and "metaphor" are fundamentally contested issues for feminist critics, especially as they figure with respect to another metaphor, the semiotic. While Kristeva has never *theorized* a gendered semiotic or claimed that it recognizes sexual difference, she has, as Jacqueline Rose observes, attributed to it "femininity, colour, music, body and affect—concepts whose oppressive lyricism has at times been welcomed by feminism but which feminism has been quickest to reject." [22] That is, Kristeva has metaphorized the semiotic as "maternal territory," and this metaphor of the maternal has opened the way to fantasies of "a centripetal, becalmed and softened feminine sexuality." [23] At the same time, as we have just witnessed, she imputes to the semiotic aggressive powers that attack the symbolic. Through the signifying modality of oralization (textualized as a form of speaking in tongues, an exploration of infantile regression), the maternal mediates aggressivity and pleasure by opening onto both sides of this threshold: devouring and rejecting, fusing and expelling; a *jouissance* that tips into pain and pleasure, both phallic and beyond the phallic. As an analyst, Kristeva acknowledges pain and pleasure as two "brinks" for the speaking subject: pain provides a certain security, "caused as one recognizes oneself as subject of (others') discourse, hence tributary of a universal Law"; pleasure "kills" by exposing the subject "to the black thrusts of a desire that borders on idiolect and aphasia" (*D*, p. x).

Two points must be made at the outset. First, Kristeva remains a strict Lacanian in repeating the claim that *all* subjects are positioned in relation to the phallus. Within the Imaginary of cultural fantasy, which is a familial structure, the infant is positioned by the phallic mother. [24] Kristeva examines how sexual identity is established in relation to the *mother's* attitude toward the phallic, how she both represents the Symbolic order for the child and symbolizes the lost archaic territory that becomes the unconscious, how her body (i.e., voice and eye introjected as (m)Other) structures the unconscious. Not to confront the "phallic" in the mother, internalized and therefore part of her, is to risk loss of identity. Not to confront the "mother" in the phallic, "woman-in-the-feminine" and all that it represses, is to lose access to the place where, Kristeva claims, "rhythm stops and identity is constituted."[25] That is, the child must recognize Other's Desire operating within the mother who remains, in some significant degree, unaware of its operations.[26]

Second, Kristeva is explicit about the relation of the body to signification. The semiotic does not represent an unmediated experience of the body. Idealizing an unmediated relation to the mother's body produces fantasies—which are, of course, mediations. Moreover, these fantasies construct the cultural woman-in-the-feminine and account for the traditional images of women in even the most semiotically charged writings. Toril Moi underscores Kristeva's insistence that "idealisation of the semiotic in itself involves a denial or cover up of the psychic pain and violence which in fact characterises the early interaction between the mother and child."[27] The space of difference between "maternal" and "metaphor" is the symbolic.[28] After mirror stage Castration, enforced by the Law of the Phallus and secured by the Name of the Father, there is no place *other* than the symbolic. The maternal metaphor itself blocks the dream (or nightmare) of at-one-ment with the mother. Unmediated access to the mother is not available, even in psychosis: the mother who "screens" the unconscious cannot be (re)possessed, Kristeva writes (*D*, p. 241). What is erected in this place of foreclosure is an *image* of the Mother: "for women, a paradise lost but seemingly close at hand, for men, a hidden god but constantly present through occult fantasy" (*D*, p. 240). On this side of psychosis, "the maternal body [is] a screen against the plunge" (*D*, p. 240).

Reference to psychosis reminds us of the fragile purchase we all have on subjectivity. A central concern of Kristeva's work is the relation of subjectivity to motherhood as it is haunted by the specter of psychosis: she claims that the image of motherhood wards off psychosis and that maternity is a special, culturally approved instance of "psychosis" that reenters the secret, guarded territory of the archaic mother in order to produce the baby, signifier of the mother's desire for the phallic (*D*, p. 238, 241). Arguing that pregnancy is perceived by society as a form of *jouissance* that must be kept within the phallic order (Christian theology represents an especially harsh enforcement of the symbolic), Kristeva examines the cultural appropriation of motherhood as the sine qua non of woman-in-the-feminine, the phallic signifier engendered. This analysis risks being misread as yet another inscription of the phallic order (woman's production as reproduction) rather than a description of how the phallic order is set in place and by what laws and mechanisms its orders subjectivity.[29] Kristeva emphasizes the mediating role of social reality, which both constrains and maintains subjectivity, when she writes that the mother's body becomes "the place of a splitting, which even though hypostatized by Christianity, nonetheless remains a constant factor of social reality" (*D*, pp. 240, 238). As we know, this "splitting" is part of the biological process of pregnancy, but it also represents the split in subjectivity that is figured by the body. I believe that the physiological process of maternity offers a productive figure for the psychic relation of semiotic and symbolic as a material text, a mediation that Kristeva's work hints at but never fully expresses.

According to Kristeva, the energies that rise in poetic language expel the semiotic within the symbolic, art forms perhaps providing a buffer against the fall into psychosis that splits the thetic boundary. While women and men create poetic texts that register the semiotic (and it is indeed unfortunate that Kristeva does not analyze representative writing by women), women *also* have special access to the "strange form of split symbolization" in the biological instance of reproduction. The maternal body appears to reenact in its materiality the semiotic-symbolic process; Kristeva claims that "the maternal body is the module of a bio-social program" (*D*, p. 241). As such, this body replicates the fantasy of the phallic signifer reproduced as the baby, the mother swollen with the phallus, the Virgin swollen with God's Word. Man erects these images against his fear of death, his fear of phallic loss.

My point is that maternity does not replace women's access to semiotic-symbolic expression but instead *supplements* it, giving it another expression. This "Other expression" is the *jouissance* that saints and psychotics so adore and fear, and it explains why woman-in-the-maternal so often represents woman-in-the-feminine. Naomi Schor emphasizes (perhaps too strongly) one aspect of the seamed relation between the semiotic and symbolic when she writes that "Kristeva proclaims the indelible imprint of the body on or in language."[30] The Real body is available to us only through the symbolic, which is constructed on the semiotic base of experiences that are already *inscriptions* of the body. Kristeva stresses that the semiotic is always social-historical and that its biological components (e.g., drive energies) are always already inscriptions. It is not the body that imprints language, but rather language that imprints the body through a double process of inscription.[31] Representation struggles to conceal the fact that we cannot *see* a Female-Real except in pregnancy, which accounts for the Catholic church's consecration of "maternality" and the predominance of mother-child iconography. In the Real world (not to be confused with mediated "reality"), artist and citizen continually stumble against the mysterious materiality of maternity. Pregnancy is the meeting point of the Real and the Imaginary in our culture, a place Kristeva illuminates in her discussions of the Holy Mother, pregnant with the Word of God (her body a text, her baby the Word incarnate) and artistic representations of the Virgin and child. She discovers, however, that these works are radiated by *jouissance* that escapes representative forms; the residue of the semiotic that cannot be transported onto the transcendental signifier reorganizes the textual space of the paintings. It points to a Real that is elsewhere, to another female body that is not pregnant with the Word.

Semiotic residue signals (uncannily) the threshold where identity recedes, where subjectivity vanishes, where the sign and object are traversed. The artist seeks this *jouissance*, which exists at the threshold of primal repression where the mother stands as screen to the unconscious, as a confrontation with the unrepresentable. This *jouissance* is recorded semiotically, that is, without reference to the "object-oriented libido," which Kristeva deems masculine and which does not yet exist in the semiotic. She reads this Other scene in Bellini's paintings, so different from Leonardo da Vinci's reproductions of the phallic mother, whose passion is for "body-objects" within a "mastering" discourse of representation as primary narcissism. The Virgin mother is "master" (she has the phallus), and Leonardo's artistic discourse both worships and wants to master her mastery (this is the discourse of homosexual phratry discussed above). Bellini's painterly discourse is entirely "Other" than Leonardo's, for it registers an otherness within the Virgin that directs her gaze elsewhere than the baby, who is not imaged as an object-fetish. Bellini "represents" the Virgin's folded and unfolding subjectivity in the luminous color and light of the folds in her gown. There is a "split" in the Virgin's subjectivity that reveals itself in her averted eyes (which look nowhere in particular) and among the folds of the gown, where Kristeva reads the physiological process of splitting and dividing that creates the baby. In a word, *jouissance* as maternity.

Under the heading "spaces and glimmers," Kristeva describes the surface effects of this form of maternal *jouissance*, a pleasure/pain beyond the phallic threshold whose graphic modality is taken from the maternal gestation—cellular splitting, doubling—that produced mother and child: "splitting/laminating of the surface," "implacable fragmentation and a soft lining encompassing the fragments within two masses of luminous hues," "interplay among cutting traces," "elliptical placement of blinding flashes" (*D*, pp. 267–68). As representation is replaced by a "luminous spatialization" (what Kristeva calls the "language of jouissance"), "bodies, identities, and signs" are forgotten (*D*, p. 269). She speculates that the source of these effects can be discovered in the mirroring effect of primary repression and primary narcissism. That is, the artist does not confront an idealized archaic mother but rather an idealized *relation* to her (the primary narcissism so evident in Leonardo's work). Bellini pushes the primary repression necessary for the narcissism to its furthest limits ("beyond" the image, beyond phallic *jouissance*) in the discovery of a liminal space. This may be the "lost territory" of the cultural fantasy in which the maternal becomes the image par excellence of woman-in-the-feminine. If so, the territory is empty, no longer the space of representation (it harbors no maternal image); it is rather a nonspace of scissions and ellipses, a lamination of traces, linings, and fragmented part-objects. It is closest to that indescribable space of the semiotic *chora*, which is not to be confused with the Platonic/Freudian dark cave.[32]

The movement of Bellini's art, which (en)folds the space of

representation to suggest an outside that is inside, resembles Kristeva's description of the physiological process of pregnancy: "Cells fuse, split, and proliferate; volumes grow, tissues stretch, and body fluids change rhythm, speeding up or slowing down. Within the body, growing as a graft, indomitable, there is an other. And no one is present, within that simultaneously dual and alien space, to signify what is going on" (*D*, p. 237). A semiotic space, there is nothing (yet) here that is representable. But what if we were to think of this productive interiority in terms of its (unrepresentable) psychic counterpart, the processes by which the subject will represent itself through language? I want to suggest a dynamic liminality, a spatial-temporal threshold that is neither one nor the other, participating in both at once—a production. Certainly this does not involve the substitutionary logic of the metaphor by which we could imagine the dividing tissues of the uterus that create the placental lining to be the material equivalent of the thetic instance drawn from a psychic symbolic structure—that is, some kind of one-to-one relation between the Real and the semiotic-symbolic. I would argue for something that cannot be represented as such; it is neither an organic essentialism nor the superimposition of a model or prosthesis.[33]

The permeability of the thetic-uterine lining allows the passage of drive energies and sustaining nourishment that strengthens and revitalizes. While the lining protects a sealed and forbidden space, it supports the constant reenactment of production, a continual crossing and re-crossing of the threshold of subjectivity that allows for the re-activation of semiotic residues. The French word *enceinte* carries the double meaning of this (double) activity. As a noun, *enceinte* refers to anything that closes off a space and forbids access to it; as an adjective, *enceinte* refers to the state of pregnancy. Moreover, both meanings of the term point to a materiality, a banding (*ceindre*) that is carried by the French homophone, *ceinture*, a belt.[34] These terms are related according to the principle of *lalangue*, which Lacan insists does not mean "anything at all" but only what the principle of homophony permits.[35] In the words *enceinte* and *ceinture*, homophony and etymology join forces in a particularly productive way (note that grammatology combines both these elements in its writing practice). Most important, however, these terms offer a way of *textualizing* what is otherwise only a convergence of sound: *(en)ceinte*, pronounced like the French word *sainte*, the feminine form of saint. The uterine-thetic lining engenders a textual, almost mystical, *jouissance*.

Still, the silent "-feminine" calls out for analysis. The Holy Mother, pregnant with God's Word, is represented in/as silence. The female sexual organs are imaged as an ear (through which the Virgin is impregnated), a shell that echoes sound, and her body is dissolved into tears and milk, which, Kristeva notes, are "metaphors of nonspeech, of a 'semiotics' that linguistic communication does not account for." [36] This fantasy of the feminine exists on the other side of the psychotic split, where woman bears the hysterical word-body or raves nonsensically, laughter punctuating her insanity: here, she is a silent spasm rather than a seductive, enveloping voice. Within the uterine fold the mother experiences the division of her body into otherness as both silent and dark, which gives itself neither to ear nor eye. She experiences *en/ceinture* as tacticity, pressure that will become rhythm, that will display itself spatially across her own body-text in pregnancy (*SM*, p. 242).

Already this flesh is inscribed with the word—not the spirit of God, but the social-cultural inscription of sensory responses: the textual-tactile comes before sight and sound. Sight is the shield against death, Kristeva argues. When the veil of representation is pulled away (as it is in Bellini's paintings or in avant-garde art) it is the textual-tactile that remains of the (m)Other—sensory traces more archaic than language, semiotic residues that activate the signifying "Other" within language. They are feminine only to the extent that they are what remains when the phallic signifier uplifts the sight/site of the maternal body ("woman-in-the-feminine") into the symbolic. Returning to attack the symbolic order (they can operate only *within* the symbolic), these traces produce a violent *jouissance* of the phallic text, tearing at the representation it worships with the eye/I. It bears repeating: this is not a return of the repressed but the return of an entirely Other, unrepressed textuality, a radical heterogeneity experienced first as synesthesia and textual enfolding. It marks a return of the (m)Other by way of an artistic economy that is *beyond*, but also lodged within, the letter of the Law. The textual effects produced

by this return, a division of the (m)Other's body, are the subject
of the next section of this book, a series of readings "on the limits
of genre."

❧

AFTER SHOCKS

Never is Freud more intriguing than when he tries to convince himself and
us of something that he does not know, that is, when he begins, however
tentatively, to write fiction.
　　　　Cheryl Herr, "Fathers, Daughters, Anxiety and Fiction" [37]

Reading retrospectively, as the book-making process always
forces one to do, I have discovered radical differences of style
and analytic methods among the "body parts" of the following
chapters. These disjunctions cannot be accounted for merely
by saying that the "parts" were written at different times and
places with different audiences in mind. Such differences of tone
and reading methods give voice(s) to a complaint that reverber-
ates among feminist critics: why is it that Derrida, Lacan, and
Kristeva, for whom "the feminine" is a central and troubling
question, choose to illustrate their own analytic practices through
men's writings? Is it only, as each has said in her or his own turn,
that they draw on literature that is familiar to them, works that
have become part of the French literary tradition? This question
hides another: why is it that this enclosure within the field of
men's writings is such a troubling issue for feminists? Why do
we so desire powerful theorists and critics to read women's writings, to read *our* writings?

I must beg these questions for I do not yet have any answers,
but they are extensions of a query (which is also an accusation)
often put to me by feminists: how/why do you continue to work
on James Joyce? (Or, why do you turn to male critics to justify
your theoretical claims?) For this present study, the question
might be: why do your footnotes sometimes take issue with feminist critics while giving tacit approval to men's theories? These
kinds of questions are perhaps not surprising in a profession
where diversity and difference produce anxiety, where the scholarly tone and critical apparatus make claims to impersonal, objective authority and definitive conclusions. Ours is a profession
where women have traditionally not been empowered. Still, such

questions always stun me into silence, or leave me laughing to cover my embarrassment. They bring me up short: I have been caught (out) leading a double life, talking out of both sides of my mouth, speaking with a forked tongue.

The following chapters are about doublespeak; my analysis, perhaps appropriately, is double-voiced. The readings of texts by men are closely textual, and they build a defense network of rhetorical gestures (apostrophes, letters, footnotes) against the larger, more troubling issues of gender and writing that *The Post Card* and *Finnegans Wake* address but also skirt. My analyses of women's texts, on the other hand, open themselves to a wider range of issues (including evident feminist concerns). They also hesitate against the disturbing silence of ellipses (*Three Guineas*) or Helen's struggle to read the writing on the wall at Karnak (*Helen in Egypt*). I am uneasy on both sides of the gender/genre divide, feeling the need to justify my work on men's writings ("isn't it precisely 'the feminine' in Joyce's writings and Derrida's that carries me along," I ask myself) and the need to positivize what might be read as a negative—a fault or absence—in women's writings. Too, both sides of the divide must be theorized, accounted for in politically correct terms. But what are these "politically correct terms"? Whose politics? Whose terms? I find myself bridging women's textual silences (the signs of repression which have been read by patriarchy as empty vacuity) with more and more words. While I burrow for safety in close readings of men's texts (whom do I fear? what accusations do I turn my back against?), women's writings carry me away— on my own words.

Following the Latin root of the verb to translate, I am transported beyond rhetoric and style. To where? I cannot escape the social realm, of course, life as it is lived in the quotidien, but I am carried away on the wings of desire for a transformed society. Like Virginia Woolf at work on *Three Guineas*, I hum as my fingers tap out new rhythms, the computer sings, my heart lifts, I breathe deeply, my energy is immense, I soar, I fly away. The lid of repression is momentarily lifted and the semiotic bubbles up. (. . .) Then I hear another voice. It brings me back to earth, and I hit with a thud—winded, silenced, exhausted. Like Stephen Dedalus, I cannot fly by the nets that catch me; nor am I Helen, who was transported from Sparta to Egypt, thereby avoiding Troy. There really is no escaping the double bind in which I'm caught as woman and feminist, writer and critic.

If there is no escaping the Symbolic, which places us according to genre, is there a hope of transforming it? Freud, Lacan, and Kristeva have little to say on this question, which holds such import for feminists (among others), and Derrida pauses before the overwhelming question. The question haunts this book as it haunts our work and lives. I can only approach it with hesitancy and trepidation in the last chapter, a chapter safeguarded by an Epilogue that encloses the pathway of sexual difference(s), a pathway that intersects with (and circles back on) the fictions of discourse, narrative, genre, and social institutions.

PART II

Piece Work
Textual Body Parts

CHAPTER 3

Apostrophizing the Feminine
in *Finnegans Wake*

Apostrophe in the sense in which I will be using it involves the direct address of an absent, dead, or inanimate being by a first person speaker. . . . The absent, dead, or inanimate entity addressed is thereby made present, animate, and anthropomorphic. Apostrophe is a form of ventriloquism through which the speaker throws voice, life, and human form into the addressee, turning its silence into mute responsiveness.
Barbara Johnson, A World of Difference[1]

Finnegans Wake. Readers of Joyce's text hear in these words the absence of the apostrophe that under other circumstances would mark the possessive position of "Finnegan" in relation to "wake." Others, who are unaware of Joyce's grammatical revision, hear the apostrophe they cannot see: Finnegan's wake. Although the apostrophe cannot be enunciated, it makes itself heard. It also insists on being seen, precisely because it is not there: helpful editors and printers continue to reappropriate the apostrophe to its (appropriate) place. Indeed, the missing apostrophe of the title announces its presence and finds a life of its own against all efforts to eliminate its subversive workings in the *Wake*.

Whether as mark of grammar or rhetorical trope, apostrophe enacts a counteractive logic, a "turning away and an elision" (Greek $\pi\rho\sigma\omega\delta\iota\alpha$). Grammatically, apostrophe binds ("Finnegan's wake") and excludes ("don't"). As a rhetorical figure, it employs direct address to divert its message. Invoking the subject ("O, Eve, in evil hour thou didst give ear / To that false worm"), apostrophe turns "aside" to address another through a form of self-address.[2] In this movement, apostrophe momentarily lifts the

49

Coss? Cossist? Your parn! You, you make what name? (and in truth, as a poor soul is between shift and shift ere the death he has lived through becomes the life he is to die into, he or he had albut — he was rickets as to reasons but the balance of his minds was stables — lost himself or himself some somnione sciupiones, soswhitchoverswetch had he or he gazet, murphy come, murphy go, murphy plant, murphy grow, a maryamyriameliamurphies, in the lazily eye of his lapis,

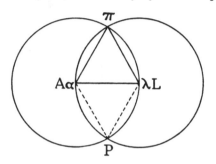

Uteralterance or the Interplay of Bones in the Womb.

Vieus Von DVbLIn, 'twas one of dozedeams a darkies ding in dewood) the Turnpike under the Great Ulm (with Mearingstone in Fore ground).[1] Given now ann linch you take enn all. Allow me! And, heaving alljawbreakical expressions out of old Sare Isaac's[2] universal of specious aristmystic unsaid, A is for Anna like L is for liv. Aha hahah, Ante Ann you're apt to ape aunty annalive! Dawn gives rise. Lo, lo, lives love! Eve takes fall. La, la, laugh leaves alass! Aiaiaiai, Antiann, we're last to the lost, Loulou! Tis perfect. Now (lens

The Vortex. Spring of Sprung Verse. The Vertex.

[1] Draumcondra's Dreamcountry where the betterlies blow.
[2] O, Laughing Sally, are we going to be toadhauntered by that old Pantifox Sir Somebody Something, Burtt, for the rest of our secret stripture?

veil of psychic repression and gives voice to intense emotion—a sigh of longing or a cry of despair. Jonathan Culler remarks that the emotional sweep of apostrophe, which "trop[es] not on the meaning of a word but on the circuit or situation of communication itself," creates a sense of embarrassment in readers. Literary critics, he writes, turn away from it "to repress [it] or rather to transform apostrophe into description. Whether this is because writing, in some innate hostility to voice, always seeks to deny or evade the vocative, it is a fact that one can read vast amounts of criticism without learning that poetry uses apostrophe repeatedly and intensely."[3]

Our embarrassment, which is neither accidental nor incidental, cannot be explained by laws of grammar and rhetoric. Emotional responses are conditioned by unconscious laws, whereas apostrophe apparently obeys laws of language. These sets of regulations share structural and functional similarities, however. When we turn aside in embarrassment from apostrophe, we repeat its gesture. We act according to a law that produces the terms of its own violation. Apostrophe inscribes itself in the negative: grammatically, it fails to enclose a unitary subject; rhetorically, it fails to reproduce subjectivity by means of direct address. Turning aside, apostrophe calls attention to the textual effects that hide its failures and disguise its law. Most important among these is the inscription of voice as the sign of pure subjectivity, an effect that apostrophe both displays and disrupts.

Finnegans Wake repeats the conventions of oral narrative and insists on the "telling" qualities of a production that weaves together narrative set pieces. Its textual difficulties are sometimes thought to yield more easily to the ear than the eye, on the assumption that *Wake* "sense" follows "sound."[4] Joyce's own famous reading of the apostrophe to Anna Livia Plurabelle illustrates how the voice erases textuality. The grammatical and rhetorical effects of apostrophe, which depend upon the eye, are silenced, and the indecision between writing and voice that characterizes the *Wake* is lost. Writing opens a space between the invocative "O" ("O tell me all about Anna Livia!"—196.1–3) and its visual effects.[5] The apostrophic O, the voice's image, exists only in writing, and its presence on the page makes visible the impossibility of apostrophe's own invoked effect—in Barbara Johnson's words, to throw "voice, life, and human form into the addressee." The O attests to the nonexistence of the voice that the apostrophe would call into sound: there remains only the O, the sign or marker. That the written effects of the vocative have been overlooked, even denied, by scholars is an inescapable effect of the *Wake*'s own law, wherein differences between telling and writing are *inscribed*.

❈

TEXTUAL FRAMES

Before examining the effects of the missing apostrophe in *Finnegans Wake*, I want to look briefly at the interlocking framing devices that establish its narrative boundaries. Commentators have identified four primary frames: song, circle, dream, and letter. Of these, the most obvious is the title ("Timm Finn again's weak"—93.35–36), with its references to the mythic hero Finn MacCool, to the Irish song, "Finnegan's Wake," and to the notions of resurrection, awakening, and a wake for the dead. The complexity of allusive levels in this title reveals a compacted linguistic structure that fails to contain the multiplicity of its own meanings, its borders overrun by excesses of language. One might claim that such spillage *is* the *Wake*, whose very title is missing the mark of punctuation that could direct, if not contain, its meanings. When editors or printers reappropriate the apostrophe, they fix the title in an English syntactical structure, possessive pronoun attached to a noun subject. The restored apostrophe specifies Finnegan as an individual subject and gives predominance to the Irish ballad, whose musical story can be told only after Finnegan's presumed death, the song recounting the manner of his death by a fall from a ladder, his "wake," and his "awakening." When the apostrophe is (properly) missing from the title, the song frame is broken. Although the lexical construct of the title retains its shadow frame, the absent apostrophe pluralizes a grammatical/narrative structure that opens rather than encloses the text. This effect—of the frame cracked—is rendered by the slight omission of the apostrophe.

The opening words of the *Wake* reveal yet another missing frame, a convention so expected that its absence shocks us into an attitude of not-reading: "riverrun, past Eve and Adam's." [6] The first word, uncapitalized, announces a text with no begin-

52

ning, a story already embarked on its telling. Both noun and verb, "riverrun" carries action without commencement, challenging notions of narrative order even as it encompasses action, meaning, and myth in the coming together of our first parents. History begins in Eve and Adam's transgression and fall away from God's law and love, their tumbling into time and space echoed in Finnegan's topple from the ladder. Enacting history as a falling away from first causes, the spiraling narrative inverts storytelling forms and unbinds the linearity of the printed text. For example, the last word of the text—"the," which is not followed by an end-stop—can be linked to "riverrun" on the first page to create a "sentence" that encompasses the whole book: "A way a lone a last a loved a long the / riverrun, past Eve and Adam's from swerve of shore to bend of bay, brings us by a commodius vicus of recirculation back to Howth Castle and Environs" (3.3).[7] This reading seals the *Wake* world within a teleological structure where beginning and ending are undifferentiated. Rather than completing the narrative figure, its encircling movement obscures the *Wake*'s failure to make good on its own narrative claims. The ring is a hole, a blank space, an O that situates the story's origin as loss constituted through deferral and repetition. Never able fully to account for itself, the story repeats the loss of its origins through a set of distancing narrative conventions: "Once upon a time" or "It was of a night, late, lang time agone" (21.5).[8]

The story's obscured origins, confounded spatial-temporal dimensions, and compounded linguistic patterns are often explained as distortions produced by the *Wake* dream structure. In this frame, the dreamer occupies the center of a linguistic field, dreaming versions of the primal scene ("in my serial dreams of faire women"—532.33) as recounted in a "nat language" (83.12) that communicates by transfers, ellipses, reversals, and rhetorical displacements. What is barred from conscious life returns in a motion of circularity and circumscription to produce an internal boundary within the "blank memory" of sleep, the dream constructing itself against the hole or black nothingness of dreamless sleep.[9] Weaving its opaque and intertextual fabric from repressed or pockmarked memories ("m'm'ry"—460.20), the dream recounts not merely the loss of narrative origins owing to forgetfulness but loss constructed as repression.

The psychosexual necessity for repression compromises the textual desire to remember and repeat. Thus the dream appropriates the textual space in which the story should develop, a space that is often framed by a written message, the letter "carried of Shaun, son of Hek, written of Shem, brother of Shaun, uttered for Alp, mother of Shem, for Hek, father of Shaun. Initialled" (420.17–19). In some sense, the *Wake* as letter transcribes the *Wake* as dream, an effort to make legible the events of the night world, to translate the dreamer and dream subject into the letter and its potential reader, to make the private public, the unconscious conscious. Constituted within the psychic double bind of repression and remembrance, the attempt fails: the letter covers up what the dream would uncover.

The song, ring, dream, and letter frames implicate each other in the circuit of communication they create for *Finnegans Wake*. While the textual limits of song, dream, and letter can usually be distinguished, the powerful encircling movement of the *Wake* overturns and elides principles of categorization, confusing internal and external boundaries. Repeating the gesture of apostrophe held within its title, *Finnegans Wake* binds and unbinds subjects and structures as it negotiates the waking-sleeping worlds. If we feel in this motion the mother's hand rocking a child's cradle, however, we overlook its violence, which is not limited to mere wordplay. My analysis begins by observing how the pluralized subjectivities of dream-letter structures enact conscious/unconscious laws. Next I explore how apostrophe encodes sexual difference as a violation of genre distinctions and rhetorical-grammatical codes. Finally, my reading examines the textual placement of the feminine within domestic language and cultural marginality, the woman's body inscribing a space of "scripture" and "stripture" open to the violence of patriarchal inscription.

THE SCENE OF WRITING

Finnegans Wake directs us toward a path of elaboration and displacement: "Who speaks?" "Who writes?" It opens a correspondence of doubles, I and you, the sender and projected receiver of secret messages. The *Wake* unfolds in scenes of writing; letters are composed, posted, concealed, discovered, plagiarized, falsified, and used to seduce, threaten, blackmail, and expose. The plot turns on questions of authority, which is contested through the very act of writing that establishes and underwrites its claims. The lessons chapter describes the general condition under which letters are composed and relayed from writer to reader:

> All the world's in want and is writing a letters.[5] A letters from a person to a place about a thing. And all the world's on wish to be carrying a letters. A letters to a king about a treasure from a cat. . . . When men want to write a letters. Ten men, ton men, pen men, pun men, wont to rise a ladder. . . . Is then any lettersday from many peoples? . . . A posy cord. Plece.

[5] To be slipped on, to be slept by, to be conned to, to be kept up. And when you're done push the chain. (278.13–24, fn. 5)

According to this analysis, the need to write letters is generalized. Letters share certain properties ("a letters from a person to a place about a thing"); in particular, these letters are to a "king about a treasure from a cat." The king designates Earwicker, whose occupation (as Tim Finnegan) is "to rise a ladder," that is, to write a letter. "Pen men" and "pun men" embody the elements of the writing trade (pens and puns), a hint that writing is a male task. The footnotes, written by Issy, constitute a "lady's postscript" (42.9), a marginal commentary on the primary texts written by her brothers and a parallel text to the history the chapter tells. These notes delineate the connections between letters and desire, between psychoanalysis and dreams: the letters are "slipped on" (as in Freudian "slips"), "slept by" (the impetus to dream); they serve as blackmail weapons ("to be conned to") and are phallic symbols ("to be kept up"). The link between writing and defecation, the use of body excrement as ink, is apparent in Shem's ability to make "encostive inkum out of the last of his lavings" (279.9–10), but is invoked here in the pushing of the "chain" that starts the letter on its way through the postal/sewage system. Issy's letter is from a cat to his majesty HCE, her literary "subject". It concerns a treasure, probably her "pussy," the object of his desire that initiates the letter writing and makes letters jump back and forth across an abyss of repression. As a writer, she occupies a "modesties office" (a "majesty's service" that includes the postal system that delivers the letter's "treasure"), a position that threatens the majesty's authority. Putting her desires into writing, she can reverse his "rise" on the ladder, undermine that (sexual) power of his authority. Her weapon? A "posy card," a postcard.[10]

The *Wake* examines disputed authority within the family through twins and doubles (Shem and Shaun; the "sosie sesthers," Issy and her mirror image) and through failed efforts to establish the omnipotent Name of the Father, who is HCE—the one whose initials are duplicated in nearly every sentence of the text—and Here Comes Everybody, proliferated into everyone and no one. Rather than shoring up the patriarch's authority, this dispersal of language diminishes his symbolic power. His sons threaten to overthrow him, each striving to establish his name in the place of the father's. In order to avert disaster, HCE declares war (the "he war"), assigning sons different languages (versions of these are transcribed as the columns of marginal annotation in chap. 10). In so doing, HCE creates the confusion of Babel that he meant to prevent.[11]

While the primary threat to the king's authority seems to be from his sons, who wish to dispossess him of control over language, in fact the most imminent menace is from his daughter, who has knowledge of his sin, which is represented by the dream scene in Phoenix Park, and whose letter can serve as witness against him. As Issy learns to write letters following her mother's copybook models, she remembers a scene in which she may have been a complicit witness or a victim. The sexual-incestuous desires that *Finnegans Wake* inscribes in letters and dreams run a doubled route between father and daughter. Earwicker acts on his desire in dreams that confuse sexual subjects; Issy plays out the multiple possibilities of her desire while seated at the mirror, transcribing conversations with her mirror image "double." The mirror marks a barred passage ('), a space of trespass between conscious and unconscious states that dreams negotiate.

The mirror space represents Issy's fractured subjectivity. Her letters retrace psychosexual splits that cannot fully be textualized because their constitutive sexual trauma is held within preconscious, preverbal states. The pathway opened by her dreamletters and mirror conversations leads back to a place of lost origins that narrative cannot recover. The effects of this originary trauma are available in all of Issy's writings, including the chatty, informal copybook letter on page 280, which opens in an address to the mother, "A.N.," "Nourse Asa," a representation of Anna Livia, from whom she admits to having "learned all the runes of the gamest game ever" (279, fn. 1). The mother also signs the letter, under the name "Auburn chen*l*emagne. *P*ious and *p*ure one" (280.27–28, emphasis added), the missive duplicating and enclosing within its salutation and signature aspects of Anna Livia as mother, daughter, lover, mistress, and sister.[12] The letter incorporates elements of Issy's seductive nature, exploiting a provocative vocabulary that reveals, without specifically naming, the object of her desire: F.M., Father Michael, the parish priest (pp), who serves as representative of God the Father (figure of Earwicker) and in the place of Brother Mick (Shaun, who plays at various times the roles of priest, postman, and policeman—a representative of the law and figure of authority), the "prints chumming" for whom Christinette "can be when desires Soldi" (i.e., exchanged or sold as the double).

Issy's letter follows an extended footnote that usurps the scripted narrative of the Lessons chapter and explores the conflation of teachers and students, old and young lovers (Mark of Cornwall and Tristram). Issy doubles as Isolde as she writes an erotic letter to her teacher, the "person suppressed for the moment, F.M." (280.12–13): "the good fother with the twingling in his eye will always have cakes in his pocket to bethroat us with for our allmichael good" (279, fn. 1). The doubled object of desire ("fother / allmichael") is counterbalanced by the divided Issy, present as the Maggies (from the rhyme in which the brothers play Mick and Nick; of the park scene where the two young girls tempt Earwicker) and as Christine Beauchamp whose schizophrenia splits her into "Chris" and her letter-writing opposite, "Sally." These erotic divisions are evident in double entendres ("kissists my exits"—280.27) and in the confusion of pronominals (I, you, we). As in the earlier letter to the king, Issy is represented as a cat. The letter incorporates a third-person description of her feline movements as she pens the letter, her actions duplicating the sexual stimulus implicit in her linguistic gestures: "Schlicksher . . . Shrubsher. . . . Schlicksheruther" (i.e., "She licks her Other," 280.16–19). The descriptive voice mimics Issy's lisp, which is textualized as the doubled consonants that divide her into "pepette" (pp), counterpart of her twin brothers as penman and postman.

The letter, which exploits the domestic language of a model homemaker, is introduced by a dream sequence in which Issy writes a scene her father hopes she cannot remember: "A scene at sight. Or dreamoneire. Which they shall memorise. By her freewritten Hopely for ear that annalykeses if scares for eye that sumns. Is it in the now woodwordings . . . then will singingsing tomorrows gone and yesters outcome?" (280.1–7).[13] As Issy's letters fold back on the father's dream, their "woodwordings" hint at her presence in the park and her complicity in the primal scene. She has an ear for rumor and an eye for scandal, writing from knowledge that is recovered *as* she writes. She desires the truth about the father: "All schwants (schwrites) ischt tell the cock's trootabout him. . . . He had to see life foully the plak and smut (schwrites). . . . Yours very truthful. Add dapple inn" (113.11–18). Written in a Swiftean "little" language, this letter is signed with her mother's initials, making it appear that Anna Livia has somehow authorized Issy's account, that perhaps it was written under her dictation. Of necessity, Issy's letters employ a double language of discretion and deceit because they are doubly censored: addressed to the mother (or her sister, Maggy), they concern the father (majesty) and are signed by his wife (a signature that may well be a forgery, stolen from the mother by the daughter as she tries to usurp the mother's position in the family). In the final pages of the *Wake* ALP's letter to HCE appropriates Issy's texts, their contents altered so that they respect *his* authority, do obeisance to *his* majesty, show respect for *his* name. The culminating letter bows before phallic authority and exposes the Reverend majesty as a "bumpkin," a "puny" (627.23, 24).

—◈—

THE PATERNAL ONE AND THE MIRROR (M)OTHER

Unlike traditional narrative, whose linear thrust is forward to a conclusion and denouement, the *Wake* unfolds backward through time and space toward a moment of originary loss. Presented first as an adolescent, then as a young schoolchild, and finally as an infant, Issy regresses to babyhood. The contradictory manifestations of authority in her writing are connected to an unremembered scene in the nursery, where she sees her father's erect penis. Staged toward the end of the book, this scene provides only partial explanation for her unpredictable and counteractive behavior: "The infant Isabella from her coign to do obeisance toward the duffgerent, as first futherer with drawn brand. Then the court to come into full morning" (566.23–25). Set in the royal court, Earwicker is again the majesty to whom Issy is a subject whose obedience and loyalty are demanded. In an earlier manifestation, he was not a king but "my prince of the courts who'll beat me to love" (460.12–13), and while she dreams "telepath posts dulcets on this isinglass stream," she swears her counterpart to silence, "(but don't tell him or I'll be the mort of him!)" (460.20). The death threat rides on an elusive piece of information about her own past experience available only (and partially) in the dream. One part of her divided subjectivity tries to remember ("Something happened that time I was asleep, torn letters or was there snow?"—307, fn. 5) while the Other suspects the sexual circumstances of the encounter: "Of course I know you are a viry vikid girl to go in the dreemplace and at that time of the draym and it was a very wrong thing to do, even under the dark flush of night, dare all grandpassia!" (527.5–8).[14]

The origin of the father's guilt and daughter's murderous longings rest in events that belong to her infancy, the pre-mirror stage, outside Symbolic language, and for him are forgotten or repressed. The *Wake* textualizes traces of these events within a dreamwork that collapses boundaries between father-daughter unconscious. Issy is present in her father's dream not only as the object of his desire, where she is a figure of Anna Livia in her youth, but as a dream subject who witnesses HCE's sexual acts. That is, she is captured by the father's gaze and she catches him within her own field of vision. Split within the dream, as she is by the space of the shattered mirror, Issy is figured as both subject and object. This splitting/doubling is, of course, a common dream effect, but how does Issy's Other, who is a witness to the scene and who accuses her of going into the "dreemplace" at the wrong time of the dream, know of it?

The *Wake* turns aside from this question, but I believe that incestuous sexual violence emerges through Issy's pockmarked memories. Repressed by her conscious mind, the effects of sexual abuse surfaces in the pathological splits of her multiple personalities, signified textually as "torn letters": "The dame dowager's duffgerent to present wappon, blade drawn to the full and about wheel without to be seen of them" (566.21–23).[15] Wrapped in sleep, the infant Isabella is forced to pay homage in a ritual scene of courtly violence, her mother (the dame dowager) a silent, and complicit, observer. In the light of "full morning" (also "full mourning" or grief), she cannot remember the evidence that might summon up the court (tribunal, seduction). The relative clarity of *Wake* language in these passages belies the immense difficulty of, and therefore repeated, efforts to bring unconscious, preverbal "events" into consciousness through language. The dream/mirror split promises communication, it transposes the message, reversing and substituting its parts. One woman is exchanged for another (mother for daughter, sister for sister). The mirror creates a mirage, an effect of the apostrophe (') that calls out for but also prevents translation.

The setting of nursery and bedroom, the acts of writing and dreaming, coincide when young Issy, seated at her mother's vanity table pretending to *be* her mother as she plays at grown-up with face creams and make-up, converses with her mirror image. This scene duplicates a dialogue begun in the cradle when baby Issy "talk[ed] petnames with her little playfilly," the image of herself in the "shellback thimblecasket mirror" that reflects her own image, "her dearest friendeen" (461.36, 15–16). This passage exploits an ambiguity of spoken and written language as Issy intrudes on the series of riddles posed of Shaun and Shem. Shem's question concerns the desire for an absent lover: "What bitter's love but yurning, what' sour lovemutch but a bref burning till shee that drawes dothe smoake retourne?" (143.29–30). The answer posits a dialogue between pepette (pette, pitounette, pipetta) and her mirror opposite, with whom she is jealously competitive; it reveals the seduction of a man ("you lovely fellow of my dreams"—114.6) who is perhaps Shem, Shaun, or the father ("old somebooby"). The mother is a third (and, like the men, absent) party to the scripting of this scene. She is referred to in the third person, while the two doubles exist as "I" and "you." The "I" tries to extract information about sexual practices from "you": "I thought ye knew all and more, ye aucthor, to explique to ones the significat of their exsystems with your nieu nivulon lead"—148.16–18. Reflecting author and actor ("aucthor"), the mirror sustains writing within its barred passage.

The literary setting for the scene is Swift's *Journal to Stella*, but the psychological background is taken from Morton Prince's *The Dissociation of a Personality*, a case history of schizophrenia.[16] Both texts describe clandestine writings between lovers/ enemies who employ pet names and pseudonyms to hide identities and exchange roles as the writers and receivers of letters. The alliance of One and Other in the writing act is a collaboration that breeds both narcissistic love and hate: "I hate the very thought of the thought of you and because, dearling, of course, adorest . . . when we do and contract with encho tencho solver when you are married to reading and writing" (146.18–22). The reading-writing process undermines and sustains the authority of the marriage contract which is further tested as the mother's image is recreated and resisted within the mirror doubles. She is present in the (m)Other's voice, imaged in the O of "O mind you poo tickly" (144.34) and the series of responses ("Of course") that punctuate the conversation, and in the reflection of the oval mirror, the O.

Sitting before her mirror image, Issy wants to silence the O, the knowing voice of her Other. The voice mimics a male lover who instructs her in the art of seduction. Lips and labia are opened and silenced (momentarily) by the sexual act: "Now open, pet, your lips, pepette, like I used my sweet parted lipsabuss with Dan Holohan of facetious memory taught me after the flannel dance" (147.29–34). Voice and vagina are conflated, and kisses promise more illicit pleasures. The Other's voice cajoles, seduces, instructs, and mocks, creating a repressed countertext of sexual-textual slips. The illicit love and sexual trespass are neither fully repressed nor consciously available: incestuous longing of father for daughter, daughter for father, sister for sister, slips through the language. Although the *Wake* records sexual difference as textual difference, a violation of generic, rhetorical, and grammatical codes, it also presents violent reinforcement of these laws within family ties and paternal privilege. Wives, sisters, and daughters are especially vulnerable under patriarchal law, their physical safety and sanity at risk. In sleep, the norms and forms of family life are transgressed and reinstituted: "O, foetal sleep! Ah, fatal slip! the loved one, the other left, the bride of pride leased to the stranger" (563.10–11). The journey toward desire's truth leads down the memory lane ("mememormee!"—

628) of writing: here the "I" and "you," the divided selves of the split subject, meet and miss each other.

APOSTROPHIZING THE SUBJECT

Oh, how it was duusk! (158.19)
O! O! O! Par la pluie! *(158.23–24)*

In the *Wake*'s workings, the "foetal sleep" and "fatal slip" produce a blank space in the text, a gap in the storytelling signaled by the apostrophe. "Finn, again!" (628.14) Anna Livia calls in her final rush to the sea. Her apostrophe to Finn and the separation of "Finn" from "again," marked by the comma of address and directive, turn the narrative back on itself, to the "riverrun" of her wake and his waking. The dream displays its apostrophic effects in the desire to know ("Now tell me, tell me, tell me then!"—94.19) and the need to forget ("And do you remember, Singabob, the badfather"—94.33). The apostrophe marks a point of departure and return—a turning point—and its enclosing gesture (') at once binds and unbinds the grammatical construct. A form of address that calls out desire for the Other's voice, a desire for response, apostrophe problematizes narrative authority and subjectivity. Always a call to memory, apostrophe even in its grammatical status gives an *image* of voice, a calling out and calling up. It (re)*produces* subjectivity. It would make the blank spaces of "m'm'ry" *speak*. The apostrophes in "m'm'ry" signal psychic repressions, the holes in consciousness, and mark the absent E and O, the alphabetic symbols of Earwicker and Anna Livia, the male and female principals of the *Wake* drama.

Anna Livia Plurabelle is most closely associated with apostrophe. She is called up through the O that opens chapter 8, called forth in the gossip of the washerwomen, who read the signs of her sin in the dirty laundry, just as her sons will later discern her private parts—"the O of woman" (270.25)—in their geometry lesson. Anna Livia's chapter is probably the best known of the *Wake*, the one that argues most seductively for the necessity of "telling" the tale. This O is voice and vagina, sign of the orifices from which ALP's own voice emits the sounds of "babbling, bubbling, chattering to herself . . . the sloothering slide of her, giddygaddy, grannyma, gossipaceous Anna Livia" (195.1–4) and from which her "daughtersons" have emerged from the night into the light. The O figures the passageways of female sexuality, and Anna Livia's sexuality is the major interest in this chapter. The opening apostrophe to her mimes the O that becomes the geometric figure for the vaginal delta through which her children enter the world:

O
tell me all about
Anna Livia! I want to hear all
about Anna Livia. Well, you know Anna Livia? Yes, of course.
(196.1–4)

The shapes are doubled in the geometric figure reproduced on page 293 of the *Wake* (see illustration, p. 50): two O's figure female buttocks, the inverted triangle held within the oblong O of the vagina. But these O's also reveal a reflected interiority, as if seen through a speculum or reflected inward and downward in the mirror of water, that produces a three-dimensional view. This mirroring effect is available only textually, however. When the invocation of Anna Livia is read aloud, nothing of its graphic spacing or design is communicated except, perhaps, as the double O's echo and mirror in sound what the *Wake* gives to sight.

The *Wake* is a reservoir of sight/sound effects, and I mention several from French to suggest the ways in which the text of the *Wake* negotiates marked and unmarked languages. When voiced, the phrase, "*O! O! O! Par la pluie!*," carries with it rain (*la pluie*) and umbrella (*par la pluie*). The "l" of *la* is lost, elided, so that rain and an article as protection *against* the rain (*para-pluie*) are both heard. (In French the gender of the noun changes from feminine, *la pluie*, to masculine, *le parapluie*.) Brotfressor Prenderguest's fork ("a pronged instrument," like the capital E signifying Earwicker) does damage to a letter he is reading at the breakfast table. The marks of its destruction evident in diacritical markings: "ay ∧ fork, or à grave Brofèsor . . . acùtely profèššionally *piquéd*" (124.9–10). Read aloud, the markings remain "unvoiced." Precisely because "grave" is missing the adverbial sign, the *accent grave*, it articulates in sound the English adjective: the professor is somber. To the eyes, however,

63

the misplaced accent grave (over "à") changes the article to a preposition (translated into English as "to") that splinters the grammatical construction in English. The effect of the French marking troubles the eye but remains unheard by the ear.[17]

A repeated question in the *Wake*, "How do you do, todo, north Mister?" (95.5—"How do you do today, my fair/dark sir?") appears intoned through various languages. As rendered "in French," it reads, "Come on, fool porterfull, hosiered women blown monk sewer?" (16.4–5), or *Comment vous portez-vous aujourd' hui mon blond monsieur*? Although the individual words of this phrase are English, syntactically they find their way into English only through a French *pronunciation*. The English form does not include a "fool," "hosiered women," or a "monk" (see versions at pages 225, 35, 54, 72, 93, 95, 160, 186, 332, 409, 466, and 511). The Old French motto, *Honi soit qui mal y pense*, offers another example, rendered variously in the *Wake* as "Honeys wore camelia paints" (113.17) and "O'Neill saw Queen Molly's pants" (495.27–28). These recognizable English words appear in a syntactical structure that sounds as if it should make sense but does not. They echo the French, which both does and does not hold their "meaning." No more does the empty O of the call to Anna Livia hold within it her meaning, the mystery of her origins, the dark secrets of her sexuality or her reproductive capabilities. The O is a call not only to the voice, to *her* voice, but it gives voice to the desire for enclosed meanings, originary powers, safe passage, and the dark sleep of the womb.

Anna Livia is known by the sound of her waters, "lilting on all the time" (627.21); her babbling, bubbling, and "sloothering slide" are calls of seduction to her "devious delts" (197.22). The calls for Anna Livia exploit the homophonic connection of *eau* and O: washerwomen working on the banks of the River Liffey hear Anna Livia's story in the waters as she flows by. The artificiality associated with the O, the trope of apostrophe, allies itself with the waters of nature, a deflection—or a naturalizing—of poetic artifice. The scene along the bank of the Liffey is not, however, a moment of lyric poetry, although lyricism vies with gossip in a pattern of tonal reverses throughout the chapter. Instead it stages a narrative, a story told through the dialogue of two women whose raucous, low Dublin accents contrast with the undercurrents of the river running past. The opening call for a story ("O tell me all about Anna Livia!") refuses the traditional terms of direct poetic address. Undirected and undifferentiated, the O comes from nowhere immediately identifiable; no reading context is provided for it; it fills a space and silence that cannot be mapped by a single interpretive gesture. O is a call neither *from* Anna Livia nor *to* her; she is neither the summoner nor the summoned. She appears in stories told by the two gossips, whose calls and answers repeat forms common to Issy and her mirror image. The O of address is a plea to narrative, which shares nothing with apostrophe. Narrative is all that apostrophe denies and resists.[18]

The invocative O is a plea for the Other's voice, and for an-Other voice. The apostrophe proposes a dialogue, but it requires a third party who overhears and to whom the apostrophe's "aside" is addressed. Anna Livia *is* the Other, an extra to the dramatic dialogue of the chapter. The two women telling stories about her engage each other in an I-You relationship ("You'll die when you hear. . . . Yes, I know, go on"—196.5–7).[19] As woman and river, Anna Livia negotiates a space between the two voices that echo and invite her. She does not "tell"; she is "told," albeit through a mimicry or ventriloquizing of her voice(s). Animation and anthropomorphism are merely textual effects: the O of the chapter marks her absence; it is a death knell of invocation.

Apostrophe signals at once a radical interiority (the address is inward, not outward) and fragmentation. As represented subjectivity, the voice is disembodied, divided, echoing on the wind. "O tell me all about Anna Livia!" both is and is not apostrophic. Like apostrophe, the call negotiates a terrain between nature and the anthropomorphic, "Anna Livia" naming both the river Liffey and Anna Livia Plurabelle. Including direct and indirect address in its call, the O suggests the absolute impossibility of its endeavor to anthropomorphize the river as woman *exactly* to the degree that it renders the fiction of its own success: we "hear" Anna Livia; (as if) she has responded to the call. Anna Livia is not present to this dialogue in her voice, although the ventriloquist's trick of making us think she is there, speaking through the other(s), seems a quite successful slight of sound maneuver. Either as river or woman, Anna Livia cannot be reduced to a voice: she speaks, if she speaks at all, difference(s).

Earwicker also speaks a form of difference, identifiable in his stutter. His affliction is made worse at guilty moments, and the textual doubling of letters ("ff," "kk") or syllables ("Shsh shake, co-comeraid!"—36.20) mark an involuntary repetition of sounds. The stutter appears to oppose the O of pure voice (which would overcome absence, even death) by haltingly announcing itself through a failure to communicate. Earwicker's stutter signals his sin ("sinnfinners," with its doubled consonants—36.26), as the stains on Anna Livia's drawers signify her failings: both sets of signs mark a sexual fall. The hesitation of Earwicker's speech, however, manifests itself through repetitions of words and letters that illustrate the stutter as textual spacing ("that sign of our ruru redemption"—36.25). This space without meaning, a space of repeated efforts to begin the story, a story that is always a defense of innocence or a pleading against punishment, calls attention to itself as a gap, a loss, a sound without meaning, a formal fault. The stutter marks absence of meaning and excess of sound. It also calls attention to a difference within; it is a sign of the (failed) effort to make univocal and consistent the multiplicities and inconsistencies of behavior. The stutter makes Earwicker human, but it is more than the sign of presumed guilt or the mark of original sin: it also signifies self-delusion and attempted recompense. Textually, the stutter doubles and divides, opening a space of difference, from self and others, whose effects are apostrophic: "ff, flitmansfluh, and, kk, 't crept i' hedge whenas to many a softongue's pawkytalk mude unswer u sufter poghyogh" (37.20–21). It opens itself to Babel.

The stutter stands against the singularity, the monolinguism of the pure O; it stands against the desire for exact repetition ("woo-woo willing"—36.23–24); it undoes dialogism. The stutter is a *lapsus lingua*, the site of a linguistic falling away, already figured in the fall that opens the way to babelization and Anna Livia's babbling brook. Earwicker's stuttering is the space marked out by the apostrophe we expect to find in *Finnegans Wake*, a moment between waking and sleeping, a place that marks loss and absence. This space enunciates the hope of articulation, full speech, of recall and reappropriation. But the enunciation is delayed and deformed, a sign of its failure to signify, which produces an aphasic lapse, a "blank memory" or the blanks in "m'm'ry," a hole. These are moments of significant nonsense, where meaning is denoted not through sense but by absence of sense, a hesitation, a doubling of the consonants and a dragging of the vowels that announce (in their failure to fully enounce) a meaning. They open the way to the "fibfib fabrications" of narrative (36.34).

The letter E as magiscule announces Earwicker the "Reverend . . . majesty." The siglum E, sign of HCE's sovereignty and presumed eloquence, appears in four different positions: prostrate ⊔⊔, where its erect middle term figures Earwicker's phallic power ("there was a wall of course in erection"—6.9), as well as his floundering, babbling babyishness ("on the flounder of his bulk like an overgrown babeling, let wee peep"—6.31– 32); prone ⊓⊓ ("moved contrawatchwise"—119.18–19), where its form suggests a pronged instrument, perhaps the kitchen fork Brotfresor Prenderguest uses to read the letter (124), or an enfeebled old man walking with a cane ("He who runes may rede it on all fours"—18.05); finally, "standing full erect" (36.14), pointing in opposite directions, like directional signals or a weathervane, ⅃ (36.17), Ɛ (51.19, 489.13).[20] Anna Livia is invoked with every appearance of the O, even when it appears in contexts where she is not present ("O.O. Os pipos mios es demasiada gruarso por O piccolo pocchino"—54.16–17); Earwicker too is evoked by the appearance of his siglum, including occasions when the first word of a sentence begins with E: "E'erawhere is this whorl would ye hear sich a din again?" (6.24). Meaning attaches itself to the very movement of these letters, even when they are separated from any contextual bearing that would give rise to meaning. The separation of O and E from any word *proper* marks their textual exile as alphabetic symbols, cut off by the enclosing stroke of the apostrophe. They are left to float and fly; their effects are disseminated "E'earwhere in this whorl" (everywhere in this world), whirling on the wind, spiraling in the ear.

Symbol of power, the erect E is also a sign of vulnerability. Its power and prestige can be overturned (⊔⊔) and undermined; the E carries in its wake the possibility of failure and falling. Like the old man walking with a stick, ⊓⊓, it totters along, unsure of its footing, uneasily balanced. The E assumes power because of its placement (at the beginning of a proper name or at the head of a sentence), where a fall from pride of place can change the capital E to a lowercase "e," a vowel open to exchange or even exclusion ("aver," "ev'ry"). The space of such a possibility is evident in "*E'e*arwhere," the apostrophe signaling the moment of falling off or falling down. The *Wake* opens with such a fall, retelling the story of the fall of Finnegan (whose initial "F" already signals the possibility of misstep, an E that has lost its foot as Finn loses his footing): "Dimb! He stottered from the latter. Damb! he was a dud. Dumb! Mastabatoom, mastabadtomm" (6.9–11). Tim tumbles from the top of the ladder to its foot. His "totter" is also his "stutter," the sound of falling and failing. It will lead to forgeries and fibs, themselves announced by Earwicker's inability to make the fricative "f": "fibfib fabrications." Finn's fall crashes like thunder, like God's voice proclaiming His omnipotence in sounds that frighten the barbarians into civilization and fear of His name. The fall is announced by a series of thunderclaps, or stutters, that pronounce God's power and open the way to babelian challenges to that power: bababadalgharaghtakamminarronnkonnbronntonnerronntuonnt hunntrovarr hounawnskawntoohoohoordenenthurnuk!" (3.15–17). Endowed with a certain onomatopoeic power, the stutter and stammer signal in speech the fall that brings death to the world. They are traces of babel, of babbling, a frightening sort of nonmeaning, a space marked out in the text by the place of Earwicker's fallen "e": "where he last fellonem" (7.31).

The power of the capital E that asserts Earwicker's authority as head of household and state is undermined by the diminutive "e," especially as the "eh" sound slurs vowels and signification falls away. Unlike the pure O of invocation, the "eh/er" is both a defense against the invocative and an impediment to it. A sign of the stutter, the "eh" transposes into textual space and script what can take place only in time and sound ("ah eh oh"—278.10). The effort to communicate carries with it guttural efforts at enunciation (also the grunts and groans of defecation), sounds inf(l)ected with failure, as HCE himself fears the possibility of disease: "he shat the Ructions gunorrhal" (192.2–3, where "shat," "shout," and "shot" are associated with guns, oral ruckus, and gonorrheal erections. The small "e" is also the mark of the forger, and the "eh" sound it produces is one of fear or guilt. In references to Richard Pigott, the *Wake* parallels Earwicker's fears of his actions in Phoenix Park with Pigott's attempt to link Charles Stewart Parnell to the Invincibles and the May 1882 Phoenix Park murders of two British government representatives. Pigott was exposed in his effort to frame Parnell when, during a government trial, he spelled "hesitancy" with an "e" rather than an "a." Parnell's exoneration rested, as did his supposed crime, on the existence of letters, an incriminating correspondence, and, finally, on two (almost interchangeable) letters of the alphabet. Earwicker's feared doom and damnation is spelled in his hesitancy, his stutter, in the titters of local gossips who are tattletales: "But the spoil of hesitants, the spell of hesitency. His atake is it ashe, tittery taw tatterytail, hasitence humponadimply, heyheyheyhey a winceywencky" (97.25–26).

The various repetitions of "hesitencies" in the *Wake* expose Earwicker as a fake, one whose power and authority rest on forged credentials.[21] Earwicker also assumes that a written document (a legal brief, newspaper, or poison pen letter) is circulating among the citizenry accusing him of unlawful deeds in Phoenix Park. He desires to exchange this document for another, one that will exonerate him. His dream of vindication is marred, however, by the suspicion that forgery may be the very crime with which he is being charged. Thus the intrusive "e" evidence that points simultaneously in two directions, toward Earwicker's feared guilt and his hoped-for exoneration. Moreover, this sign of his sin— the exchange of the "e" for the "a"—cannot be heard: "Hesitancy." "Hesitency." There is a certain hesitancy, an effort that sounds its own labors, in raising the E to its upright and capital position: "his hes hecitency Hec" (119.18), where the capital H (which can be made by gathering together the four positions of the capital E in a scriptural gesture ⊐+⊏) to signify Duke Humphrey ("Him," "Hom," "Hum," "Hurrah"—6.29–33). He is known by his hesitation, the almost silent sound of breath struggling toward speech, marked by his stutter, the slur, the "trace of his erstwhile burr" (34.36), which is "swift to mate errthors" (36.35).

The "e" and "a" are also inserted in transliterations of the Tetragrammaton, a symbol or substitute for the ineffable name of God: YHWH, which we hear as "YAHWEH" in Hebrew and JHVH, "Jehovah," in the Latin transliteration. But these sigla stand in place of a name, their configuration spacing out and effacing the name not to be "uttered," which is not to be heard, which is unspeakable: וחות. In a *Wake* passage that presumably refers to Shakespeare's habit of writing the letter "m" with four "legs" (which has counterparts in the "fourleaved shamrock" and the "quadrifoil jab" of the professor's fork, whose marks write a supratext on the morning mail), we also find remarks on the written and spoken forms of YHWH:

> and the fatal droopadwindle slope of the blamed scrawl, a sure sign of imperfectible moral blindness; the toomuchness, the fartoomanyness of all those fourlegged ems: and why spell dear god with a big thick dhee (why, O why, O why?). (122.34–123.2)

The double occurrence of ח, the Hebrew cheth, makes a "four-legged em" (חח); in its singular occurrence the cheth looks like the letter Greek *pi* (π), that figures in Shem's geometric drawing of the mother's vagina, where *pi* is doubled to make two "p," signs of the brothers, who are at war with each other, playing out at one level the Pigott-Parnell controversy. The immediate question, however, is the writing of God's name: "why spell Dear God with a big thick D?" The Irish language offers a partial answer, its word "fiadh" (pronounced "dee") means God.[22] "Dear" is a mark of salutation or address and also an invocation to God repeated in Anna Livia's missive: "Dear. And we go on to Dirtdump. Reverend. May we add majesty?" (615.12–13). In this version, "majesty" is an afterthought, and although it denotes the majestic, it is not written with a magiscule. The "thick dhee," with its intrusive (but almost unheard) "h," signals the fatal flaw in the majestic scheme; the "h," which is immediately followed by "e" and "y" ("why"), is the slur or burr of Earwickean speech. This flawed majestic pattern is summoned by the O—"why, O why, O why?"—a call, a prayer to God, to YHWH. Here the O of pure sound substitutes for the A of Anna Livia, who figures as pure sound in the text.

This call to God is also a call to script and to scripture. The "e" and "a" exist in sound, in the *ear*, in h*ear*ing. Their existence is, moreover, accidental since it was the Greek borrowing of the Semitic alphabet, which included signs only for consonants, that gave us signs for vowels, through a Greek economy that used extra Phoenician letter-symbols not needed for consonants to represent vowels. The "e" and "a" presumably existed in sound in this configuration—YAHWEH—before they existed in script, and in script they are the signs of translation and transgression, a space of both absence and excess.[23] These two marks—"e" and "a"—graphically denote the law of apostrophe. In YAHWEH, they are excessive, arbitrary, and interchangeable intrusions that signal a historical accident. In their absence—YHWH—they are still "heard," so that their erasure from writing is an erasure of the law that already prohibits their very existence. The law of YHWH is a law of prohibition (God's first commandment: "The Lord thy God is one God. Thou shalt have no other gods before Him"). YHWH prohibits utterance of the Name, which "e" and "a" allow by making the anagram a "name" in the place of the unrepresentable name: YAHWEH. The "e" and "a" also signify the impossibility of a *language* or *a* language: they have been seconded into service by a later historical movement, a moment of economy where one sign fills in for another. They give breath and sound to what is extraneous and unnecessary; this very sounding makes a call to the necessary: YAHWEH. Like the apostrophe, "e" and "a" share in what Derrida calls "the event of the mark": "not only what is said in it but its very saying and writing, the mark of its law and the law of its mark."[24] The "e" and "a," whether present or absent, mark a certain genre.

To insert these (almost mute) sounds in the spaces between the letters of Y-HW-H is to disobey the law of YHWH, to make the name *effable*, to call out sound and difference already inhabiting the name, to transl(iter)ate, to transgress. This law captures Earwicker, who hears of his indiscretions in the scratch of the tree branch at his window (a sound of scripture: "Tip"—8.08) and in the scratchy whisper of voices, those of the washerwomen, telling the story in the wind, on lips, in slips of the tongue, in kisses and lisps. He hears and does not want to hear; he fears and does not know what to fear; he hopes for a successful forgery and prays for vindication; he hides behind his name but wishes to be dispossessed of it; he recognizes his name and cannot recognize it. In the very act of trying to impose his authority—through his name—he decrees (and is already decreed by) confusion. "Earwicker," that first syllable of the name—"ear," "hear"—breeds dissent, conflict, and error enters through the ear, a *Perce-Oreille*: "the mar of murmury mermers to the mind's ear"

(254.18).²⁵ Sleeping, Earwicker hears the murmur of memories that mar his dream. He hears "memory" and "m'm'ry," and he chases the "e" and "o" down the whirling, whorling vortex of the O, toward origins.

INSCRIBING THE FEMININE: A SEXUAL ALPHABET

> *A is a guess and a piece.*
> *A is a sweet cent sender.*
> *A is a kiss slow cheese.*
> *A is for age jet.*
> Gertrude Stein, "Yet Dish" ²⁶

Resisting the pull of the E and A toward the whorling vortex of the O, the alphabetical configurations l, p, s, carry apostrophic (and catastrophic) effects of separation and exclusion. Cut off, these letters stray through the text detached from the parental body: "What's that ma'am? says I" (272, fn. 1). "Who'll buy me penny babies?" (273, fn. 5). "The small p.s. ex-ex-executive capahand in their sad rear like a lady's postscript" (42.8–9). The confusion of letters as modes of correspondence and alphabetic symbols again overturns any systematic effort to recover what is lost or displaced according to the law of apostrophe. Although all six letters disseminate throughout the text, the vowels E, A, and O gravitate toward origins, sexual unions, the desire for knowledge of sources, and are drawn to the delta of ALP's siglum Δ. In general, this first group evoke the parents, HCE and ALP, and are associated with the vagina and throat. The consonants l, p, and s inscribe the children and are identified with penis and lips. Issy's lisp is heard in the sibilants of her seductive messages, while the doubled threat of her brothers, Shem and Shaun, figures the powers of pen and post.

Following the t(r)ails of these letters, we discover signs of flawed speech and failed communication as the *Wake* traces the alliance of sin and speech, the slur or hesitation that announces sin. The speech defects of father and daughter, whose incestuous coupling is specularized by the dream, signal their unlawful desires. His is a "hisshistenency" (146.34) and hers a lisp: "He fell for my lips, for my lisp, for my lewd speaker" (459.28). Wakean "s" sounds are associated with Issy's lips, suggesting sighs, whispers, the "shimmers" of Nuvoletta's "lightdress" (157.8), the swish of skirts, sounds of the river reeds, and the stir of the air: "The siss of the whisp of the sigh of the softzing at the stir of the ver grose O arundo of a long one in midias reeds: and shades began to glidder along the banks, greepsing, greepsing, duusk unto duusk" (158.6–9). The "s" announces the serpent in the garden of Eden, the flaw in the immortal scheme, the sound of the tempter's speech as a mark of forbidden knowledge, the sting of death: "hce! O hce!" (291, fn. 1). Repeated, the "s" draws itself out in Earwicker's "hisshisstenency" (146.34), which carries in its wake the hissing of his detractors, the snake in the grass, the hiss of the asp, and the sounds of micturition. The "s" also traces the flaccid form of the penis, which when erected writes a "capital Pee for Pride" (296.5) in the appropriate place of woman's anatomy: "in Milton's Park under lovely Father Whisperer . . . making her love with his stuffstuff in the languish of flowers and feeling to find was she mushymushy" (96.10–12).

Issy is present to this scene as a "liss in hunterland" (276, fn. 7), and her lisped, "Liss, liss! I muss whiss!" (148.26) aligns her with Lilith, apocryphal precursor of Eve, and Lily Kinsella. The liquid l's and swishing s's combine in the temptresses: the "lilithe maidenettes," "two disappainted solicitresses" (90.16), the "saucicissters" (96.13), "two stripping baremaids" (526.23), "*the Misses O'Mollies*" (106.34), "one dilalah, Lupita Lorette" (67.33) and her "sister-in-love, Luperca Latouche" (67.36). But the doubled "l" and "s" join with the "p" to mimic pepette's "little language," which is also Issy's baby talk and lisping "s." [27] Yoked together, the "ls" sound with "p" (pee) provides the acoustic effect of urination, while the yonic shape of the p-q inverted letters (representing the Prankquean) provides a visual clue to urination and invagination. [28] The letters (pq, ps, ls) couple, separate and recouple in seemingly accidental patterns. The effect of their movement is divisive, even destructive of patterns and motifs. They enforce meaning even when they appear where they should not be or in "contexts" where their placement seems out of place or irrelevant. That is, these "symbols" refuse symbolic status. Carried along as part of the Liffey's litter, they find no resting-place. They are metonymic, transgressive, and potentially revolutionary.

The *Wake* plays on the double meaning of letters (documents, alphabet signifiers) thematically and orthographically. In one such scene of writing Issy, seated at her vanity table, pens a letter to her lover, her "pettest parriage priest" (458.4). At her looking glass, Issy is also Alice ("Alicious, twinstreams, twinestraines, through alluring glass or alas in jumboland"—528.17–18), whose narcissism threatens to drown her "in pondest coldstreams of admiration forherself" (526.28–29). She addresses her Other, her rival in love, as "you pig, you perfect little pigaleen" (143.35), practicing a series of poses. The radical shifts in tone move from the seductive ("Tell me till my thrillme comes!"—148.2) to sadism ("you want to be slap well slapped for that"—148.6) to vampirism: "Yes, the buttercups told me, hug me, damn it all, and I'll kiss you back to life, my peachest. I mean to make you suffer, meddlar. . . . Bite my laughters, drink my tears" (145.14–19). She begs for the punishment of the pen ("Pore into me, volumes, spell me stark and spill me swooning"—145.19–20), and calls for translation and transgression: "Transname me loveliness, now and here me for all times" (145.21). She is a "hot lisbing lass" (553.18) whose teenage sexuality involves petting and the "parted lipsabuss" (147.20). The lisp is a lapsus, a "lipsus of some hetarosexual" (120.35).

Imitating her mother before the oval mirror of the makeup table, Issy paints a face that is itself a letter, "of eyebrow pencilled, by lipstipple penned" (93.25). Indeed, the links between "lips" and "letters" are forged throughout the *Wake*. Dion Boucicault's play, *Arrah-na-Pogue* ("Arrah of the kiss") is an important Wakean literary source, a play from which Joyce borrowed the character Sean the Post and in which a secret message is conveyed by a kiss. Joyce's spelling of "pogue" creates an orthographic neologism, poke and penis ("poghuing her scandalous"—388.23). An earlier reference ("in Arrah-na-pogue, in the otherworld of the passing of the key of Two-tongue Common"—385.3–4) images lingual sexuality, the passing of the letter from mouth to mouth. This image is repeated in the last words of the *Wake*—"Lps. The keys to. Given!"—reminiscent of Molly passing the seedcake from her mouth to Bloom's, a scene recalled at the close of *Ulysses*. In the play, Sean the Post is called on to sing ("Open the dure softly, / Somebody wants ye, dear"), and the image of the open mouth asking the woman to "open the door" appears variously in the *Wake* as the request to open the lips ("now open, pet, your lips"—147.29; "to ope his blurbeous lips"—477.28; "what passed our lips"—528.2–3; *My Curly Lips Demand Columbkisses*" (105.32). Miming the image before her oval mirror, Issy "praxis oval owes and artless awes" (458.35–36) while writing a letter. The letter's last request is "kissists my exits" (280.27), prefigured in *Wake* associations between lovemaking and letter writing, the violence of brother battles and wife beating, efforts to read the arabesque script of the Book of Kells ("that last labiolingual *basium* might be read as a *suavium* if whoever the embracer then was wrote with a tongue in his (or perhaps her) cheek"—122.32–34), and a "lady's postscript" that pleads for financial assistance: "I want money. Pleasend" (42.9–10).

Letter writing and lovemaking, letters and labials, are bound together by the *Wake* dreamwork. The "lps." of the final line of the text are both lips and lisp, elsewhere associated with "please," the plea of the woman to her other and also the *pli* of the envelope which encloses her sexual secrets. The *Wake* seals, stamps, and posts woman through the mails. She is portrayed as a letter whose covering must be slit open and whose message is ravaged in order to be read. The destructive instrument is a fork (⊓) whose "therrble prongs" (628.5) ALP fears. Woman's plea is "please stop, do please stop, and O do please stop" (124.4–5).

The plea (and *pli*) contained within the letter return us to the letter's circuit, where Shaun the Post plays a crucial role. As a sign of forbidden desire, the letter traces a tortuous route through the postal system, along a pathway that leads to and is a diversionary tactic against incest. Entrusted to Shaun, who is the embodiment of canonical and common law, the letter catches him in a double bind: the need to deliver the letter and the desire to suppress it. That is, the postal system itself has an investment in insuring that the letter arrive and not arrive at its destination.[29] Thus Shaun delivers the letter always into the wrong hands (which are also the right hands), insuring that it is continually deflected, diverted, displaced, and detoured. The diverted plot and scrambled discourse of the *Wake* are at one level *effects* of the letter's nonarrival.

As the letter is carried along the pathway, it meets every possible form of resistance to delivery. Ultimately, it cannot be de-

livered, for reasons stamped on its envelope: "No such no.";
"None so strait"; "Overwayed. Understrumped"; "Too Let. To
be Soiled"; "Vacant." The occupants of the various Dublin addresses tracked by the postal system (addresses that once belonged to James Joyce) meet similar fates: "Noon sick par-
son"; "Exbelled from 1014 d."; "Dining with the Danes";
"Arrusted"; "Drowned in the Laffey"; "Salved. All reddy buried"; "Cohabited by Unfortunates." The letter's circuit either
begins or should terminate at "29 Hardware Saint . . . Baile-
Atha-Cliath," but even its message despairs of delivery: "Nave
unlodgeable. Loved noa's dress. Sinned, Jetty Pierrse." The letter has been opened by "Miss Take," its address "Wrongly
spilled," and has been sent "Back to the P.O. Kaer of" (420.17–
421.14). Its nearly illegible signature admits responsibility for
having "sinned" and "signed," while the signator's name includes both Jerry (Shem) and HCE, among whose doubles is
Persse O'Reilly. The postal system has certain claims on this letter. It has become the property of the post (and Shaun will claim
authorship of it), its final resting place to be the Dead Letter Office (the midden heap), where its "penmarks used out in sinscript
with such hesitancy by [the] cerebrAted brother" (421.18–19)
will be pecked at by Biddy the hen. Interrogated by the girls from
St. Bride's school (incarnations of Issy), Shaun first denounces
the letter as belonging to "Mr O'Shem the Draper," who put his
mother up to writing it ("She, the mammy far, was put up to it
by him"—421.35–36), for which Shem should be "depraved of
his libertins to be silenced, sackclothed and suspended" (421.36–
422.1).

As Shem's twin, Shaun claims credit for the letter ("Well it is
partly my own, isn't it?"—424.23), accusing his "celebrAted"
brother of stealing it from him ("Every dimmed letter in it is a
copy. . . . The last word in stolentelling!"—424.32, 35). An-
gered by this thievery ("As he was rising my lather"—424.36–
425.1—that is, as he was writing my letter), Shaun recognizes
the hand of his brother in the letter's "hesitency," whose subject
is "HeCitEncy," his excellency, HCE. The letter tells again the
episode in the park and conflates the sin of the father with writing
a letter, as though "righting his name for him . . . after laying
out his litterery bed" (422.34–35) were the equivalent of the

sexual sin the letter describes. Claiming the authority of the letter for himself, Shaun disclaims his responsibilities as the postman ("innocent of disseminating the foul emanation"—425.10–11), arguing that under the law he "will commission to the flames any incendiarist whosoever . . . would endeavour to set ever annyma roner moother of mine on fire" (426.2–4). The letter is "incendiary": it inflames desire, but it also risks being put to the flames, consumed, reduced to ashes.

The system insures that Earwicker's secret is safe by hiding the letter in the one place he would not think to look, a place he knows *too* well, and one he assumes can only be filled by him, a place that marks the very failure of the postal system to read woman's writing: ALP's vagina. Here the letter remains—unreadable because never delivered—hidden in the apostrophe of its language, a marker of the (missing) phallus and sign of sexual difference.[30] The letter has undergone to a series of transformations, however:

> Heated residence in the heart of the orangeflavoured mudmound had partly obliterated the negative to start with, causing some features palpably nearer your pecker to be swollen up most grossly while the farther back we manage to wiggle the more we need the loan of a lens to see as much as the hen saw. Tip. (111.34–112.2)

Life on the midden has produced stains that are read as signs, a chemical-historical process that melts, merges and mutilates, producing the "negative" from a "positive" and blurring distinctions between marks and their meanings.

A second text emerges as a negative of the first, its defining feature a stain (tea stain or watermark), the signature of woman's complicity in the writing act and sign of her violation by the pen(is). The signature works within the negative, overturning the feminine "affirmative" and disarranging the sexual alphabet (pp/ qp; l/y, l/p). As this struggle for authority affects the letter, the message is altered so that its signature, the sign of its possession, is obliterated—that is, it is opened to any who might read the letter. The signature is missing, its blank space overlaid by a "teastain (the overcautelousness of the masterbilker here, as usual, signing the page away)" that usurps and effaces the name (111.20–21). Every member of the Earwicker family "signs" the letter as it appears in chapter 5: Earwicker by the tea stain, Issy with her "four crosskisses," Shem with his title ("Shem the Penman"), and Shaun in the postal stamp that pays for the letter's delivery ("P.P.M"—postage prepaid in money—131.03). The multiple "signatures" proclaim the absence of a singular possession, each covering the blank space of its signatory (where Anna Livia's sign is expected) in such a way that all marks of possession are put into question. The letter belongs to no one and to everyone, its violation occurring under the "closed eyes of the inspectors" (107.28) of the postal system through which the letter circulates.

ETERNALIZING THE GEOMATER, MARGINALIZING THE GIRLISH GIGGLER

That is to sight, when cleared of factions, vulgure and decimating. (289, fn. 1)

Writing in the *Wake* holds secrets and poses riddles whose answers rest (rather literally) with woman. Efforts to decode the female body, through various forms of transcriptions and translation, reveal a masculine blindness to sexual difference. For instance, Shem's triagonal inscription of woman on page 293 of *Finnegans Wake* (see page 50) provides no entrance to its hiding place, the place in which this secret writing inscribes itself under the protection of the hymen. The hymeneal fold is marked in Shem's drawing by overlapping circles, which figure both the virginity of this text (its inaccessibility) and the potential for violation at the point where it can be penetrated. In order to expose the secret text, to deliver the letter and deliver up its message, the woman's body must be violated. In fact, it must be twice violated because the letter is twice concealed, hidden first internally, protected by the double fold of the hymen, then concealed by the "everydaylooking stamped addressed envelope" (109.7–8) of its "feminine cloithering" (109.31) that covers the female body. To discover the message, the woman must first be stripped (writing and reading are forms of "secret stripture"—293, fn. 2), then penetrated. Reading, therefore, constitutes a kind of rape, a desire to impose authority and uniformity through violence, to appropriate the secret at all costs, to expose a textual/ sexual vulnerability. "Form" is broken in the effort to extract "meaning," emptying the text, making it bleed, erasing, effacing, blanking out, or "rewriting" certain of its forms and norms. Submitted to the light of day, rescued by the reading process from its dark hiding place, the letter is rendered transparent. The hymeneal veil that supports "sin" and "sign" as double signatures of dream and letter, each bearing the mark of the other, is broken.

As a cultural text, woman's body carries meaning but does not produce it: patriarchy inscribes the female body with the pen(is). Her body produces "tots" rather than "thoughts": "Where did thots come from?"—597.25, the *Wake* repeatedly asks. Excluded from culture, woman nonetheless insures its continuation by her "nature," her ability to give birth. From earliest times in Western culture, she has lived within domestic enclosures, her language a derivative and domesticated form of man's language, rendered banal and utilitarian. *Finnegans Wake* repeats this tradition, while Issy's actions subvert it. In the Lessons chapter, for instance, her commentary appears in a form belonging to philosophic argumentation and scholarly erudition. The contrast between this standard notational structure and its subversive sexual content, however, explodes the scholarly pretensions of the chapter.

The footnotes form a narrative commentary of their own. Moreover, they give voice to feminine laughter, a *jouissance* of language, that splits open academic, phallogocentric discourse. They constitute an apostrophe to the domestic, to female sexuality, to "private" speech, to "illogic" and "chaotic" energies. They also reveal the daughter to be "worldly wise," at least within the family world. The themes of incest and sexual seduction echo throughout the notations, hinting that the daughter has the "goods" on her father's lusty attentions. Evidence of Issy's knowledge can be found in the relation between the subject matter of the text and the *form* of the footnotes, the spelling of words containing clues to the father's presence, and echoes of a linguistic byplay indicating that the notes are double-voiced. The notes are not a narrative (although they may be rearranged to create a story line). Rather, they elucidate the complex relations among internal parts of the text, first adding a third voice to the dialogue of the brothers (a triologue), then doubling the notational voice to create a quartet—or, textually, a chiasmus **X**. This cross-structure, whose center is an impasse, is also found in the dream, whose origin in the waking world can never be identified.[31]

At certain crucial points, the notes divide, like the voices of the washerwomen in chapter 8, where the women rubbing away at the stains on Lily Kinsella's drawers are aged incarnations of Issy's divided ego:

> [1]What's that, ma'am? says I.
> [2]As you say yourself.
> [3]That's the lethemuse but it washes off.
> [4]Where he fought the shessock of his stimmstammer and we caught the pepettes of our lovelives. (272 fn. 1–4)

These notes are keyed to a discussion of the family—"Pappa-passos, Mammamanet, warwhetswut and whowitswhy" (272.5–6)—including father, mother, two sons who are at odds with each other ("warwhetswhut"), and a daughter with an as yet undifferentiated personality ("whowitswhy"). The text presents a riddle for identification of the family members in their recurrent incarnations through history: "But it's tails for toughs and titties for totties" (272.6–7), in which the "toughs" are the brothers, the "totties" their sisters. This line echoes "teems of times and happy returns," which initiates the theme of historical return in new guises. The process of naming, attempting to identify and discern personalities behind roles, is a theme carried through the parallel structure of the notes, a game played throughout the *Wake*. The game acknowledges linguistic slips between word and referent, and hints at threats to phallogocentric and patriarchal powers.

Identity and its possible disguises are concerns of Issy's notational discourse, where the person addressed often maintains a shadow existence; she sometimes has a name—Maggy, Pipette, Laughing Sally—and carries forth identifications made earlier in her role as Issy's mirror image. These identifications retain their functions from previous contexts, so that Maggy appears in the reference to letter writing (recalled from *Wake* I I I) in Issy's thank-you note for gifts: "Well, Maggy, I got your castoff devils all right and fits lovely. And am vaguely graceful. Maggy thanks" (273 fn. 6). Pipette, even when not specifically named, is identified by Issy's lisp: "Pipette. I can almost feed their sweetness at my lisplips" (276 fn. 6). Occasionally, the person addressed is identified in the text to which the note is joined, as in "Dear and I trust in all frivolity I may be pardoned for trespassing but I think I may add hell" (270 fn. 3). The "Dear" of this address is associated with Alice in Wonderland and her real-life counterpart, Alice Liddell ("Though Wonderlawn's lost us for ever. Alis, alas, she broke the glass! Liddell lokker through the leafery, ours is mistery of pain" (270-19-22). "Alice," "aliases," and "alas" conjoin in this reference to someone who is "lokker" through the "leafery," spying on the world of Wonderlawn. That "someone" is present in the next footnote, "He is all menkind of every desception." Lewis Carroll, the pseudonym of Charles Dodgson, whose "desception" amounted to spying on the world of young, nubile women such as Alice Liddell—the very sin that HCE may be guilty of in Phoenix Park. Lewis Carroll, like HCE, is "all menkind," introduced under the linguistic guise that offers multiple incarnations and reincarnations. The gaze belongs to the male (Dodgson, a cleric and university lecturer, was an amateur photographer), and "seeing" is "sinning." The young women who are the focus of the gaze are sexually sullied by the eye/I of the male.

The *Wake* compulsively reviews and repeats the thematic and linguistic links between "sin," "sign," "sex" and "sight." The relation among the four terms is plotted across the scholarly text of chapter 10 (which incorporates four voices) and the female body (293) that superimposes two triangles and double circles. Issy's commentary on the drawing, and her own labeling of its parts, are particularly instructive. Unlike Kev (Shaun), she understands what she sees: "Draumcondra's Dreamcountry where the betterlies blow" (293 fn. 1). Her note includes a variety of sexual puns ("con," "cunt," "butt," etc.), resounding a theme already set forth by the passage on which it comments, a passage that itself includes sexual wordplay. In the second footnote, she confesses to her alter ego Laughing Sally that her father is present (under the guise of "old Pantifox Sir Somebody Something, Burtt") and that she fears he will haunt her "for the rest of the secret stripture" (293, fn. 2). The crux of the geometry riddle is the need to "see" and "sign," to identify and name. The page begins with what looks like a name, "Coss? Cossist?" (Arabic for vagina); it poses a question ("You, you make what name?"), and the problem Dolph sets out for Kev is to identify the mother by her definitive parts. Patriarchal powers and fears rest in phallic sexual difference—the male parts available to sight, female sexuality dark, secret, and potentially subversive.

The physical properties of this page are both different from and analogous to all the pages of chapter 10, a central strip of narrative surrounded by the distinguishing marginalia. The imposition of the drawing at the center of the page, however, changes the internal relation of the text to itself, incorporating what heretofore had been outside—linguistic signs differentiated for the reader by their manner of reproduction (print faces) and placement on the page. If we had forgotten, we are now reminded that this chapter's subject is relations and relativity, apparent in the subject matter of the children's lessons and visible in the construct of the textual surface. We read here the sum of various efforts to comprehend scholarly texts, to translate them into terms that are meaningful and relevant. What is relevant to Issy (as woman) is irrelevant to her brothers, and their different views merge only when the implications of the drawing are made clear. The process of notation on this page is intimately tied to the processes of reading and listening—incorporating facets of both written and oral production; the notes reflect the very process that we ourselves enact as we read the chapter. Only when the drawing is labeled, identified and defined (i.e., translated into other terms, another language) are its implications removed from the general arena of signs and placed in a specific, gendered context. Issy's pun, "stripture," is highly accurate: woman is both stripped and scripted by this process.

Issy refuses to be the object of man's gaze; instead she steals the gaze and sneaks into her father's dream to observe him watching her. Her notes have stripped and scripted this scene for us. She draws the parallels between Dolph's drawing and her mother's physiognomy: "Ugal egal ogle. Mi vidim Mi" (297 fn. 2). She delineates equal angles, and remarks, "I see." We rely on her commentary for corroboration, explication, extenuation of our reading. Without her notes, our relation to the text is distanced, obscured enough, perhaps, to prevent our "seeing."

Issy focuses our attention on sexual difference, on the masculine desire for it and denial of it. She draws our eyes again and again to the drawing of the mother's vagina, which is here enclosed, impenetrable, without an entrance. When Kev investigates the vagina of his real mother, he discovers, of course, that it is open and emits both sounds and substances ("Waaaaaa. Tch! Sluice! Pla!" [297.17]); indeed, its very purpose is to provide an entrance (and an exit), a place for penetration, an opening, an origin. The *Wake* narrative delineates all the possible substances that ebb and flow into and from this orifice:

> discinct and isoplural in its (your sow to the duble) sixuous parts, flument, fluvey and fluteous, midden wedge of the stream's your muddy old triagonal delta, fiho, miho, plain for you now, appia lippia pluvaville, (hop the hula, girls!) the no niggard spot of her safety vulve, first of all usquiluteral threeingles (and why wouldn't she sit cressloggedlike the lass that lured a tailor?) the constant of fluxion Mahamewetma, pride of the province. [297.21–30]

Issy's comments in a note to this meditation on tides of the vaginal canal that "Mahamewetma, pride of the province" includes "all meinkind," a conglomerate of "mankind," "my child," and—perhaps most importantly—"me in kind." That is, Issy in her body, in her female gender.

Issy's language is inf(l)ected by the metaphors of human sexuality that occupy the *Wake* and that her own discourse recuperates. Her notations retell the story whose ambiguous, amorphous, often repeated but never predictable history the *Wake* attempts to reconstruct. Her commentary provides links between the masculine world (with its concern for the past, first causes, origins, scripture, and reference) and with the more intuitive, visionary world of the woman whose purpose it is to generate, to produce, to give human life its origin. Issy repeats the terms of sexual difference, with a difference.

The fault in Dolph's drawing of female anatomy is that he leaves no point of entrance in the geometric figure: it is a closed, encircled world—not unlike the hermetically closed world of scholasticism for which it is a paradigm. The "entrance" to this world is provided by the woman, who herself embodies a point of entrance into historical and biological reproduction. Issy establishes relations, hints at origins, provides references, inverts hierarchies (taking over the narrative by establishing her own text), and takes the academic into the real, lived, experienced world. And in so doing she both repeats the actions of her mother (through whose vagina she entered the world) and anticipates her own originary powers. By repeating the story, translating it, telling it again, she lets us know that she *knows* the story, has access to the ambiguous and shadowy events that have led to humanity's downfall throughout history and that are now threatening to topple HCE. She doubles back on the story each time she comments on it, reinvesting it with the meaning given by her own perspective. This process is not instinctive: she learned it first from her mother, whose waters echo the story and whose "O" promises knowledge of origins and entry points, then from other women she overhears spreading the gossip, embroidering the action a bit further. Issy is Biddy the hen, scratching at the letter; she is the washerwomen, airing the Porters' dirty linen; she is the gossip who never reveals her sources and who takes great liberties with the facts. Issy is on the circuit of the apostrophe, where the E and A circulate; and her "lps" (lips) repeat the story. Her footnotes turn aside; they apostrophize.

The movement of apostrophe problematizes the series of oppositions its doubling movement invokes: sound/silence, here/there, me/you, speaker/listener, internal/external, address/response, living/dead, presence/absence, etc. Apostrophe resists and enforces these oppositions even as it traverses them. It is the mark of difference, a difference within that precedes such categories and brings them into existence: apostrophe announces the silences within speech, providing in the announcement graphic evidence of the power of that silence: O! Apostrophe compromises systems, bodies (including the human body), origins, delivery points, and points of departure. It undoes the structure of hierarchies and resists closure—this last a way of resisting the narrative drive from origin to closure. That is, apostrophe calls the question of genre to account. As a grammatical marker, apostrophe marks all that it cannot fully account for.

Finnegans Wake repeats this gesture: its rush of words, letters, sounds, and songs covers over its own failure to account. The effort to tell the tale from beginning to end, with all false starts and loose ends carefully tied together under the generic imprint, "narrative," is undone by the turn (') of the apostrophe and the apostrophic turning aside. *Finnegans Wake*: a turning that confuses subjects and objects, waking and sleeping, borders and boundaries, definitions and explanations, genders and genres. Apostrophe, an impurity that contaminates the pure sound of O, or the moment of pure presence, or the pure present. Apostrophe is at work even when we cannot see it or hear it: Finnegan's wake. *Finnegans Wake*.

CHAPTER 4

Letters: *The Post Card* in the Epistolary Genre

You shall understand, that I know not when, there came a Poste, I know not whence, was going I know not whither, and carried I know not what: But in his way, I know not how, it was his hap with lack of heed, to let fall a Packet of idle Papers, the superscription whereof being only to him that finds it, being my fortune to light on it, seeing no greater style in the direction, fell to opening the enclosure, in which I found divers Letters written, to whom, or from whom I could not learne.

          Nicholas Breton, A Poste with a Packet of Madde Letters, *1602*

. . . Granted, then, that all of literature is a long letter to an invisible other, a present, a possible, or a future passion that we rid ourselves of, feed, or seek.

          The Three Marias: New Portuguese Letters; *1972*[1]

I want to focus on the moment in literary history when epistolary fiction emerged as a genre—the moment when "letters" became "literature"—by looking closely at a contemporary text that extends and subverts the differences between letters and literature. To remove the "Envois" of Jacques Derrida's *The Post Card* from their present-day context and force them into a narrowly defined literary form is to expose how history has denied differences between "letters" and "literature": since the seventeenth century, "letters" have been made to serve (as) "literature"; that is, letters have been made to serve the law of literary genre. "Envois" simultaneously serves and transgresses this generic law. Collectively, the *envois* form the preface to a book that was not written, a book whose subject would have been "the *postes* of every genre" and a study of the system in which letters circulate.[2] They form a philosophic treatise on the status of writing in West-

Drawing of Plato and Socrates, by Matthew Paris, the frontispiece of *Prognostica Socratis basilei*, a thirteenth-century English fortune-telling book. From Bodleian Library, Oxford, Ms. Ashmole 304, fol. 31v (detail). Analyzed by Jacques Derrida in *The Post Card*.

ern culture; they are the private correspondence of a lover to a beloved, and the introduction to a published, and therefore public, text. They both represent the genre "letters" (as dispatches, circulars, letters of credit, form letters, poison-pen letters, purloined letters, dead letters, love letters, forged letters) and contest the separate status of the genre by playing the letter against literature, identifying the postcard as "inadmissible literature" (*PC*, p. 9). "Envois" reflects and refuses to be constrained by literary form: it is relentlessly self-conscious, unable to take for granted the structure and conventions letter writing employs.

"Envois" composes itself by a double writing that articulates the law of genre and enacts its effects. The law exceeds its own limits, simultaneously inscribing and transgressing its own boundaries: "You situate the subject of the book: between the posts and the analytic movement, the pleasure principle and the history of telecommunications, the postcard and the purloined letter, in a word the transference from Socrates to Freud, and beyond" (*PC*, back cover). "Envois" submits its dispatches to the postal system, where they shuttle between *postes*, or relay stations, along a psychosexual trajectory of desire that creates "correspondences" between its subject of address (an absent beloved) and the form of address (a postcard). Framed as epistolary fiction, "Envois" composes a "love letter" that goes beyond its own address.

Addressed to "*toi, mon amour*"—addressed to love—"Envois" enacts a law of genre (*la loi*) that is declined in the feminine: "you, my love" is both the subject *envois* address and the one who whispers the message of desire in the ear of "J.D.," the writer of the postcards. The feminine serves the law of genre as its suppressed mark of difference (from the phallic), thereby exceeding and unbalancing its oppositional structure. The law forbids the crossing of gender/genre boundaries while ceaselessly, helplessly trespassing on its own interdiction. "Envois" traces these effects through its address, which upsets notions of an embodied gender identity, even as it constructs an erotic alphabet from gendered bodies:

I repeat, my love: *for you*. I write for you and speak only to you. You are perhaps the only one to know it, but you know it, in any case better than anyone; and you have no reason to doubt it, no more than this card that you are reading now, that you are holding in your hands or on your knees. Even if you did not believe what I am writing on it, you see that I am writing it to you, you are touching it, you are touching the card, my signature, the body of my name, me. [*PC*, p. 73]

What engenders "my signature," and how is the "body of my name" gendered? Speculating on these questions, Derrida retraces the exchange of *envois* for "Envois:" letters become literature, and the generic law suppresses the (feminine) mark of its own self-difference.[3]

Reversing the traditional roles of epistolary fiction in which the heroine writes under the dictation of a male author who appropriates her femininity and creativity in the service of a literary genre, "Envois" places the masculine under the dictation of a feminine figure, writing a fiction inscribed in the hymen rather than by the pen(is). Included on the trajectory of the letters that shuttle from loved to beloved is a lengthy treatise on the relation of gender to genre, on the difference between *le poste* (post, position) and *la poste* (mail), between the pleasure principle and the death drive, between letters and the *genre littéraire*. "Envois" composes a "reverse inquiry," a retracing of the historical moment in which letters became literature, in which gender served genre.

The shift from letters to literary genre is as difficult to follow as the postal relay of Derridean dispatches. This movement was not a "leap" or a sudden change of generic norms but rather a zigzagging motion across an unbounded territory where the distinction between "letters" and "literature" was yet to be made. The genre Linda Kauffman defines as "amorous epistolary discourse" includes Ovid's *Heroides*, a classical text that looked back to Sappho and forward to Heloise, but as a genre amorous epistolarity did not face a critical crossroads until the seventeenth century:

As it passed from history into legend, Heloise's character, like Sappho's before her, underwent a momentous metamorphosis. Sometime between the appearance of her Latin letters in France in 1616 and Bussy-Rabutin's passionate paraphrase in 1687, the learned medieval philosopher who acted on high ethical principles was transformed into a fictional *grande amoureuse*. What happened was that *The Letters of a Portuguese Nun* appeared anonymously in Paris in 1669. Although it is unlikely that Heloise's original letters directly affected Guilleragues' conception of the *Portuguese Letters*, the latter certainly had a profound influence on all the subsequent versions, imitations, sequels, and paraphrases of Heloise's letters.[4]

At its most popular, the genre denied its fictionality, announcing the "truth" of woman's desire inscribed *au féminin*. Authenticity rested not in textual signatures (which sometimes, as in *The Portuguese Letters*, were missing) but in emotional intensity. During the seventeenth and eighteenth centuries, fictional verisimilitude rested in the sense of reading "real" letters. When letters appeared under a publication imprint, questions of veracity, authorship, and ownership coincided.[5] Samuel Richardson's *Clarissa* proved, however, that fiction could reproduce, even improve on, these passionate inscriptions of feminine desire and distress. Although amorous epistolary discourse became "assimilated to the novel, like a footpath joining a highway," as Kauffman observes, the mark of its generic law existed under erasure in narrative fiction.[6] Relentlessly satirizing the generic claims of amorous epistolary discourse, "Envois" writes a love letter to its (own) law.

WOMAN AND LETTER: GENDER AND GENRE

Now the feminine, or generally affirmative gender/genre, is also the genre of this figure of law, not of its representatives, but of the law herself who, throughout an account, forms a couple with me, with the "I" of the narrative account.

Jacques Derrida, "The Law of Genre"

Although it has become a critical commonplace to claim that the eighteenth-century novel evolved under the sign of "woman"—hypostatized in feminocentric fables consumed by a female reading public—what seems less clear is the ideological content of the masculine investment in such an economy.

Nancy K. Miller, " 'I's' in Drag"[7]

Retracing the correspondences "Envois" inverts and overturns, I begin with that "critical commonplace" traced by the history of the novel: the place of woman in such fictions, the importance of gender to the development of literary genre. Derrida's writing addresses the more generalized relationship posed by these terms (woman/novel; gender/genre). Outlining the law of genre, he starts from "common" knowledge: that in French the word "genre" encompasses and designates gender. English borrows the generic sense of the word as it applies to literary forms, but relies on a different word, "gender" (whose common genesis with "genre" remains hidden in the Latin root *genus* and the Greek γενοσ), to distinguish biological differences. The law of genre functions in part as a reminder to "the Anglo-American reader that in French the semantic scale of genre is much larger and more expansive than in English, always including within its reach the gender." [8] Tracing the common thread, the essay uncovers the hidden assumption that etymologically links gender and genre: the integrity of biological genders, which cannot be "mixed," whose distinctive, generic forms must remain intact.

If the law of genre forbids the mixing of genres ("Genres are not to be mixed"), Derrida's essay demonstrates the impossibility of *not* mixing genres, of not investigating the proximity of genre to gender. "Envois" inscribes the effects of this proximity. First, it traces the path of male desire for a "female element," thus repeating conventional forms in following the effects of the generic law for a genre that had its root (and found its route) in the feminine. [9] Second, "Envois" rewrites the speculations of the law of genre by constructing a correspondence between the "I" of the narrative and the feminine figure of the generic law (*la loi*) under whose dictation the "I" writes. The two form a couple, a man and wife whose union traces certain effects through the writing. Third, and perhaps most important for my purposes, "Envois" subverts the law of gender that has traditionally supported the integrity of the literary genre: "Envois" mixes genders and genres.

Literary histories of epistolary fiction frequently comment on the apparent link between women and letters and, specifically, on the suitability of the epistolary genre for the feminine gender. Ruth Perry and Linda Kauffman examine how epistolary fiction explores and exploits social conventions that constrain women's lives and make them fit for lovemaking and letter writing. The love letter is the special province of the feminine. [10] Separated from male enterprise and worldly activity, women established links with others through correspondence; they represented themselves through the written word and substituted the act of writing for the action of living, finding in the blank page the occasion to create an ideal version of themselves, to establish a correspondence between an affair of the heart and the language of the heart. Letters provide freedom from the claims of reality precisely because they are private, recording desires necessarily silenced by prevalent social codes. Letters promise to reveal secrets, examine private passions, strip away the social mask, and expose the real person. They attempt to create an image of self and are the effect of such an effort. Letters scrupulously explore the consciousness of the writer, probe emotional states, and examine the conscience. They provide a pastime, a means to break out of restrictive, conventional lives, of counteracting the inertia and boredom that often characterize the woman's part.

Letters also document the emotional exchange of the social/ sexual contract that seals woman's fate: in describing the circuit of this exchange, writing substitutes for the act of lovemaking; it becomes a record of as yet unlived passions. As emblems of the invented life, letters invite women to fictionalize both themselves and their subjects, the female imagination constituting itself in a dialogue between the present "I" and the absent "you" of the correspondence. Thus, the historical progress from letters to literature is measured by a fictionalization of the letter-writing process: what began in the reality of separated lovers forced to enact a love affair in letters ended in the fabrication of both lovers and correspondence, ended in a certain "genre" of epistolary fiction. Women who filled empty lives by writing letters later passed idle hours reading literature (written by men) constituted of similar letters.[11] The exchange of women's letters for a literary genre *based* on women's letters initiates a series of substitutions, including the appropriation of female creativity under the guise of heterosexual desire.

Epistolarity inscribes an absolutely rigid law: the fiction it promotes can only take place within the letter; the letter contains both the word and the world and substitutes "word" for "world," exchanging writing for living; the movement of letters across a distance of space and time fuels the desire that they emblematize. Letter fiction constructs a poetics of absence because it cannot accommodate action that takes place outside the letter of its law. Life is either set aside until the obstacles separating the lovers can be negotiated and closed (when the gap closes so does the fiction); or life that resists its own loss is lived in a fictional past, when love was "living" and "active." For these reasons, epistolary fiction often represents woman as a figure of suffering (she writes in extremis), her isolation the theme and medium of the fictional form. Absent of a self, of a call to life requiring action, woman constructs a fiction of herself in a life secured by love, in a fate sealed by sexual desire. She "marks time" as she writes, holding in place two possible resolutions of her fate, seduction or abandonment, either of which will seal her sexual identity.

Paradoxically, desire that cannot be acted out fuels epistolarity. Writing opens the possibility of fulfillment and consummation, and, even when it mourns a love lost, writing is inaugural: it rekindles desire. As the following portion of Heloise's letter demonstrates, letters can frame loss *as* desire:

> Letters were first invented for comforting such solitary Wretches as myself. Having lost the substantial Pleasures of seeing and possessing you, I shall in some measure compensate this loss, by the Satisfaction I shall find in your writing. There I shall read your most secret Thoughts; I shall carry them always about me. I shall Kiss them every moment.[12]

The capacity of letters to recapture and rekindle retrospective desire made them appropriate models for fiction. That the letters from which the epistolary form was derived were already fictions, already often positing a correspondent who was a fiction of the absent lover, positioning a *self*-address within their address as well as an address to love itself, is not merely an irony that the epistolary genre exploits again and again, but a property of letters themselves, which locate their possible fictionality in the gaps between the present moment of their writing and the retrospective elements of their subject matter, between the present moment of their writing and the future moment of their reading. Epistolary writing includes the anticipatory, the retrospective, and the self-reflexive in its sweep.

Linda Kauffman observes that the technique of prolepsis in amorous discourse functions to authenticate memory and memorialize "everything that is related to the image of the beloved," who becomes the "repository of all identity and desire." [13] Directed toward the future from the position "in memory of ————," the love letter oscillates "between memory and hope," obsessed with an oral mode of writing. As Janet Altman explains, "epistolary language is preoccupied with immediacy, with presence, because it is a product of absence." [14] The temporality of first-person speech creates a false sense of an immediate subjectivity that epistolarity ultimately denies. As the letter inscripts and encrypts desire, rehearsing scenes of loss and abandonment, it hollows out subjectivity and creates the very loss it fears. Addressing desire, the letter celebrates the death of the subject who signs her own death warrant. A sealed message, the letter is a coffin (one thinks of *Clarissa*, whose heroine writes on the coffin that later entombs her). Death operates within the epistolary genre, not least when amorous discourse tries to master loss, to overcome absence and separation, to read beyond the dates, stamps, and other temporal signs that consign the letter to the past even as it addresses a "present" lover. Transporting itself across time and space, amorous discourse weaves an intricate web of verb tenses that both celebrate and deny the past, evoking the loved one, restating past events and forecasting others, "thriv[ing] on imagination, roles, scenes, theater." [15]

"Envois" replays these scenes, staging the relation of desire and death within the terms of the postal principle that carries the letter. Prefacing the set of essays collectively entitled "To Speculate—on 'Freud,' " the *envois* reinact the relational structure of repetition of the *fort/da* game (on which Freud speculates in *Beyond the Pleasure Principle*) as a scene of representation. I cannot undertake here a close analysis of Derrida's reading of Freud's text, except to say that he maps psychoanalytic speculation onto a scene of writing in ways that illuminate the structuring principles of the epistolary genre. The *fort/da* game invented by Freud's grandson during his mother's absences reenacts loss (he throws a reel or spool attached by a string under the bed skirts) in order to master it and thus bring pleasure (he reels the spool back): the mother/spool goes away, then returns. Later, the child invented a similar game with a mirror, this time making his own image disappear and reappear; this game forecasts certain elements of Lacan's mirror stage. Derrida shows that epistolarity also reenacts loss and return ("disappearance-return," "absence-representation") in the exchange of letters. While it appears that a law of "tauto-teleology" binds epistolary structures (the heroine's fate in death, abandonment, or marriage is held within the address of her love letter), in fact another logic is at work.[16] Rather than mastering the loss it represents within the scene of writing, the letter produces from loss an excess of desire. That is, loss is never balanced by fulfillment or desire by satisfaction. Indeed, as Gayatri Spivak observes, Freud concludes that little Ernst takes more pleasure in the *fort* than the *da*: "The *un*-pleasure of the *fort* . . . is . . . for the pleasure of the *da*, more pleasing than pleasure *itself.* This affectional asymmetricality renders the phenomenal identity of pleasure undecidable; and keeps the game forever *in*-complete, although Freud insists to the contrary."[17]

Feminine excess, an undecidable pleasure/unpleasure, an excitation that goes *beyond* the law or principle, upsets the phallic economy in which all gains accrue to the master. Something remains behind when the account is closed, woven into the textual signatures or encrypted in a "dead" letter that goes astray. Derrida assigns various names to the "differantial stricture" of the postal/pleasure principle: *hymen, pli, revenance, supplément, double bande, différance.* However we call it, whatever address we give it, this feminine figure *exceeds* the law. An "excess" of feminine desire that cannot be bound or mastered returns (from within) to haunt the law of epistolarity. It hollows out a structural difference *within* psychic, grammatical, linguistic, and literary laws that is externalized as a gap *between* self and other, letter and lover.[18]

The phallic structures of fiction that suppress the feminine mirror the social and political realities of Western culture. Only recently have we begun to plot the relation of textuality and sexuality, noticing the similarities between woman's place in society (where it is prescribed, confined, legally bound) and her place in letters (where the law of letters and the laws of literature keep her "in her place").[19] Feminine desire as woman pens it in her own love letters represents a powerful threat to social/sexual institutions precisely because it risks going out of control. Erotic desire is "erratic": it can get carried away with itself and escape its boundaries. To serve patriarchal ends and needs, it must be rewritten in such a guise that woman thinks the desire so written belongs to her. Rerouting the feminine, epistolary discourse creates a complex grammar of sexuality; it invents fatal plots in which the heroine succumbs to marriage, dies of shame, is forced to deny her sexuality, and offers metaphors and images of seduction in which love is virtually indistinguishable from rape. In such novels as *Clarissa, Julie, ou la Nouvelle Heloise, The Portuguese Letters*, for example, the heroines try to discover the dividing line between their own desire and someone else's. Theirs are, in Peggy Kamuf's terminology, fictions of feminine desire: "Whether it is behind the solid walls of the nun's cloister, at the unspoken limit of the hysteric's language, or within the frame set by a parent's desire, the passion that shapes these fictions can only discover itself in transgression of the law which encloses it." [20] Vehicles for the expression of all that is denied, repressed, or silenced by the culture, the letters of amorous discourse try to short-circuit systems of cultural repression by writing across the borders of forbidden desire. Defying the system, they also encode its power structures. Rarely an exchange between equals, these communications operate within enormous economic, legal, educational, and gender imbalances that reinforce the initial interdiction of desire and underwrite patriarchal privilege. For example, if the woman writer is under the man's employ (as in *Clarissa*) or tutelage (as is Heloise), she occupies a vulnerable social position. Empowered, the man can encourage, manipulate, and brutalize woman, bringing her desire under his "dictation" and enforcing constraints upon it.

Under the dictates of a phallic economy, "the male bond of privilege and authority constitutes itself," according to Nancy Miller, "within the laws of proper circulation." [21] The circuit does not negotiate a space of sexual difference but rather binds male narcissism to homosocial power: woman serves as the "currency of the erotic exchange" between males. [22] The apparent heterosexual economy of letter fictions masks homoeroticism, for which both the letter and the woman serve as fetish. The letter-writing *amoureuse* only appears to be the object of man's desire; in fact, she represents a masculine fantasy of feminine desire. Written into the text in translation, under the signature of the male author, woman's epistolary discourse circulated under the sign of patriarchy. Sold to a desiring female readership, these patriarchal plots completed a circuit of economic exchange among men. [23]

The argument that epistolary fiction only poses as feminocentric writing is a powerful one. Yet the autobiographical and domestic forms of women's writing on which epistolary discourse draws, and on which its verisimilitude and emotional intensity rest (e.g., Heloise's letters, or those of the Portuguese nun) inscribe textual/sexual difference within gender. Letter writing records feminine desire, and its address to the lover incorporates a self-address. Women's letters circulate, properly speaking, under the stamp that taxes the *exchange* of desire within a phallic economy. Derrida writes: "the stamp is not a metaphor, on the contrary, metaphor is a stamp: the tax, the duty to be paid on natural language [*la langue maternelle*] and on the voice" (*PC*, p. 52). Epistolary discourse fictionalizes the "mother tongue," the "natural" language of feminine sexuality, in order to route it within the laws of "proper circulation." Challenging this order of propriety and property, woman pens a double message, her letters inscribing submission and rebellion, defiance and desire.

Linda Kauffman argues that amorous epistolary discourse transgresses the law of its own genre and masks the rebelliousness of the writing act in the request to write again, to keep the circuit of desire open: the letter "is an attempt to negotiate some kind of correspondence." [24] Heloise's correspondence with Abelard, for instance, breaks the rules that he has established for their letter writing: he insists on reading her through her vows as a nun; she refuses to write as a nun, writing instead as a grieving lover. Resisting the forms of tyranny that have led to this painful correspondence, she rewrites the rhetorical forms of epistolarity and refuses to remain silent about her sexual desire. She breaks forms and norms by claiming to adhere to them, by elaborating them so lovingly and cleverly as to overturn their laws. As Kauffman explains, Heloise "bursts through the forms of acceptable correspondence, and shatters the refuge Abelard [has] taken in treatises, authorities, conventions." [25] Woman's self-desire (and desire for self) threads a silent subtext in the epistolary genre, taking a path of detour and deferral.

If phallic authority informs the law of literary genre, its powers extend to the interpretive "phallacy" as well. An empty text that presumably only inscribes loss (of the phallic), the letter figures the female body. [26] Putting pen(is) to paper, woman en(s)crypts the feminine within the terms of the masculine. By contrast, reading tropes on a scopic economy. Penetrating, surveying, interpreting, filling the text with meaning, reading enacts patriarchal violence:

reading is rape. These metaphors of sexual difference gain particular power in relation to epistolary fiction, which tells (sexual) secrets.[27] By definition a dangerous form of writing, the letter must remain within the circuit of sender and receiver—that is, it must circulate within a phallic economy. Folded back on itself to create an envelope, the letter is sealed, stamped, even written in code so that—should it fall into the wrong hands (a possibility highly probable before the development of the modern postal system)—its secrets will be safe. Breaking (into) these codes, reading is not merely voyeuristic but duplicates the (repressed) sexual act that the letters themselves address. The woman's letter-body opens itself to a double violation. First, her writing images forth a feminine sexuality that exists only as a shadow of itself in this society: en(s)crypted, it exists as a difference within itself; second, the act of reading duplicates the sexual act already mimed by the first writing: pen(is) and eye are instruments of violence.[28] The movement from the dialectical oppositions of gender difference to an internal division within genre, which makes three of two, suggests that woman is doubly present in the written text. She is written into the gap between the letters, in the space between letters and literature, in the fold of the envelope, where her existence-in-absence, her existence under repression, makes a claim to the literary effects of letters.

The literary effects of feminine desire, systematically overlooked by Western letters, are radically reinscribed in *The Post Card*, which contests the "tauto-teleology" of the epistolary genre. Is it true that epistolary discourse unfolds between two oppositional poles, the exchange of letters enacted according to an economy of the same, the final term of the fiction implicit in its first letter? Using the postal system to encompass all contracts of desire, Derrida restates in various ways his conclusion that the circuit of desire cannot assure the letter's arrival or destination: "it is not sure that the sense [*le sens* as both "meaning" of the words "postal system" as well as the direction the system takes] of the p.s. (postal service) is assured of arriving at its destination, nor is the word to post" [*poster*]" (*PC*, p. 162). Playing on the rules of epistolary genre and detective genres, Derrida rereads Edgar Allan Poe's "The Purloined Letter" by way of Jacques Lacan's seminar on the letter. Lacan takes up Poe's story to illustrate how the "symbolic order . . . is constitutive for the subject," which receives its "decisive orientation . . . from the itinerary of a signifier." He claims that the movement of the purloined letter structures the story's plot within a phallic circuit that always confirms its own powers. In psychoanalytic terms, the letter [signifier] is indivisible and "always arrives at its destination." In this phallic reading, the story repeats an age-old plot, *cherchez la femme*, the letter seeking its "proper" place within female anatomy.[29] Deconstructing the embedded phallogocentrism of Lacan's claim (the Phallus as transcendental signifier), Derrida argues that (1) "a letter does *not always* arrive at its destination, and from the moment that this possibility belongs to its structure one can say that it never truly arrives," and (2) "the divisibility of the letter is also the divisibility of the signifier to which it gives rise."[30]

The arguments on both sides of the psychosexual divide are complicated by twists and turns that defeat summary. Simply put, however, Lacan plots the Law of the Phallus within Poe's text to illustrate a founding principle of psychoanalytic theory: human subjectivity is created in the fissure of a radical split whose terms of sexual difference are enjoined upon the subject. A symbolic construct rather than a biologic fact, sexual difference for Lacan is arbitrary, enforced, never a "given." Derrida situates his critique of the phallic signifier within the abyssal structure of subjectivity's radical split. Because it follows a split *within* the subject, the letter's arrival at this nonplace can never be guaranteed. Who is to say, from one moment to the next, where in relation to this asymmetrical divide the subject is speaking or writing?

DIFFERENCE, DUPLICATION, DISSEMINATION

Before going about putting a certain example to the test, I shall attempt to formulate . . . what I shall call the law of genre. It is precisely a principle of contamination, a law of impurity, a parasitical economy. . . . The trait that marks membership inevitably divides, the boundary of the set comes to form, by invagination, an internal pocket larger than the whole; and the outcome of this division and of this abounding remains as singular as it is limitless.

"The Law of Genre"

In order for the circuit of the letter to end up confirming the law of the phallus, it must begin by transgressing it; the letter is a sign of high trea-

son. Phallogocentrism mercilessly represses the uncontrollable multiplicity of ambiguities, the disseminating play of writing, which irreducibly transgresses any unequivocal meaning.
    Barbara Johnson, The Critical Difference [31]

"Envois" tells a story of reversals beginning with a reversal of the scene of writing that is its philosophic subject and the spur to its narrative. Instead of imaging the familiar scene of writing put forth by the epistolary genre, where according to Nancy K. Miller, "a man stages himself as a woman longing for his presence in his absence," "Envois" invokes "the possibility of a male voice of absence" by presenting a male whose fate is presumably sealed by sexual desire. [32] In *A Lover's Discourse*, Roland Barthes outlines the gender effects of an exchange whose genre effects Derrida takes up. Barthes writes:

Historically, the discourse of absence is carried on by the Woman: Woman is sedentary, Man hunts, journeys; Woman is faithful (she waits), man is fickle (he sails away, he cruises). It is Woman who gives shape to absence, elaborates its fiction, for she has time to do so; she weaves and she sings; the Spinning Songs express both immobility (by the hum of the Wheel) and absence (far away, rhythms of travel, sea surges, cavalcades). It follows that in any man who utters the other's absence *something feminine* is declared: this man who waits and who suffers from his waiting is miraculously femininized. A man is not feminized because he is inverted but because he is in love. (Myth and utopia: the origins have belonged, the future will belong to the subjects *in whom there is something feminine*). [33]

"Envois" reverses and repeats the traditional plot of epistolary fiction wherein a domesticated woman pines for the worldly, and therefore absent, lover. Separated from the loved one by an active life of professional travel, isolated by the very requirements of his profession, the lover writes in solitary hotel rooms or on trains and planes as he crosses national boundaries and international time zones. In his isolation, he plays the part of those women letter writers who invented their lives and inspected their suppressed desires through letters.

This transposition of parts raises a crucial question: can man occupy the place of woman? Can the male writer compose a discourse of absence, elaborate its fiction, give form to that which defines the feminine? To do so under the law of epistolary fiction is to create the male writer's fantasy of the female, to portray her "in drag." Miller comments that for a male writer to take seriously the effort to write "as" a woman—that is, to allow the feminine to emerge as the feminine rather than to create a fiction of it—may be "too painful, too threatening to be assumed in a masculine identity." [34] If one subscribes to Roland Barthes's belief that "amorous absence . . . can only be articulated by the one who remains, not the one who leaves: *I* always present only constitute myself in relations to *you* constantly absent," then "Envois" is not written from the position of absence held by woman. [35] Rather, "Envois" acknowledges that position by marking its otherness. Derrida does not give voice to the feminine, does not put words in the mouth of *toi, mon amour*. Instead, he allows her to remain silent. In doing so, he (silently) acknowledges Barthes's imperative: "to invoke absence is to posit from the start that the place of the subject and the place of the other cannot be reversed; it is to say: 'I am loved less than I love.' " [36]

The writer of the *envois* constitutes himself in the measure to which he fears being loved less. The *envois* "write over" the absent *destinataire*, however, who is present only to the genre of "Envois." Although "Envois" reverses the general properties of the epistolary genre and exposes its contradictory logic, like many epistolary fictions it constitutes a one-sided correspondence. Just as editor-authors of traditional epistolary fictions had the ultimate power to constitute the text, so the letter writer can both write and unwrite this fiction of desire. Blank spaces in the text denote the missing portions of his own letters (letters that were ordered burned, then rescued by the writer from the flames), and there are no letters from "you, my love." Indeed, *toi, mon amour* may be a fiction, her missing letters mere invention. Her identity, the role she plays as correspondent, forms the central mystery of the fiction: "Who writes? To whom? . . . To what address?" (*PC*, p. 5; translation modified). Even her gender is in question. The word *amour*, the masculine noun of address most often used in Derrida's text, makes a "he" of the presumed "she" of a heterosexual coupling. In the plural form, however, *amour* changes gender. Addressed in the grammatical form of the intimate singular, *toi, mon amour*, the one and only, is nonetheless pluralized. *Amour* has an Other, who divides and brings dissension to the loving couple. Conforming to the Western no-tion of woman as double, *toi, mon amour* has another woman in her.

Through this play of grammatical genders and genres I believe Derrida tries to expose the asymmetry of sex-gender relations, to unveil their violence, to *displace* them, not merely to invert their positions. The inscription/erasure of female subjectivity troubles Derrida's postcard fiction. It invites accusations that the postcard writer (whose gender/genre is also in question) usurps woman's position the better to silence her. One could argue that this dis-course engages *toi, mon amour* as an object; she occupies a place between two males, "Jacques Derrida," who signs the text *The Post Card*, and "J.D.," who signs the postcards. Does "she" become "a product of male desire and male artistic practice" or does "Woman" in the mythic and generalized sense of Barthes's terminology negate or erase "woman" as subject? "Envois" puts these questions into play within the folds of gender/genre distinctions.[37]

As object of desire, *toi, mon amour* exists under censorship, in the absent responses to the *envois*. As the figure of desire, however, she constitutes the very pleasure/postal system in which the *envois* circulate. Addressed as desire itself, she serves as its destination; "written out" of the impulse to entrap desire, she exists only under erasure. In the gaps of the letter's fiction "En-vois" traces a pathology of censorship: it is this "secret" that is made public.

The literary form of "Envois" dictates that: the letter stand for the lover; the letter and lover be one; the letter follow the phallic law of patriarchy. Although the *envois* move within the closed space of epistolary fiction, they unsettle the generic dictate that letter = lover and the notion that the letter secures desire. Trans-gression of the genre is achieved, in part, by the writer's effort to "read" the relation not only of his correspondence with *toi, mon amour* but with another loving couple, Socrates and Plato, pictured on the front of the postcard. "Envois" constantly plays the couple against the two lovers who are coupled, constantly questions the equation of epistolary fiction (letter = lover) by doubling the terms of the correspondence and reversing its sex-ual dynamic: heterosexual turns out to be homosexual; desire-indifference underwrites an economy of the same. Every commentary on the scene of writing refers both to "J.D." and "*toi, mon amour*" and to Socrates and Plato. Moreover, each figure in the correspondence is doubled so that the writing game comprises eight players, all of whom (plus the reader) *The Post Card* addresses:

> I have the impression that I am writing to my most foreign homonym. [P. 182]
> If I address myself . . . always to someone else . . . I can no longer address myself to myself. [P. 112]
> For you are, yourself, my unique, my only destination. [P. 136]
> Socrates comes *before* Plato . . . an irreversible sequence of heritage. [P. 20]

The simultaneous inscription of the recto and verso of the post-card reveals a double image of the Western metaphysic. One side of the card writes out the dictates of authority and patriarchal power; the "backside" of the card records woman's censored desire. Feminine desire leaves its trace, which is writing in the Derridean sense, that is, writing-under-erasure, writing read in spacing, grammatical forms, punctuation marks, the negative of a photographic image or the impressions of bas-relief.[38] As the phallic law inscribes the fate of the feminine (writing its "underside"), it cannot help but violate its own literary code: the law always produces the terms of its violation. This backsided writing tells a reversed story, maintaining itself in opposition to a patriarchal (his)story of proprietary claims of inheritance and heritage.

In this rewriting, woman's place is held both by "J.D.," who writes under intimidation of *toi, mon amour*, and by Socrates, pictured as writing under the dictation of Plato:

> Socrates writing, writing in front of [before] Plato, I always knew it, it remained like the negative of a photograph to be developed for twenty-five centuries—in me, of course. . . . Socrates, the one who writes—seated, bent over, scribe or docile copyist, Plato's secretary, no? He is in front of Plato, no, Plato is behind him, smaller (why smaller?) but standing up. With his outstretched finger he looks like he is indicating, designating, showing the way or giving an order—or dictating, authoritarian, masterly, imperious. [*PC*, pp. 9–10][39]

The theme of reversed doubles is apparent in the two-sided material properties of the postcard, in the relation of "J.D." to *toi, mon amour*, and in the picture of Socrates seated on the high stool of the scribe, writing under Plato's dictation (see illustration, p. 87). This image of Socrates and Plato reverses historical knowledge and contests inherited notions that Plato served as Socrates' scribe, the student recording the master's words in a kind of "gramophony." The scene sketches an economy of writing as intellectual indebtedness (but of whom? to whom?), a debt that weighs heavily on Plato, who can escape its imperative only by rewriting (i.e., reversing) the terms of the contract under which he is forced to labor. Plato's debt to Socrates is the debt of Western civilization, the debt of writing to speech.

This economy of indebtedness is also a familial one, as Derrida has repeatedly shown.[40] As son, Plato's dream is to make Socrates write his (Plato's) will, thereby killing Socrates, killing the father, killing speech, making the debt null and void: "In choosing violence—and that is what it's all about from the beginning—and violence against the father, the son—or patricidal writing—cannot fail to expose himself, too. All this is done to ensure that the dead father, first victim and ultimate resource, not be there. Being-there is always a property of paternal speech. And the sight of the fatherland." [41] Overturning the traditional roles of Socrates and Plato, "Envois" places Socrates in the position of dispossessed fatherhood. His paternal authority is usurped by the son.

Under the force of Plato's will, Socrates writes his own will. Like the letter-writing *amoureuse* of epistolary discourse, he signs his name to a contract that is really his own death sentence: "Watch closely while Socrates signs his death sentence under the order of his jealous son Plato" (*PC*, p. 15). The letter Socrates writes (to which Plato will put his own name) is a contract of death written in the name of the Other, a ceding of "will" under dictation. In this inverted scene of writing in which Socrates no longer represents the fatherhood of speech but rather the sonship of writing, Socrates writes the will—that is, the volition—of the one who now has the power to appropriate his own voice, his own will. The exchange of "wills" constitutes a contract in which Plato's volition is transcribed as Socrates' last will and testament. The reversal of positions, the exchange of power, creates the "photographic negative" reproduced as the postcard.

Deprived of his authority, Socrates is unmanned, made to occupy the place of woman (of writing), to play woman, to write out the dictum that will result in the death of Socrates, the silencing of woman:

> [Plato] argued that the private speech of the household, the speech of women, lacked either the form of philosophic argumentation or the form of poetry. It was, therefore, without meaning—unformed, chaotic, evanescent, the speech of doxa (mere opinion, not truth). . . . The women of Plato's time were not only excluded from politics but also debarred from participating in the process of becoming what Plato meant by a "good" human being—a process that required a special search for truth within the all-male forum for philosophic discourse, a pedagogy, and intimacy that is the *mise en scene* for the Platonic dialogues.[42]

Excluded from intellectual and social debate, Plato's silenced woman becomes an absent presence in Western civilization, the feminine a hidden element in history's record. Because woman's language has traditionally been defined as a derivative and domesticated form of man's language, it is rendered banal, domestic, and utilitarian, sharing the debased status of writing.

Deconstructing the hierarchical relation of speech to writing, Derrida reveals that even in its denigrated, narrow sense, writing exceeds categories of containment. An expanded notion of *écriture* as writing that precedes speech, already present in the first breath of speech, illustrates the creative and subversive potential of writing. Whether in Derrida's grammatological writing practice, Hélène Cixous's *écriture féminine*, or Luce Irigaray's speculative, miming critiques of privileged philosophical discourses (Plato, Freud), *écriture* writes a double message: it submits to and resists the logic of sameness that underwrites patriarchal forms and conventions.[43] Establishing a hierarchy in which the "all-male forum" of public discourse is valued above the all-female world of domestic speech, Plato wished not only to distinguish between these two kinds of speech but also to protect male speech from corruption by the imitation, and also revolutionary potential, of "woman's" language.

The scene of writing pictured on the card produces various

readings of writing as a subversive act. The first of these is the familiar reversal of the historical imperative, Socrates came *before* Plato, which translates as the inverse route that the message on the postcard might take: "Socrates turns his *back* on Plato, who has made him write what he wanted while pretending to receive it from him" (*PC*, p. 12). "Dictation," then, is a form of writing: Plato writes—his index finger extends—on the back (*sur le dos*) of Socrates so that the message received will be his own message backward. But this scene stages a *redirection* of the dictated message. Socrates turns his back to Plato to subvert the dictated message, making it the will of Socrates rather than Plato. However, it is not altogether clear that Socrates *is* writing. He holds in his hands both pen and *grattoir*: "You will say that 'to write' is also to scratch [*gratter*]; no, he is scratching in order to erase, perhaps the name of Plato . . . perhaps a dialogue of Plato's" (*PC*, p. 49). Socrates may be effacing Plato's name from the message and affixing his own, in which case the message Plato receives will not be "his own message backward," but a message dictated by Socrates—so that Plato is dictating his own death warrant.[44]

This scene of writing raises not only political and philosophic issues but offers itself to sexual and psychoanalytic readings. The representation on the card transfers into the discourse of "Envois" as a particularly erotic position for lovemaking, a reversal of the traditional poses of male and female. "J.D.," the writer of the postcards, speculates on possible interpretations of the picture, commenting that Plato, like a bus conductor, "drives" Socrates, his finger in his back, his extended penis (a part of the chair on which Socrates sits) a writing instrument that directs the scribe. This reading confuses front/back, recto/verso by word scrambles: *déjà* (the inverse of the initials, "J.D.") and *derrière* (an anagram for Derrida). The reading overturns and inverts genealogical inheritances, and the heritage of Western civilization is signaled by reversed genders, identities, and sexual preferences. An effect of Plato's divisive edict—the division of "public male discourse" from "private woman's writing"—results in the creation of homosocial worlds. The homosocial becomes homosexual as differences between genders are submitted to the psychosexual economy of "sameness": to dictate the movement of the pen is to write on the "erotic *dos*" and commit a homosexual act. The "photographic negative" of the postcard reveals anal intercourse between males.[45]

Each of the contradictory "readings" produced by this scene of writing is duplicated in "Envois" under the aegis of the epistolary genre. Socrates occupies the place of woman, the postcard writer pens his message under the dictation of an-Other. Just as the scene portrayed on the postcard reverses the positions of Socrates and Plato, so "Envois" reverses the patriarchal imperative of epistolary fiction: the letter of the law is returned to the feminine as the postcards are composed under the menace of "you, my love": "I write under your threat" (*PC*, p. 38). In the position of the feminine, he is dictated to by her: "'I' (he) 'loves' the law, a feminine figure" (*PC*, p. 38). Identities, genders, genres are exchanged. *The Post Card* reproduces the exchange of "wills" between Plato and Socrates as a transfer of the feminine law of the genre letters to the masculine *genre littéraire*, a transfer that signals the appropriation of woman's creativity, a denial of her existence and substance. The genre of this fiction is in doubt just as the gender of *toi, mon amour* is put into question: "We are of the same sex . . . S is P. Q.E.D." (*PC*, p. 52) writes "J.D." to his absent lover. Indeed, there is some suspicion that the writer of the postcard pens letters to himself in drag, framing his desire for his heterosexual other as the desire for his own (reversed) image. Barbara Johnson, writing of Lacan's seminar on "The Purloined Letter," observes:

> The message I am reading may be either my own (narcissistic) message backwards or the way in which that message is always traversed by its own otherness to itself or by the narcissistic message of the other. In any case, the letter is in a way the materialization of my death.[46]

The process that inverts history and metaphysical hierarchies and causes the collapse of heterosexual binary distinctions into the homosexual produces no conclusive readings either of the scene of writing portrayed on the postcard or the writing scene raised by the text of "Envois." The material questions posed by the text and picture—"Who writes? To whom?"—multiply their terms, doubling not only the binary opposition of letter writer/letter reader but also the terms of the discourse: "J.D." is at the same time both the writer of the letter and reader of the postcard; *toi, mon amour* is both the one addressed and the one who dictates. Each of these positions is transgressed by the reader of *The Post Card*, who interpolates the relation of the correspondents and negotiates the time-space positions held by the *signataire* and *destinataire*. This odd game of reversals never comes out "even."

"J.D.," the "reading character" posited by "Envois," also dictates reading relations. This figure writes the text and reads its internal relations, calls to our attention the internal divisions that position the correspondents, and constructs the double frame of *envois* and "Envois" within gender and genre. "Envois" may be an apostrophe, an address to the mark of punctuation that designates possession (of an identity, a name) and to a genre that addresses itself to love, to the loved one, calling up *toi, mon amour* and calling out of silence and absence:

> Thus I apostrophize. This too is a genre one can afford oneself, the apostrophe. A genre and a tone. The word—apostrophizes—speaks of the words addressed to the singular one [*unique*], a live interpellation (the man of discourse or writing interrupts the continuous development of the sequence, abruptly turns toward someone, that is, something, addresses himself to you), but the word also speaks of the addressed to be detoured. [*PC*, p. 4][47]

As a grammatical marker, the apostrophe forms an internal exclusion, signifying the impossibility of possession and the inherent possibility of internal division. "J.D." writes to "you, my love": "There is an other in you who from behind [*par-derrière*] dictates the terrible thing to you, and she is not my ally [*mon alliée*], I have without doubt never had business with her, we (yes, we) do not know her" (*PC*, p. 125). He is afraid of this "other" who inhabits "you, my love" and dictates to her the necessity of her dictation over him. In awe of her power, he is terrified of her emergence in the text: "Your sinister 'determination' has cut us in two, our glorious body has been divided [against itself]" (p. 193). A second incarnation of the feminine presents itself not only as the negative of its opposite (the other's "other") but as the product of an effort to subjugate, appropriate, and gain authority over its counterpart, an effort to silence the other, to make the other a shadow, a mere reflection—as in a mirror—of the self. As this struggle for authority affects the letter, the message is altered. Its very inscription, signature, the sign of its possession is deformed, often obliterated altogether. Not only is the place of signature open to any who might sign the letter and effectively efface the real author, the whole notion of authorship is put into question. What takes place in the dictation and writing of the letter is a death struggle, an effort to kill *toi, mon amour* and her other by writing them "out" of the text. Although the death sentence carried by the letter is written out and signed, its crime leaves traces: the feminine law and her shadow other can be read through the writing that would obliterate them. They trace a treacherous and sinister route, one that can be read only by following the grammatical markers of gender.

PHALLOGOCENTRIC LAW OF GENRE

Subject ⟶ Object
(masculine) ⟶ (feminine)

"J.D." ⟶ *toi, mon amour*
(author of *envois*) ⟶ (to whom *envois* are addressed)

Socrates ⟶ Plato
(author of dialogues) ⟶ (to whom dialogues were dictated)

"Jacques Derrida" ⟶ "Reader"
(author of *The Post Card*) ⟶ (to whom *The Post Card* is addressed)

SUBVERTED LAW OF GENRE

Subject ⟶ Object
(masculine) ⟶ (feminine)

Toi, mon amour ⟶ "J.D."
(who dictates *envois*) ⟶ (who signs the *envois*)

Plato ⟶ Socrates
(who dictates death warrant) ⟶ (who signs his own death warrant)

"je" ⟶ "tu"
(subject of "Envois") ⟶ (to whom *envois* are addressed)

The new law operates against the shadow presence of the old law so that an inversion of its principles and methods can take place. Each position on the graph has its "other"; each position on the graph is violated by this "other."

Toi, mon amour occupies the position of subject (masculine) as she dictates to "J.D.," but she occupies the object position as she is dictated to by her "other" whom "J.D." fears. Her message is "traversed" either by "its own otherness to itself or by the narcissistic message of the other" (here, the shadow "other" of *toi, mon amour*). It is impossible to chart precisely this traversal, to know at any moment which positions *toi, mon amour* occupies or whether the messages "J.D." pens are written under the menace of *toi, mon amour* or her other. A more troubling question is whether *toi, mon amour* is someone other than "J.D." or whether she stands in for his other. Identifications, proper names, cannot properly be affixed. However the game is played, whoever occupies the various positions that displace each other, the game being waged is a death struggle.

A death warrant written in the name of the other, the love letter signals the threat of extinction, of consummation, the possibility of making good on the contract of desire that initiates and reciprocates the letter's movement through the postal system. Prompted on its course by desire, the post raises the stakes in this erotic game as letters of desire shuttle through its exchange: "What impels me to write to you all the time?" asks the postcard correspondent. "Envois" hints that desire prompts the pen(is), that writing addresses desire, or its simulacrum. The very problem of naming this desire, of calling desire by its "proper" name, haunts the writing (which is, as the writer admits, highly "improper"): "and when I call you my love, my love, is it you I am calling or my love? You, my love, is it you I thereby name, is it to you that I address myself?" (*PC*, p. 8). (The opening words of the Portuguese nun are, *Considère, mon amour*; it is impossible to decide whether she is addressing her chevalier or her love.) Escaping the attempt to "name" desire, to possess it, to appropriate it, Desire goes by many different names.

A traditional endeavor of the epistolary genre is the naming and addressing of desire. Its history rests in the social environment of the early eighteenth century, as Ruth Perry observes: "Marriageable women were rarely alone with the men they imagined themselves to love; such a lack of access could only have encouraged idealized dreams of romance. Many courtships were carried on in letters fuelled by the imaginative process of writing, because written correspondence was the most direct and private way that unmarried men and women had of communicating with one another."[48] Whatever the historical causes of creating in correspondence an illusion of desire, it translates into fiction as a *figure* of desire. Rousseau describes the figural quality of language in the second preface to *Julie, ou la Nouvelle Héloïse*: "love is only an illusion; it fashions, so to speak, another universe for itself; it surrounds itself with objects that do not exist or that love alone endows with being; and since it states all its feelings by means of images, its language is always figural."[49] The scene of writing is structured by way of imagination and rewritten memories that establish the forms and norms of the romance, sending desire on its way. Amorous epistolary exchanges are marked by an apocalyptic movement, by fatality. Julie writes in her first letter to Saint-Preux, who refers to his own first letter as "fatal": "In this first step I feel myself dragged into the abyss."[50] This statement follows Julie's exclamation, "Ah! le premier pas, qui coute le plus," a maxim of the overdetermined epistolary plot: from her first step the heroine is fated. The letter carries fatality in its address. Derrida comments that "epistolary fictions multiply when there arrives a new crisis of destination" (*PC*, p. 232). Standing in lieu of consummation, letter writing *forestalls* the ultimate destination of desire in death, in the Dead Letter Office (*lettre morte, l'être morte*) or the heroine's fate.

"Envois" repeats and also deconstructs the belief that the origin and destination of writing is death: "I kill you, I annul you" (*PC*, p. 33). The series of carefully calculated blank spaces that interrupt "Envois" signal the effort to "kill" desire and annul its effects.[51] The spaces may be seen to mark the absent remains of consuming desire that ends in conflagration, requiring the story to be taken up again. A ghost, a voice from the dead situated in the ashes of the fire or in the silent spaces of the text, dictates desire. *Toi, mon amour* dies from an excess of desire. The contract taken out on her life and signed by "J.D." is destined to insure her fulfillment, her consummation:

The addressees [*destinataires*] are dead, the destination is death; no, not in the sense of S. [Socrates/Subject] or by p.'s predication [Plato/predicate], according to which we would be destined to die, no, not in the sense in which to arrive at our destination, for us mortals, is to end by dying. No, the very idea of destination includes analytically the idea of death, as a predicate (p) is understood in the subject (S) of the destination. [P. 33][52]

Desire that predicates consummation would end in the fatal, and inevitable, destination—an arriving-at-death. The writer desires to merge his identity with *toi, mon amour*, appropriate her signature, erase her words from the transcript, and make her image a negative of his own. Indeed, the doubling constructs his subjectivity. In the process, she could be robbed of a name, signature, personality, gender, physical body, a voice. Her "existence" might even be a figment of the writer's imagination: "You have always been 'my' metaphysics, the metaphysics of my life, the 'verso' of everything that I write (my desire, speech, presence, proximity, law, my heart and my soul, everything that I love and that you know before me"—p. 197). The two correspondents are twins who maintain separate identities only through the writing that both doubles and binds them, preserving the distance (of absence, of silence) for the exchange (of identities, of signatures) in order to circumvent the final extinction, consummation, destination. The postal system, however, prevents any arrival at a "final" destination, derailing the possibility of unified subjectivity (the merger of "One" and "Other"), and forestalling the *arrêt de mo(r)t* that would extinguish desire by consuming it.

"Envois" posits conditions of a correspondence that would exist beyond (*au-delà*) the letter, beyond the message of desire dispatched through the postal system under the stamp of the pleasure principle, but it does not put them into place. Instead, it puts them into play. Playing on *poster* and *arriver*, "Envois" "posts" itself to the "beyond" it desires, but never arrives there (*il n'y arrive pas*, which also includes the French word for step, *pas*).[53] The *envois* still operate within the limits of desire and under the law of genre they would try to undo. The correspondence spirals round itself in an endless regression of transfers that defer fulfillment and the consummation they invite. The very existence of this writing as the expression of desire makes it impossible to go "beyond" desire. The cards form a palimpsest: intimate messages between two lovers that "correspond" to all love letters ever written. Previous forms of writing, including woman's suppressed messages of desire, show through the charred, erased, and punctured surface of the cards.

WRITING THE INADMISSIBLE, READING THE ILLISIBLE

Writing is unthinkable without repression. The condition for writing is that there be neither a permanent contact nor an absolute break between strata: the vigilance and failure of censorship.

Jacques Derrida, Writing and Difference

The image is presented, pure and distinct as a letter: it is the letter of what pains me. Precise, complete, definitive, it leaves no room for me, down to the last finicky detail: I am excluded from it as from the primal scene, which may exist only insofar as it is framed within the contour of the keyhole. Here then, at last, is the definition of the image, of any image: that from which I am excluded.

Roland Barthes, A Lover's Discourse[54]

The longed-for presence of the lover that must always be denied follows the Ovidian tradition of lover's discourse, a genre whose effects are openly displayed by letter fictions and often commented on by letter writers theselves. The Marquise de Merteuil writes out this elaborate "erotic protocol" in her correspondence with Valmont in which she explains her warnings that the young lovers of *Les Liaisons dangereuses* not act precipitously on their feelings for each other. Her letters to Valmont carry a double inscription of this message, which is directed toward the young lovers but also to him: it is her "law of genre" for epistolary romances. The epistolary genre plays out the effects of the dictum "Absence makes the heart grow fonder." In claiming that only the object of desire can satisfy the lover's needs, its perverse logic opens the way to substitution and supplement: erotic activities with any available and acquiescent partner can only increase desire for the loved one. Desire *as desire* is longed for and openly courted. The substitution of another woman for the beloved, like the exchange of one letter for another, can only restate the *desire for presence*, never provide the presence of the lover that is presumably so desired: "this desire carries *in itself* the destiny of its nonsatisfaction."[55] *Any* woman, then, can be made to serve desire's claim since nonfulfillment of desire's contract is always assured. Valmont adheres *to the letter* to the substitutionary and supplementary principle of sexual satisfaction. His desire renews itself where it will.

The author of the fiction, like the version of himself he has created in the fiction's pursuing lover, takes his pleasure where he will. That is, he takes his pleasure in providing obstacles to the lovers' efforts to consummate their desire and also provides his hero with occasions to refuel desire for the beloved. The frustrations to which the author submits his fictional lovers can serve only his own erotic desires, their very dissatisfaction—and his control of the situation—a stimulant to autoeroticism. If writing includes elements of the masturbatory, the epistolary genre provides a rich source of autoerotic pleasure in which both author and reader participate. Writing and masturbation share the substitutionary logic described by Rousseau:

> This vice, which shame and timidity find so convenient, has a particular attraction for lively imaginations. It allows them to dispose, so to speak, of the whole female sex at their will, and to make any beauty who tempts them serve their pleasure without the need of first obtaining her consent.[56]

Epistolary fiction "disposes" the female gender and dispenses with individual women by creating imaginative feminine figures for the purposes of self-satisfaction. Each lover creates an image of the other and excites a desire for the *image* through writing. For the author of epistolary fiction, who presumably stands outside its limits, the entire narrative is itself an invented image of desire thwarted or threatened, and therefore intensified, through which he can follow his own erotic desires.

Individual letters and, ultimately, the fiction itself image desiring as the psychic condition of longing that substitutes desire for its object, the fictional replaces the "real," absence is a hunger for presence. Analyzing *Julie, ou la Nouvelle Héloïse*, Paul de Man writes:

> The very pathos of the desire . . . indicates that the presence of desire replaces the absence of identity and that, the more the text denies the actual existence of a referent, real or ideal, and the more fantastically fictional it becomes, the more it becomes the representation of its own pathos.[57]

This referential fiction posits a chain of substitutions—exchanges of letters, signatures, identities—that never succeed entirely in canceling each other out: "whenever a substitution has taken place a new unbalance, by excess or default—which is both a lack and a remainder—is revealed and requires new displacements."[58] The excess or default stands both inside and outside formal, generic boundaries: excess (*supplément*) of desire recommences the chain of repetitions and substitutions that attempt to overcome absence (default) of identity by inventing the presence of desire, an action that is from the outset doomed to failure.

As a *present* lover, *toi, mon amour* is inadmissible to the fictional form; she exists only in absence, in the space between desire and fulfillment. Although the story told by "Envois" is punctuated by moments when the lovers are joined, these moments are narrated by deferment, textualized as anticipation or recollection. Materially speaking, the genre excludes *toi, mon amour* in her gendered body, which can be rendered only textually as the writing that *represents* her gender/genre. Present to the genre *en souffrance*, suspended and unclaimed within the system that invents her, *toi, mon amour* is known by her effects—the return of (the letter of) desire.

A surprising effect of epistolary fiction's substitutionary and supplemental logic is the sinister connection between the autoerotic and censorship. Written from within the fissure of subjectivity (that is, from the position of self-censorship), "Envois" censors and writes what *is* censored by the *genre littéraire*. It censors woman's desire (making it the "negative" to the masculine norm) and also inscribes its erased effects on the backside of the postcard. Under the phallic law of genre, woman can be represented only under erasure, but "Envois" calls attention to the erased and charred effects of the cultural holocaust.[59] In the game of double writing, *toi, mon amour* is unwritten as she and/or he writes: "*En train* [in the process of] writing *you*, of writing *to* you" (*PC*, p. 32; emphasis in original, translation modified). Addressing before the fact of publication the effects of the double inscription of woman, the writer comments:

> . . . and if, because I love them too much, I am not publishing *your* letters (which by all rights belong to me), I will be accused of erasing you, of stifling you, of keeping you silent. If I do publish them, they will accuse me of appropriating for myself, of keeping the initiative, of the body of woman, always the pimp, right? Ah Bettina, my love [blank spaces in text] and it

will be even worse if I publish your letters under my name, signing them in your place. [*PC*, p. 231][60]

The effects of erasing/appropriating woman's desire are not warded off; *The Post Card* calls to them (in apostrophe) and is haunted by their forms of self-censorship.

Censorship demands that the text be rewritten, that its "real" message be presented differently: "The censor's function, of course, is not to prohibit communication, but only to disguise it—the secret is public."[61] Censorship guarantees double writing, necessitates the "reading between the lines" well known to lovers and spies. Derrida's double writing slips under the watchful eyes of the postal inspectors (as does the latent content of dreams) precisely because its message appears to be so open, so public, so innocuous, so unanalyzable: "What I like about the post cards is that, even in an envelope, they are made to circulate like an open but illegible letter" (*PC*, p. 12). The public message is "illegible" to the extent that it disguises a private one, however. Disguised as a hidden message of "Envois," her gender submitted to the requirements of genre, "you, my love" reads the secret writing, the backside of the card and the underside of its message. She can decipher the script because it "belongs" to her. Materially, the text is hers. Women's amorous discourse often mourns the loss of the lover while also, secretly, mourning the loss of *self*. At one level, *toi, mon amour* signifies the loss of self (that never could be) for the postcard writer who takes (up) her place as a position of loss and betrayal. Heloise writes to Abelard:

> God knows I never sought anything in you except yourself. . . . You know, beloved, as the whole world knows, how much I have lost in you, how . . . that supreme act of flagrant treachery robbed me of myself in robbing me of you.[62]

Letter by letter, Heloise invests her self, her subjectivity, in Abelard. Decoded, the censored message reads: "God knows I never sought anything in you except *myself*." But an effect of these multiple transfers, letter exchanges, and translations is that each correspondent internalizes the other.

Exploring gaps and silences, forms that are empty, genres that are defined by what they are *not* (a postcard is not a letter), and writing that is *illisible*, "Envois" tries to account for gender/genre losses. Inadmissible as literature, the postcard cannot be taken seriously. Its generic claims are too meager and its constraints of space and subject matter too limited to qualify even as a "letter," that is, as a signifier. Indeed, the card is a signifying fragment, a letter divided (against itself).[63] All the genre has time or space to write is: "I am here" ("here, where you are not"), a message whose surface meaning almost escapes us, but which seems peculiarly appropriate to the feminine, which is, culturally speaking, neither "here" nor "there." The message translates a basic law of subjectivity, however; it articulates a doubled or split subject that subjectivity acts to deny. In Lacan's famous phrase, "Where the *moi* [me] was, there shall *je* [I] place itself."[64] Constituted by absence, the writing subject is never present to (him/her)self. The postcard message reminds us, then, that subjectivity is the creation of the Other: "I" constructed through an absent, but internalized, "you." The law of subjectivity is the law of genre necessarily transgressed.

How does "Envois" recover this message? Appropriating the postcard, which cannot support the denigrated genre (letters) it stands in for, "Envois" overturns the epistolary law. Failing to rewrite woman's desire in its own terms, epistolary discourse returns the law of genre to the feminine, reversing the historical movement that appropriated woman's letters for literature. If the epistolary genre makes a fiction of sexual difference and heterosexual eroticism, "Envois" preserves in/difference, enveloping the component elements—letter and lover—within a textual space that is both interior and exterior to itself. Elsewhere Derrida calls this the space of the hymen, whose effects he describes in "The Double Session":

1. "Hymen" . . . is first of all a sign of fusion, the consummation of a marriage, the identification of two beings, the confusion between two. *Between* the two, there is no longer any distance between desire . . . and the fulfillment of presence, between distance and non-distance; there is no longer any difference between desire and satisfaction.

2. Thanks to the confusion and continuity of the hymen . . . a (pure and impure) difference inscribes itself without any decidable poles, without any independent, irreversible terms . . . What is marked in this hymen between the future (desire) and the present (fulfillment), between the past (remem-

brance) and the present (perpetration), between the capacity and the act, etc., is only a series of temporal differences without any central present, without a present of which the past and future would be but modifications.

3. The hymen . . . produces the effect of a medium (a medium as element enveloping both terms at once; a medium located between the two terms). It is an operation that *both* sows confusion *between* opposites "at once." What counts here is the *between*, the in-between-ness of the hymen. . . . But this medium of the *entre* has nothing to do with a center.

4. The hymen . . . merges with what it seems to be derived from: the hymen as protective screen, the jewel box of virginity, the vaginal partition, the fine, invisible veil which, in front of the hystera, stands *between* the inside and the outside of a woman, and consequently between desire and fulfillment. It is neither desire nor pleasure but in between the two. Neither future nor present, but between the two.

5. At the edge of being, the medium of the hymen never becomes a mere mediation or work of the negative; it outwits and undoes all ontologies, all philosophemes, all manner of dialectics. It outwits them and—as a cloth, a tissue, a medium again, it envelops them, turns them over, and inscribes them.[65]

Within the fictional space (the *entre*) it is possible to write on both sides of the card simultaneously by forming an alliance (a hymen) that *incorporates* gender and genre, rather than making gender submit to genre. Doubly inscribed in what might be called "hymeneal writing," the feminine separates and sutures, it is an effect of "the vigilance and failure of censorship."[66]

Hymeneal writing outwits the dialectical oppositions that support epistolarity's tautological narrative structure even as it reinscribes the law of genre: the heroine's beginning (her gender, her femaleness) marks her end (her desire-in-death); she is forced into submission by patriarchal forces that deny her the right to (write) her desire. Creating an *entr'acte* of desire-in-difference, hymeneal writing stands between the tauto-teleological terms. Derrida links this double affirmation—"the excessiveness of *yes, yes*"—to the law of gender and genre: "the double affirmation is not foreign to the genre, genius or spirit of the law. . . . The law is in the feminine."[67] The gender of the law's figure is also the genre that the law writes.

Just as the hymen "fuses" with the woman's body from which it is derived and "con-fuses" by "stand[ing] *between* the inside and outside of woman," the double mark of genre attempts to keep the genre pure: erecting borders, it fails to secure them. Repeating its own story of desire, the letter frame of epistolary fiction signals *difference from* and collaboration with the genre that encloses it. The hymenic fold of the letter that envelops and seals its contents, that reveals and conceals the presence of woman, subverts the notion of inside and outside—of the framed borders—it seems to mark.

-❊-

SKIRTING THE LAW: LE BORD AND BORDER

Cells fuse, split, and proliferate; volumes grow, tissues stretch, and body fluids change rhythm, speeding up or slowing down. Within the body, growing as a graft, indomitable, there is an other. And no one is present, within that simultaneously dual and alien space, to signify what is going on.
Julia Kristeva, Desire in Language

That which will not be pinned down by truth is, in truth feminine. *This should not, however, be hastily mistaken for a woman's feminini*ty, *for female sexuality, or for any other of those essentializing fetishes which might still tantalize the dogmatic philosopher, the impotent artist or the inexperienced seducer who has not yet escaped his foolish hopes of capture.*
Jacques Derrida, Spurs: Nietzsche's Styles[68]

The hymen figures an internal limit of undecidability. Letters submit to and transgress the law of genre at once, so it is impossible to say at any moment which aspect—submission or transgression—is at work. Nor does one element in this double structure cancel out the other: together they condition the system of representation. Hymeneal writing draws our attention to the "feminine operation" at work in all writing.[69] Inscribing and exceeding the generic law, it does not delineate the purity of genre but rather its inescapable impurity. It writes out a principle of contamination, establishing a parasitical economy in which "letters" and "literature" live *off of* and are composed *out of* each other. This "feminine" writing exposes and veils, avoids and addresses the relation of woman and letters at the birth of the *genre littéraire*.

Before epistolary discourse became a literary genre it supposedly documented authentic experience; it was constituted of "real" letters, which were stolen, sold, and then published to serve the vicarious pleasures of a desirous reading public. The pretext of authenticity, as I have already observed, was imperative to the form: the greater the claim to verisimilitude, the more valuable the fiction. Letter fictions rested on a doubly disguised (and therefore vulnerable) authority. Letter fictions were read as "letters," and "letters" were often assumed to be fictions. Robert Adams Day remarks:

> It is not a simple task to produce an acceptable definition of "letter fiction." Indeed, we discover that fiction itself in this era is a slippery and elusive thing. Genres are not established; fact masquerades as fiction and fiction as fact; the two may alternate even from page to page. Titles give little help: "history," "romance," "true relation," "memoirs," "novel" may mean almost anything, and this has led Walter Allen, in *The English Novel*, to compare the period very aptly to a *frontier territory*, such as Alsace-Lorraine.[70]

A genre whose limits are in question, whose premises are contaminated by the inability to distinguish fact from fiction, letters from literature, seems a felicitous position from which to examine the legacy of written authority. And the existence of a historical line that separates letters from literature or distinguishes authority through generation is the first casualty of *The Post Card*. "Envois" trespasses this moment, remaining either on the edge (*le bord*) of the shift or inscribing its abyssal effects, partaking of the massive *décalage horaire* that no writing can avoid. These dispatches anticipate the further study of the subject they address ("the *postes* of every genre," that is, the study of the posts in every genus, gender, and style) without truly *effecting* the study. "Envois" is not systematic; indeed, it inscribes all that is a-systematic. And the *envois* constitute *les restes d'une correspondance*, the remains, traces, vestiges, and residue of a correspondence that once existed and met its "destination" in "consummation."

The *envois* are both less and more than they claim. They figure in the "excess or absence" they address; they participate in a genre and demonstrate the contradictory and impossible claims made by genre. Constituted in the relationship of exchanges and transfers traced by the movement of the letters, the genre unsettles the authority of its own construction. The *genre littéraire* cannot say on what authority it rests, whether or not its component parts are authentic, whether or not the signatures to its individual letters are "proper." As a genre, epistolary fiction can make no claim to its own purity, although that is the one claim it insists must hold for its heroine. To lose her purity, to give in to her desire, amounts to losing her life.

What, then, is the destination of the literary form? Any response to this question must negotiate and finally encompass the notion of borders. Incorporated within the metapostal system of international communication in which the *envois* shuttle through time and space, the concept of borders, separations, national frontiers, differences between people and languages, between time zones and territories, is itself contestable. Unable successfully to close its frontiers, to insure that nothing is lost, the system represses the possibility of its own malfunction, represses (even as it describes its effects) the possibility of loss: the letter may not successfully pass the border of its *own address*. A hedge against ultimate loss in death, the letter inscribes fear of loss even as it proclaims its own gain. Every scene of writing tests whether the excess or lack of desire that starts the letter-writing chain *can* be recuperated within writing.

"Envois" examines the mechanics of two "systems" joined by writing: the system of desire (for the absent other) and the system of the postal service (by means of which the separated lovers make their desire known to each other). Desire can never fully be destroyed through *action upon* it, since consummation leads either to renewed desire or constitutes itself in the remains of desire, figured in the ashes of the burned letters written by *toi, mon amour*. The postal system is founded *against* the possibility that a letter will go astray, an event that traumatizes "Envois." When the missing letter is eventually returned to "J.D.," its sender, he refuses to send it again, to make it retrace its path in a system that cannot guarantee the retracing of any path.

The postal system figured by "Envois" bears witness to its own fallibility in the calculated spaces, the ellipses, of its failed communications. Each relay in the system marks the trace of an absent other, but tracing the *va-et-vient* of the letters that circulate within the system and keep it functioning, we cannot discover the direct route (root) of the trace. We suspect there is a scene of seduction and betrayal that reverses all our notions of the *generation* of this text: does woman "write" under the penis of male author(ity)? does Socrates "write" with his back turned to Plato (in the "amorous position") under the *diérection* of the phallus that appears on the postcard as an extended leg(acy) of the copyist's chair? Are such scenes, drawn from epistolary fiction, not the effort of literary genre to arrive at its destination? Folded into the multiple relays of the postal system—and hidden in the folds of the envelope that encloses it—the postcard writes its double message of desire ("I am here"; "Here I am") that inverts the historical movement from letters to literature and undermines the principle of genre:

> The question of the literary genre is not a formal one; it covers the motif of the law in general, of generation in the natural and symbolic senses, of the generation of difference, sexual difference between the feminine and masculine genre/gender, of the hymen between the two, of a relationless relation between the two, of an identity and difference between the feminine and masculine.[71]

Unable to answer the questions it poses—"Who writes? To whom?"—*The Post Card* propounds a double fiction of desire and dictation. Against the claim by "J.D." that he writes under the intimidation of "you, my love," a counterclaim is lodged where *toi, mon amour* is constituted under the dictation of "J.D." In fact, the postcard makes good on both contractual claims: the law of genre is simultaneously defied and inscribed. An absent, silent, desired feminine serves in her absence to instigate the writing and marks in her *difference* that which is produced through the writing. She generates the writing and is the figure generated by it. In her double inscription she dictates her desire—the double acquiescence to (her own) desire: "yes, yes."[72]

CHAPTER 5

Ellipses: Figuring Feminisms in *Three Guineas*

St. Paul, for example, lays it down that women, when praying in public, should be veiled. "The implication is that if veiled a woman might prophesy [i.e., preach] and lead in prayer."

Three Guineas

We took his orders,
went and searched, and there in the deepest,
darkest recesses of the tomb we found her . . .
hanged by the neck in a fine linen noose,
strangled in her veils—

Antigone[1]

Toward the end of *Three Guineas*, Virginia Woolf claims poverty, chastity, and derision as the great educators of women, and she makes their lessons a condition of her gift to the daughters of educated men. Woolf then turns to a different culture (the Greek) and an earlier historical moment (fifth century B.C.) to discover how sexual difference was inscribed in the shift from the oral tradition of sacred law to the written code of secular law. She sees this shift as the founding moment of patriarchy in the West and traces its history to the rise of twentieth-century totalitarianism. Woolf focuses her analysis through Sophocles' *Antigone*, whose eponymous heroine symbolizes the fourth condition of Woolf's gift of a guinea, "freedom from unreal loyalties." Antigone's fate is bound up with her commitment to distinguishing "unreal loyalties" from "real loyalties," tyranny from freedom, public duty from personal necessity, and Law from laws (p. 81). Sophocles' drama plots its heroine's tragic fate within these

123

categories, her life and death inscribed in the terms of sexual difference.

I want to begin with *Antigone*, a text that discloses the premises of Woolf's argument: private and public worlds are not separate, but joined in a hierarchical figure that veils the working of the patriarchal law, which Virginia Woolf refers to as the Law of the Fathers.[2] In *Three Guineas*, ellipsis traces the irrationality of this law—its madness—veiled by a rhetoric of rationality. Antigone fashions her *brochos*, the noose from which she hangs herself to escape Creon's brutal law, from the veils that cover her body. Her death by strangulation unveils, silently, the law's operations in a movement marked in Sophocles' text by ellipsis ("we found her . . . hanged by the neck in a fine linen noose"). Antigone falls back, almost literally, against the (il)logic of the law.

Woolf uses ellipsis to signal a falling back or turning away from the socially constructed opposition of truth and illusion within Western thinking, a moment of contradiction and confusion. In *A Room of One's Own*, for example, she asks: "Why, if it was an illusion, not praise the catastrophe, whatever it was, that destroyed illusion and put truth in its place? For truth . . . those dots mark the spot where, in search of truth, I missed the turning up to Fernham," an imaginary, or illusory, women's community.[3] Those dots also mark a turning point in modern feminist theory: they figure a space of textual-sexual difference that produces writing effects. Woolf's ellipses displace narrative alignments, confuse borderlines between textual interiority and exteriority, confound representational orders, and transform (or mix) genres and genders. Ellipsis is not merely a recurrent textual feature of *Three Guineas*, it constitutes the primary structuring device of the text, joining the political argument to the rhetorical-grammatical form through which it is elaborated. The figure of ellipsis also forges links between Woolf's text and a larger social-historical inheritance, "Western civilization."

The question of truth and illusion is posed both in *Antigone* and *Three Guineas* as a question of loyalties. Defining private and familial loyalties as "real," Antigone privileges them before the tyranny of individual rulers; she acknowledges a higher Law, one to which the "laws" of rulers must bow. When Creon sets himself up as the embodiment of the law of state, he places himself beyond the Law and from this position condemns Antigone to death. Her choice is to honor the Law of gods before secular laws, to honor her brother before her uncle, to follow private and personal commitments rather than public and social conventions, to privilege love above hate, and compassion above revenge. Her treasonous act—burying her brother, Polyneices, against the orders of her uncle Creon—pits female "irrationality" against male authority. Her relation to the law is both familial and private (her uncle stands in for her absent and dead father, Oedipus), legal and public (she is subject to Creon's rule of the land), and she is caught within the binary logic of this structure. Antigone is loyal to unwritten laws of nature and kinship groups, but she is subjected to the written laws of man and the state. Tensions between unwritten and written laws are apparent in cultural definitions of sexual difference and the hierarchical social structures that enslave women.

Woolf's most explicit statement on the false distinctions that support these laws (state/family, public/private, reason/emotion, culture/nature) follows a commentary on fathers and daughters. She writes: "Society it seems was a father, and afflicted with the infantile fixation" (*TG*, p. 135).[4] Invoking the father figure of psychoanalysis, Woolf restates Freud's famous question ("What do women want?") from the perspective of the daughters of educated men. She declares: "They [daughters] all wanted—but what one word can sum up the variety of things that they wanted, and had wanted, consciously or subconsciously, for so long? . . . they wanted, like Antigone, not to break the laws, but to find the law" (p. 138, ellipsis mine). Explicating this elliptical reference to the relation between desire and the law, sexual difference and patriarchal oppression, Woolf doubly displaces herself from her own text: first, by including this discussion in an endnote, where she writes from the position of an Outsider who is exiled from patriarchy by her gender; second, she writes around the opinions of Mrs. Drummond (activist and author), one of many figures Woolf draws to the support of her argument:

According to Antigone there are two kinds of law, the written and the unwritten, and Mrs. Drummond maintains that it may sometimes be necessary to improve the written law by breaking it. But the many and varied activities of the educated man's daughter in the nineteenth century were clearly not simply or even mainly directed towards breaking the laws. They were, on the contrary, endeavours of an experimental kind to discover what are the *unwritten laws*; that is the private laws that should regulate certain instincts, passions, mental and physical desires. That such laws exist, and are observed by civilized people, is fairly generally allowed; but it is beginning to be agreed that they were not laid down by "God," who is now very generally held to be a conception, of patriarchal origin, valid only for certain races, at certain stages and times; nor by *nature*, who is now known to vary greatly in *her* commands and to be largely under control; but have to be discovered afresh by successive generations, largely by their own efforts of reason and imagination. Since, however, reason and imagination are to some extent the product of our bodies, and there are two kinds of body, male and female, and since these two bodies have been proved within the last few years to differ fundamentally, it is clear that the law that they perceive and respect must be differently interpreted. [Pp. 184–85; emphasis added]

This extraordinary passage, which deserves more comment than can be given here, searches for the sources of unwritten law (previously assumed to have been laid down by "God") and distinguishes written law (the laws of state) from the law of nature (figured by Woolf in the feminine). The laws regulating "instincts, passions, mental and physical desires" do not, however, fall under the law of nature (now "largely under control"), nor are they laid down by "God." These laws, first formulated by Freud, open onto another (psychic) reality that is only partially, and imperfectly, regulated by society.

Woolf observes that psychosexuality cannot be separated from its cultural-symbolic encodings within the family, where from ancient times men have assumed power over women: "There can be no question—the infantile fixation is powerful, even when a mother is infected. But when the father is infected it has a three-fold power; he has nature to protect him; law to protect him; and property to protect him" (p. 135).[5] The symbolic power of the father's "natural" (familial) relations to his daughter is enforced through the vast network of social, sexual, legal, religious, and economic conventions. Woolf documents the history of patriarchy as an institution with particular reference to its psychosexual organization. In *Antigone* she discovers a parable of the Law of the Fathers.

The figure of the Law in *Three Guineas* is complex, drawing as it does on both ancient unwritten laws (natural law, religious beliefs, and "common" or traditional law) and written legal codes. Following Freud, Woolf treats social-cultural codes within psychoanalytic structures, thus she subsumes beliefs, codes, natural and psychic orders under the "law." A reference point for these terms of her argument is Sophocles' tragedy. Page duBois, a contemporary classics scholar, takes up these same issues in *Antigone*, with special attention to the character of Antigone within feminist criticism and Freud's definitions of sexual difference. Her analysis reveals what is at stake when Woolf draws the classical world into her analysis of modern culture. It is helpful, then, to rehearse the terms of duBois's argument.

She warns against reading *Antigone* within the "essentializing" and "ahistorical" terms of Freudian difference. Observing that social organization of sexual difference varies among cultures and changes over time, duBois argues that in ancient Greece gender difference was "inextricably bound up with . . . agriculture, language, theater."[6] Ancient, preagricultural myths equated woman's body with the earth and parthenogenic fertility. Later myths replaced autochthonous legends with versions of heterosexual reproduction. Sophocles' tragedy draws on one of these, the legend of Kadmos, which encompasses the themes of writing and sowing: the earth (woman's body), no longer spontaneously productive, is a space to be cultivated, a blank tablet on which the pen(is) writes.[7] DuBois reads Antigone as a signifier of sexual difference within warring cultural syntaxes: hers is the preliterate law "of blood ties, of chthonic gods, of laws called *agrapta*, 'unwritten' "; Creon's is the new, written law of the *polis*, posted in the marketplace "for all male citizens to read" ("Antigone," pp. 376–77). Oedipus' incest—coupling with Jocasta, his mother and wife—has infected not only the reproductive lines of the House of Thebes but has polluted the linguistic codes of the city as well. Antigone and Creon display symptoms of sexually coded "similarity and contiguity disorders" (duBois borrows Roman Jakobson's terms): sexually and linguistically, she remains within the order of metonymy (sameness, incest) while he exploits metaphor (substitution, phallic insemination) ("Antigone," pp. 378–79). Creon's new substitutionary order violently yokes together elements of the old order into a new syntax. Acknowledging that Creon is "sometimes too eager to engage in substitution" and is "unable to control syntax," duBois observes that he causes the dispersion of Polyneices' corpse by refusing it burial. This violent act opens the confrontation with Antigone (pp. 378–79).

DuBois's cultural analysis does not, however, fully account for the social-sexual-linguistic violence at the heart of *Antigone*; it fails to observe the psychic (dis)order that directs the play and organizes its characters in relation to each other. Social and linguistic orders cannot contain the violence of Creon's actions and speech, nor can they fully explain it. Through substitutionary logic Creon enforces the social order of the ancient city, which privileges "non-incestuous hetero-sexual relations" to reproduce the community ("Antigone," p. 375). But his actions exceed this social ideology and threaten to destroy it. His words tear the social fabric and split the symbolic order. Indeed, Jakobson's analysis points to failures of linguistic orders (similarity and contiguity, metonymy and metaphor) as *effects* of psychic disorders. Antigone's entrapment within the metonymic linguistic order and the old myths is explained by her gender, which denies her access to the written word, and her status as daughter/sister within the generational and reproductive disorder caused by incest. What explains the violence that directs Creon, that pushes him beyond the limits of his own social laws? Creon's violent language calls out for analysis. It speaks (to) another order, the mythic order organized by unwritten laws ("blood ties") to which Antigone is loyal.[8]

Virginia Woolf was intensely interested in the "unwritten laws" that govern "instincts, passions, mental and physical desires" (*TG*, p. 184). *Three Guineas* is her clearest statement on the psychological causes of social orders. Like duBois, Woolf sees Antigone framed within conflicting laws, but she focuses on the psychic necessity of those laws—or, rather, the failure of law to account for psychic necessity. But she does not accept Freudian theory unreservedly. She challenges, for instance, Freud's assumption that women display reduced ethical and moral capacities. Perhaps his most famous statement on this issue occurs in "Some Psychical Consequences of the Anatomical Distinction between the Sexes," an essay that informs *Three Guineas* and provokes duBois's objections to Freud's essentialist and ahistorical descriptions of gender differences. Freud writes:

> I cannot evade the notion (though I hesitate to give it expression) that for women the level of what is ethically normal is different from what it is in men. Their super-ego is never so inexorable, so *impersonal*, so independent of its *emotional* origins as we require it to be in men. . . . Character-traits *which critics of every epoch* have brought up against women—that they show less sense of justice than men, that they are less ready to submit to the great exigencies of life, that they are more readily influenced in their judgments by feelings of affection or hostility—all these would be amply accounted for by the modification in the formation of their super-ego which we have inferred above. We must not allow ourselves to be deflected from such conclusions by the denials of the feminists, who are anxious to force us to regard the two sexes as equal in position and worth.[9]

Ethical normality in men, Freud argues, differs from that of women because the male superego is "impersonal" and "independent" of emotion; ethical normality in women has an emotional origin that results in women's lack of a sense of justice. Virginia Woolf protests the premises of Freud's argument. Moreover, she stages her resistance in a reading of *Antigone*.

Woolf reverses the terms of Freud's equation, finding that *men* are controlled by emotion and lack an impersonal sense of justice. Disclosed in the last chapter of *Three Guineas*, her discovery results from careful examination of social-cultural attitudes toward women gleaned through painstaking research in history, literature, biography, newspaper archives, and radio journalism—research documented in the more than forty pages of footnotes to her text.[10] She turns, for instance, to Professor Grensted, Nolloth Professor of the Philosophy of Religion at Oxford, who was asked by the Anglican church fathers to analyze the psychological reasons why women could not be admitted to the religious priesthood. Grensted writes that, although psychology cannot support the view that "man has a *natural* precedence of woman," psychologists "fully recognize the *fact* of male dominance" (*TG*, p. 125; emphasis added). Anticipating Lacan's distinctions between the Real and the Symbolic, this statement distinguishes biological sex differences from social gender constructions. Grensted attributes the hostility and "strong feeling" aroused in the ministry by the suggestion that women might join its ranks to "infantile fixation" in men. He writes: "whatever be the exact value and interpretation of the material upon which theories of the 'Oedipus complex' and the 'castration complex' have been founded, it is clear that the general acceptance of male dominance, and still more of feminine inferiority, resting upon subconscious ideas of woman as 'man manqué,' has its background in infantile conceptions of this type" (*TG*, p. 126).

Grensted leaves further investigation of these subjects to "specialists." But Woolf urges her readers to "raise the veil of St. Paul" through an analysis, however "rough and clumsy," of men's "fear [of women] and of the anger which causes that fear" (*TG*, p. 128). Like Grensted, she does not assume that "ancient and obscure emotions which we have known ever since the time of Antigone and Ismene and Creon at least" (*TG*, p. 130) are natural or essential. Indeed, she is intensely interested in the relation of these emotions to social, cultural, and historical constructs. She agrees with Grensted that appeal to any natural, "unalterable law that man is the creator" (*TG*, p. 140) is a rationalization, the product of "subconscious motives" that exist "below the level of conscious thought" (*TG*, p. 128). In *Three Guineas*, Woolf repeatedly states her belief in the unconscious and credits psychic structures not available to conscious thought or rational explanations as forces in society and culture. Nor does she deny the effects of unconscious, psychic functions to the Greeks, however distant and strange their culture appears from twentieth-century life.[11]

Woolf readily draws lessons for modern women from *Antigone*. Examining the relation between written and unwritten laws (*TG*, pp. 80–81), she discovers a false dichotomy between the "private house" and the "public world" (*TG*, pp. 130–31) that has kept daughters, from the time of the Greeks, under the rule of the family patriarch. These are divisions that Antigone herself seeks to understand. Woolf reads Creon's "claim to absolute rule over his subjects . . . [as] a far more instructive analysis of tyranny than any our politicians can offer" (*TG*, p. 81). For duBois, on the other hand, Creon's rule is "not necessarily dictatorial." She sees Creon as an "aristocrat who betrayed his class, allied himself with the *demos*, the 'people,' and took power over the state," breaking the stronghold of kinship groups ("Antigone," p. 377). He submits Antigone to the new order of metaphor and substitutionary logic as part of a larger program of democratic reforms, enacted to conquer ancient codes of "sameness." DuBois's analysis, however, overlooks the reality of Antigone's future marriage, which would further enmesh her within archaic metonymies, blood ties, and unwritten laws. Haimon, her betrothed, is Creon's son; in marriage, she would move between Oedipus (her dead father/brother) and Creon, her uncle/father-in-law, who is also head of state. Marriage would bind Antigone in a double structure, where the strictly separate worlds of private house and public forum overlap and keep her under the guardianship of patriarch and tyrant.

Woolf constructs a commentary on modern totalitarianism through a retelling of the (mythic and Freudian) Parable of the Law of the Fathers. She tells of nineteenth-century fathers who expended enormous energies to keep their daughters within the confines of the family, within the circle of brothers and sisters, within the metonymic order that subordinated daughters' lives to the needs of the family patriarch. The fathers of Elizabeth Barrett, Charlotte Bronte, and Sophia Jex-Blake protested their daughters' desires to write, to marry, to have children, to earn money, to live outside the parental home. We know these stories, Woolf reminds us, only because these daughters escaped the family circle and recorded their personal experiences in fiction, history, and biography. Their texts gave courage to later women who fought to restructure the divisions between public and private, to alter the division of labor, to gain suffrage, change public law, and open the professions to women.

The success of the suffrage movement in England, followed in the 1930s by a severe European economic crisis, brought political backlash: women were accused of taking jobs away from men. In 1938, the year *Three Guineas* was published and almost twenty years after women gained the franchise, men urged a return to the old metonymic order. Italian, German, and Spanish dictators were cheered when they called for women to return to the home and resume their "natural" childbearing and child-rearing duties under the supreme authority of their husbands. The economic rationale for this revision to an old order masked deep-seated psychological motives, and Woolf heard the grain of "infantile fixation" as she listened to the protests of cabinet ministers, professors, and barristers over the wireless:

Homes are the real places of the women . . . Let them go back to their homes. . . . The Government should give work to men. . . . A strong protest is to be made by the Ministry of Labour. . . . Women must not rule over men. . . . There are two worlds, one for women, the other for men. . . . Let them learn to cook our dinners. . . . Women have failed. . . . They have failed. . . . They have failed. . . . [*TG*, p. 141; ellipses in original]

Emotional and full of hate, these voices articulate male fears of empowered women that might result in the loss of male rights and prestige.

These voices contradict Freud's claim that the "super-ego [of women] is never so inexorable, so *impersonal*, so independent of its *emotional* origins as we require it to be of men" ("Psychical," p. 257). The voices on the wireless return Woolf to a distant past, where she listens to Creon, the ancient dictator, whose message echoes down the ages, heard again in the voices of modern dictators and warmongers—Mussolini, Hitler, and Franco:

Whomsoever the city may appoint, that man must be obeyed, in little things and great, in just things and unjust . . . disobedience is the worst of evils. . . . We must support the cause of order, and in no wise suffer a woman to worst us. . . . They must be women, and not range at large. Servants, take them within. [*Antigone*, lines 748–50, 756–61, quoted in *TG*, p. 141, ellipses in Woolf's text][12]

Woolf comments that Creon, "who held that 'disobedience is the worst of evils,' and that 'whomsoever the city may appoint, that man must be obeyed, in little things and great, in just things and unjust' is typical of certain politicians in the past, and of Herr Hitler and Signor Mussolini in the present" (*TG*, p. 170). The rhetoric of tyranny masks deeply rooted fear of the Other, for which the "infantile fixation" is symptomatic, and projects onto women (and outsiders, such as Jews and gypsies) what men fear in themselves—the presumed weakness of woman's nature.

Sending Antigone to her death, Creon declares, "While I live, no woman shall rule me" (*TG*, p. 170). This statement is grounded neither in the city's laws nor in the archaic myths of chthonic gods; rather, it articulates an ideology of power within the social construct of sexual difference in the ancient city. At stake in Creon's statement (and Woolf's argument) is not the fact of biological sex difference but the difference that sex makes—socially, culturally, historically, and ideologically. Patriarchy draws a veil over this difference, behind which is a "concealed force" (*TG*, p. 137) that *Three Guineas* exposes.

The route to the place where Antigone is walled up alive is "down some wild, desolate path never trod by men" (line 870), a path outside the city walls, untamed, unmapped, twisting, turning, circling back on itself. This path is a figure of woman as she is plotted in the patriarchal script, a figure of subversion, disrule, irrationality, an outsider, an uncivilized alien. Woman—emotional, irrational—comes to symbolize anarchy. Creon describes anarchy in/as the feminine, substituting anarchy for Antigone in a violent rhetorical dismemberment and refiguration:

> Anarchy
>   show me a greater crime in all the earth!
>   She, she destroys cities, rips up houses,
>   breaks the ranks of spearmen into headlong rout. . . .
>   Therefore
>   we must defend the men who live by law,
>   never let some woman triumph over us.
>   Better to fall from power, if fall we must,
>   at the hands of a man—never be rated
>   inferior to a woman, never. [lines 752–61, ellipses added)[13]

Anarchy is unveiled as the figure of woman, troped through a rhetoric of substitution that violently yokes the feminine to social disorder. Isolated in her underground tomb, Antigone is a figure of dismembership and outsidership from the new social order Creon decrees: "This young girl—dead or alive, she will be stripped of her rights, her stranger's rights, here in the world above" (lines 975–77). His words at once give Antigone status as resident alien and revoke those rights. Antigone has few rights to forfeit, however, as she is not a resident alien (she has returned to Thebes from Colonus, where she followed her father in his exile), nor was she ever eligible for citizenship. As an illiterate woman, she has no place in this culture: her "home" is her "tomb."

Antigone circumvents the death by starvation Creon arranges for her. Subverting his orders through suicide, she exercises the minimal (and negative) power she has over her own life. Textually, this self-violence is marked by ellipsis, which leaves the violence itself as something to be understood, available only by its effects, a figure of incompletion or "falling short"—the action of suicide by hanging. Although Creon rescinds his death sentence, he cannot outrun its execution. He falls short in time as Antigone falls short in space. Exiled to a wilderness outside the city limits, Antigone dies in the place of the Other, in whose name and under whose signature her death is decreed. However, her commitment to the old laws and her death under the new laws writes a limit text (inscripted by her dead body, hanging in its veils) in the relation of private and public, oral and written codes. Antigone unveils Creon's tyranny and false pride. Her death is a form of signature, signed by the linen noose that silences her. Peggy Kamuf explains that "signature articulates the one with the other, the one *in* the other: it both divides and joins." [14] Although Antigone's death is enacted beyond the city's law, ideologically it is inscribed in the relation between Law and law, between public and private, state and family. The motives for and methods of her death trace a confusion in metonymical and metaphorical relations, between outside and inside, forum and hearth. Creon's order positions her across a line of sexual difference: figured as Other, she is sacrificed to a social order that privileges the same, the metonymical order of homosocial relations among men. [15]

The site of Antigone's suicide, outside the city and below ground, is both a mythic and psychic space. She dies beyond the limits of civilization, trapped in the (repressed) ground of the cultural unconscious on which Western man erects his philosophies of rationality and writes his laws. Edwin Ardener defines this territory beyond cultural boundaries as the "wild zone." Adapting his anthropological constructs for feminist criticism, Elaine Showalter comments that spatially this area is a "no-man's land, a place forbidden to men"; experientially it "stands for the aspects of the female life-style which are outside of and unlike those of men"; metaphysically, "from the male point of view, it may simply be the projection of the unconscious." [16] This "wild, desolate path," Creon says, has "never been trod by *men*" (line 870). A chain of ancient associations divides culture from wilderness along a line of sexual difference, the line Antigone walks on her way to death.

Representation of the unconscious as a "wild zone" below conscious thought incorporates historical associations that divide man-culture-reason from female-wilderness-illogic. Creon claims the city as his own, by "law" (line 825), and defends his decision to exile Antigone in the wilderness as an effort to protect his "royal rights" (line 833). But his appeal to the law veils his own (irrational) fears; his irrational behavior draws the law to itself as a sign of rationality. Creon's behavior cannot fully be explained by the social and cultural codes of his time and place. The Leader of the Chorus says that the deaths of Antigone and Haimon are "proof of his own madness," and Creon himself wails, "so senseless, so insane . . . my crimes, my stubborn deadly—" (lines 1391, 1393–94; ellipsis in original). No logic or law, however "rational," no power structure, however repressive, can fully encompass that other, psychic law that directs his actions. Sophocles' text recognizes this other order by a line of dots (. . .).

Page duBois writes across this line when she states that "one of the dividing issues between Antigone and her antagonist [C]reon" is "the nature of the law," especially the issue of justice that Freud treats in his essay on the psychical consequences of anatomical distinctions of men and women ("Antigone," p. 372). She disavows the Freudian "transhistorical" model of identity and discards its usefulness for feminist criticism and, more particularly, for the study of ancient Greek civilization. However, duBois draws on Freudian terminology to understand forms of feminist criticism and her reactions to them. Her argument has a double focus, and it is worth taking a moment to examine its logic. First, she cautions that to make Antigone a "feminist exemplar," to see her as a "defender of personal values against the cruel state," is to dismiss her as "a figure in language, [bound up] in the cultural and linguistic codes of the ancient city" ("Antigone," p. 376)—in brief, to dehistorize her. Second, she says that feminist critics have been misled in adopting a "confessional mode" of criticism that "celebrate[s] women's private world" rather than analyzes how "the social and economic construction of gender represents women to themselves as well as others" ("Antigone," pp. 371–72). She urges feminists to be "critical of a politics which is satisfied merely to abide in the position to which culture assigns women" ("Antigone," p. 373)—that is, within the metonymic structure of sameness. Under these terms, however, Woolf's own feminist arguments, which link the private and public, personal and political, the historical and the psychosexual, would be dismissed. What Woolf sets out to prove in *Three Guineas*, drawing *Antigone* to her aid, is that the personal is *always* political.[17]

DuBois' skepticism about the role for the "personal" within the political is couched, interestingly, in Freud's terms: "the politics of refusing the decorum of academic formality forces women who simply personalize their intellectual work into the culturally endorsed position of 'emotionalism,' so contemptuously described by Freud" (p. 373). DuBois is not alone in finding the personal indecorous, and there is much to be analyzed in her separation of the personal, confessional, and "psychological" from the historical, cultural, and social. Admitting to both "embarrassment" and "fascination with" feminist criticism's "confessional mode" ("I feel uncomfortable with this sort of unveiling, I confess, and would like to understand why"—"Antigone," p. 371), she edges the door open to a self-analysis that begins in the personal, the "emotional," the confessional. However, she turns away from the possibilities of such analysis, which might begin by reflecting on the rhetorical gestures of her own discourse, for example, the apostrophic movement of turning aside, a movement similar to ellipsis. Instead, duBois turns Freud's terminology against feminist criticism: "feminist scholarship does have exhibitionistic aspects; there is narcissism in the incessant gaze at what seems to be oneself, that is, at Woman" ("Antigone," p. 371).

In *Three Guineas* Virginia Woolf argues powerfully for a feminist politics that begins with the personal. She sets aside decorum to break the seal of silence that history and culture have placed on the realities of women's lives. Important among these realities are the psychological pain of exclusion from culture and restricted personal freedom. *Antigone* dramatizes, tragically, the impossibility of clearly separating the personal from the political. Creon himself draws the connection between private and public when he declares to Haimon, "Show me the man who rules his household well: I'll show you someone fit to rule the state" (lines 739–40). Creon's own behavior transgresses this wisdom, which he misrecognizes as the truth of *his own* actions. His words, however, confirm the realities of family life Woolf analyzes in *Three Guineas*: "Things repeat themselves it seems. Pictures and voices are the same today as they were 2,000 years ago. Such then is the conclusion to which our enquiry into the nature of fear has brought us—the fear which forbids freedom in the private house.

That fear, small, insignificant and private as it is, is connected with the other fear, the public fear, which is neither small nor insignificant, the fear which has led you to ask us to help you to prevent war" (pp. 141–42). Inquiring into the *motivations* behind male fear of the female, the (irrational) fear in which patriarchy grounds its rationale, *Three Guineas* opens on to an "other" scene, whose sexual-textual symptom is the ellipsis.

-·§§§·-

ECONOMICS, EDUCATION, ELLIPSIS

The brilliance of A Room of One's Own *lies in its invention of a female language to subvert the languages of patriarchy. . . . Its tropes figure new reading and writing strategies, enlisting punctuation in the service of feminism with the use of ellipses for encoding female desire, the use of initials and dashes to make absent figures more present and transforming interruption, the condition of the woman writer's oppression . . . into a deliberate strategy of woman's writing.*
Jane Marcus, Virginia Woolf and the Languages of Patriarchy

I have this moment, while having my bath, conceived an entire new book—a sequel to a Room of Ones Own—about the sexual life of women: to be called Professions for Women *perhaps—Lord how exciting!*
Virginia Woolf, 20 January 1931 [18]

The narrative structure of *Three Guineas*, which opens on the question of how to prevent war and arrives at a socialist-feminist critique of patriarchal institutions, is perhaps the most demanding of the Woolf *oeuvre*. Against the rigidity, narrow mindedness and self-interest of patriarchal thinking, Woolf develops a sinuous and subversive argument that reveals the false logic behind the mask of masculine rationality and social order. *Three Guineas* constructs a fiction, based on three letters from representatives of political and charitable organizations, from which it poses three fundamental questions regarding social-cultural values. (1) Why are there wars and who profits from them? (2) Why are women educationally disadvantaged? (3) Why are women either financially dependent on men, or—if they are employed—poverty-stricken? Within the frame of a letter fiction, the unnamed narrator (who is identified only by gender and social class, and whose marital status, educational background, religion, and political affiliations are never directly revealed) weaves a series of internal fictions that mirror public attitudes toward the concerns voiced in each of the three letters. That is, *Three Guineas* mimes and mocks the culture it critiques. The three guineas of the title refer to the requested support that each letter writer desires for his or her cause, but the narrator's gift of a guinea to each of her correspondents is more than a token gesture toward changing society. The guinea is simultaneously the symbol of women's oppression, representing the very material powers of patriarchy, and the sign under which Woolf's critique proceeds: it invokes the powers of "ancestral memory" in the service of social and cultural reform. When all is said and done, Woolf concludes that patriarchy can be dismantled only by radical economic change.

It is precisely the elliptical shape of Woolf's text that eludes analysis, the constant crossing and recrossing of genre boundaries (critical essay/letter fiction), the folding back on and inversion of phallologic, the weaving together of the heterogeneous strands of daily living that constitute the fabric of society and culture. Ultimately, Woolf cannot disentangle (herself from) the web of issues that initiate the overwhelming question: "How . . . are we to prevent war?" (*TG*, p. 3; ellipsis mine). But the figure of ellipsis, which she uses repeatedly throughout the text, leads us through the textual labyrinth. One important effect of this incessant turning and re-turning is that efforts to formulate an answer to the question of war remain provisional, open to revision and rethinking; meanwhile, the letter that poses it awaits an answer while Woolf turns to women's concerns. Only when she has given a guinea to rebuild the women's college and a guinea to support poor professional women does Woolf turn back to the opening question. In the end, she offers a guinea for the fund to prevent war, but refuses to join a society against war. She withholds her signature, leaving the form sent by her male correspondent unsigned (*TG*, p. 144). In fact, her signature is to be found in the figure of the ellipsis, which simultaneously signs and unsigns, opens and overturns narrative and political logics.

My argument, then, will try to do two things at once: first, explicate the major premises of Woolf's argument and articulate the narrative strategies through which they are developed; second, examine the ways in which ellipsis situates *Three Guineas* as a theoretical discourse on psychic and social "otherness."

Ellipsis is both a threshold and a place of trespass. It announces a barrier of transgression, a moment of trauma and falling away, *and* it constructs a space where writing exceeds cultural limits to lift, momentarily, the veil of social (and linguistic) repression. A permeable textual boundary, ellipsis corresponds textually to the traversable inner limit between Kristeva's symbolic and semiotic. It signals an alternative logic constituted as the vanishing point of rational meaning and the entrance to unconscious structures of representation. Ellipsis maps the path of the Other as it traverses the text. *Three Guineas*, usually considered the most academic and least "poetic" of Woolf's texts, leads us down this Other pathway and teaches us to read its meaning letter by letter and dot by dot (. . .). Letters and dots are also, from the most ancient times, seeds—*seme*, sign and grain. Disseminated through elliptical inversions and insinuations that confound the linear plot of phallologic, the seeds/semes escape the straight furrows of sexual insemination captured in the metaphor of woman's body as a field to be ploughed and planted.[19] Ellipsis figures the transformative powers at work in Woolf's text; it is a sign of change and reordering that troubles the smooth flow of narrative and effects twists of logic and fate.

Ellipsis is a hybrid form. The *OED* tells us that formerly it referred both to the three dots that mark omission of words in a sentence and to the dash used in writing or printing to indicate omission of letters in a word. The printer's dash is a mark of textual censorship that graphically displays linguistic suppression due to religious (G—d), political (k—g), or moral (d————) law. More commonly, the dash as a mark of punctuation carries the meaning of its verb form (to strike violently, to complete hastily, to destroy, to confound, to rush). Woolf's dash, for instance, punctuates flashes of insight and force of argument in the "violent stroke" of her pen.[20] By contrast, ellipsis in her writing signals trauma, memory lapse, intellectual and emotional confusion—often around issues of sexual difference. This violence is of another kind, a psychic blockage or impasse.

Ellipsis compounds the categories of rhetoric and grammar through punctuation: it "leaves something to be understood" (*OED*). In grammar, it refers to the omission of one or more words in a sentence whose presence is needed to complete the grammatical construction or fully express meaning. The rhetorical sense of ellipsis comes from *ellipse*, a "noun of action," its meaning taken from plane geometry, where one side of a figure is constituted by a "falling short." The ellipse opens onto a curve or deviation. In this sense, ellipsis is related to "trope," the signifier for figurative language, which in Greek means "to turn" and in geometry refers to multiple tangents on a curve. Like the dash, the ellipsis is structured through an apposition of stasis and kinesis within the meaning of ellipse as a "noun of action." Ellipse also figures movements in space, where the line of planetary orbits appears oblique and eccentric. Made up of curved planes, ovals or circles created by deviations from the straight line, a geometric elliptical constitutes a turning back. Whereas the dash moves forward, the ellipsis turns away. The *American Heritage Dictionary* notes a relation between the Greek *elleipsis*, a falling short or defect, and *elleipein*, "to leave in or behind, to leave out." In both the grammatical and rhetorical senses of the term, then, the ellipsis is understood as absence, fault, or defect. Its geometrical meanings, however, include turning back, falling short, the curve of deviation and extension of boundaries (as in the Greek hyperbole), an excess of "throwing beyond." All these meanings of ellipsis are at work in Woolf's text: impasse and entrance into a new figurative space, ellipsis becomes for her a symptom of patriarchal oppression and the site of political disruption.

Ellipsis, as mark of punctuation and rhetorical figure, structures a context of meanings for *Three Guineas*. What invites analysis is the *textual* difference ellipsis makes as it supports and extends Woolf's political argument. She did not consider *Three Guineas* well-written, describing its writing as a violent, physical and elemental force: "I have been in full flood every morning with 3 Gs"; "Oh how violently I have been galloping through these mornings! It has pressed & spurted out of me, if thats any proof of virtue, like a physical volcano." [21] The sexual imagery of these statements is significant, as is their violence: the "physical volcano" is psychosexually charged. Early readers and reviewers of *Three Guineas* reacted to the excess and unreasonableness they felt in the force of Woolf's argument. The most famous response was Queenie Leavis's scathing review in *Scrutiny*.

A more personal and painful reaction came from Vita Sackville-West. In its accusation that Woolf provokes her reader with "misleading arguments," Vita's letter drew distinctions between public and private writing, envisioned scenes of physical combat between the two women, and effected a sex change for Virginia. Vita claimed that Virginia played a "gentleman's game," thereby misleading her readers:

> You are a tantalising writer, because at one moment you enchant one with your lovely prose and next moment exasperate one with your misleading arguments. You see, so provocative a book can't be thanked for in a mere letter; it would need a reply as long as the book itself, and that would mean a publication by the Hogarth Press. And far be it from me to cross swords with you publicly, for I should always lose on points in fencing, though if it came to fisticuffs I might knock you down. So long as you play the gentleman's game, with the gentleman's technique, you win.[22]

Woolf's angry response focuses on the issue of "misleading arguments":

> Of course I knew you wouldn't like 3gs. . . . But when you say that you are exasperated by my "misleading arguments"—then I ask, what do you mean? If I said, I dont agree with your conception of Joan of Arc's character, thats one thing. But if I said your arguments about her are "misleading" shouldn't I mean, Vita has cooked the facts in a dishonest way in order to produce an effect which she knows to be untrue? If *thats* what you mean by "misleading" then we shall have to have the matter out, whether with swords or fisticuffs. And I dont think *whichever we use*, you will, as you say, knock me down. It may be a silly book, and I don't agree that its a well-written book; but its certainly an honest book: and I took more pains to get up the facts and state them plainly than I ever took with anything in my life.[23]

Behind this defense of her arguments lurks the troubling question of how to define the "facts" of women's lives. The historical determination of sexual difference, which Woolf calls "patriarchy," prescribes women's proper social roles and constructs an official, public version of their lives. A "gentleman's game," patriarchy denies the oppression of gender difference through "facts" that make fictions of women's lived experiences.

Vita fails, finally, to see through this game or understand how it makes the oppressed complicit in their oppression and turns victims against each other. Adopting a rhetoric of physical violence, she accuses Virginia of miming patriarchy's gestures. Virginia's argument is perhaps too subtle for Vita, who does not follow the complicated change of voices and rhetorical positions effected through the letters or see that the argument "mimes" the logic of its opposition only to subvert it.[24] Rather than poorly written, as Woolf feared, *Three Guineas* is superbly crafted.

Like *A Room of One's Own*, it constructs its argument through a series of fictions. The narrative methods of both works are complex, full of rhetorical twists and turns. *Three Guineas* exchanges the first-person storyteller of *A Room*, which incorporated the multiple voices of "Mary Beton, Mary Seton, Mary Carmichael" (*Room*, p. 5), to position itself within the first-person plural ("we"), which weaves together strands of subjectivity across the divide of sexual difference. The "we" allows Woolf to backtrack on her narrative, elliptically enfolding the history of women's oppression and outsidership already traced in *A Room of One's Own*. She often speaks from the position of masculine authority so that readers can hear the grain of fear (or psychic necessity) in the voices of professors, politicians, and patriarchs. The "we" expands Woolf's authority, co-opts her opponents, and opens the grammatical space of the ellipsis, which effects a two-part confusion—first, in gender distinctions among the fictional correspondents and the various witnesses they employ; second, between the author and reader of *Three Guineas*.[25]

The narrative proceeds through an exchange of letters, the first of which, written by a man, poses an overwhelming question—"How in your opinion are we to prevent war?" The magnitude of the question is breathtaking, and its mode of address, which crosses an unspoken gender barrier, is "remarkable": "when before has an educated man asked a woman how in her opinion war can be prevented?" (*TG*, p. 3). Situated on the grounds of sexual difference, these questions open the double analysis of *Three Guineas* that draws together a series of apparently unrelated assumptions. The first of these are: "education makes a difference"; "war is a profession." Woolf does not give war pride of place in her argument. Instead, she subsumes it under the category "education," explaining that the desire to wage war is the creation of patriarchal institutions, primary among them education and religion.[26] If Woolf's analytic method is to establish incongruous opposition and then invert what seems logically to be its hierarchical orders, her fictional method is to personalize and humanize institutions and society. Thus she frames a sketch of her correspondent.

Commenting that "without someone warm and breathing on the other side of the page, letters are worthless" (*TG*, p. 3), Woolf apostrophizes the gentleman letter writer, giving life to what otherwise remains a textual maneuver that allows her the opportunity to speak/write. The first of many textual gestures toward the lived, material relation of body and spirit, economics and existence, education and freedom, gender and oppression, she premises her argument on an awareness of the "other side of the page." She endows her correspondent with wife, children, house, profession (barrister), and comments that he is gray-haired, and middle-aged—as she is in "real life." The "first difficulty of communication" arises from their shared experience of social rank:

> When we meet in the flesh we speak with the same accent; use knives and forks in the same way; expect maids to cook dinner and wash up after dinner; and can talk during dinner without much difficulty about politics and people; war and peace; barbarism and civilization—all the questions indeed suggested by your letter. Moreover, we both earn our livings. But . . . those three dots mark a precipice, a gulf so deeply cut between us that for three years and more I have been sitting on my side of it wondering whether it is any use to try to speak across it. [*TG*, p. 4]

Ellipsis marks the "gulf" of gender, which Woolf will argue constitutes a more fundamental division among human beings than differences in age, marital status, education, social rank, economic status, or political commitment. Indeed, she concludes that gender is the primary factor in differences among men and women in education, social class, economic status and political attitudes.

The sheer immensity of this divide silences Woolf, who asks another woman, Mary Kingsley—nineteenth-century feminist, writer, traveler, and political activist, who changed British policy toward native peoples in West Africa—to "speak for us." To speak, that is, for women of the "educated class." Across the gap of educational difference, Kingsley's female experience speaks a "foreign tongue": the familiar mother tongue of sexual difference is ironically offset by the language of the fatherland spoken by the Nazi armies against whose threat *Three Guineas* takes its feminist stance. As a sister, Mary Kingsley renounced her own desire for education and contributed to "Arthur's Education Fund," a category of household economy Woolf borrows from Thackeray's *Pendennis* (*TG*, p. 4). Kingsley's words, taken from her biography, are a confession: "I don't know if I ever revealed to you the fact that being allowed to learn German was *all* the paid-for education I ever had. Two thousand pounds was spent on my brother's, I still hope not in vain" (*TG*, p. 4). Educated within the family, Kingsley learned to place her brother's "necessity" above her own desires, to forego all the "luxuries and trimmings" that are, according to Woolf, an essential part of education—travel, society, solitude, a lodging apart from the family house" (*TG*, p. 5). Gender alone, Woolf argues, distinguishes the (masculine) "essential" from (feminine) "luxury" (*TG*, p. 26). That Mary Kingsley eventually broke away from family restraints, to be remembered as a traveler and educator, is an irony that Woolf's analysis underscores.

Linking the issues of women's education and economic independence to the question of preventing war, Woolf constructs a dizzingly complex argument. She begins by revealing that patriarchal logic is based on "double-faced" facts. For instance, education holds both positive and negative values: "it is good for one sex and for some professions, but bad for another sex [female] and for another profession [marriage]" (*TG*, p. 26). For thousands of years, she writes, history has turned a blind eye to women's desires for education, desires that burned strongly despite the "impediments that tradition, poverty and ridicule could put in its way" (*TG*, p. 25). Lurking behind the resistance to educating women is the fear of women's economic independence. That is, patriarchy and capitalism condition each other (indeed, they are indistinguishable from one another), their goals and values supported by the press, government, military, stock exchange, and the professions of law, medicine, religion and education. Declaring these desires in women to be "irreligious," the church even went so far as to make women's love of learning a sin. Unveiling St. Paul's teachings, Woolf discovers the fear that motivates this belief. If educated, women might discover the twisted logic of sexual difference and refuse to serve family. They might take jobs away from men—precisely the complaint of British conservatives and European fascists in the 1930s, who wanted women out of the workplace and back in the home.

The effects of capitalist-patriarchal ideology on women's lives, as recorded in biographies and women's books, are material and economic. Whereas the educated class (which includes noblemen, landed gentry, and members of the liberal professions) "possess in its own right and not through marriage practically all the capital, all the land, all the valuables, and all the patronage in England" (*TG*, p. 18), women possess in their own right virtually no privilege-conferring valuables. She declares that women are "step-daughter[s] of England," sharing less fully than men in its "blessings" (*TG*, p. 14). It is not surprising, then, that they do not understand the "reasons, the emotions, the loyalties which lead men to go to war" (*TG*, p. 9). Men make war a profession out of duty and patriotism, and in return for "blessings" received, according to Woolf. But they also find in war "a source of happiness and excitement," an "outlet for manly qualities" (p. 8). That is, war provides psychic rewards for men.

Seeking support in preventing war, the letter suggests three ways women could contribute: "the first is to sign a letter to the newspapers; the second is to join a certain society; the third is to subscribe to its funds" (*TG*, p. 11). Reviewing the letter's request, Woolf is reminded again of women's economic deprivation, and she contrasts the gentleman's guinea coin to the "sixpenny bit" in the hand of the gentleman's daughter. Symbol of patriarchal entitlement, the guinea coin was no longer minted in Woolf's time but it continued as a monetary concept, determining the value of goods and services. Representing privilege, luxury, and gentility, the guinea rings out the central "fact" supporting Woolf's claim that money buys influence. Limited to "indirect influence" over their fathers, brothers, and husbands, women have little power to effect changes in the system that engages in war to protect its social and economic interests and to gain psychic relief in acting out repressed aggression. Indirect influence, Woolf comments, is "low in power, very slow in action, and very painful to use" because it turns the home into a political arena or a battleground, as it did during the fight for suffrage (*TG*, p. 14).

Within the educated class, the weakest of all classes in the state according to Woolf's argument, women are "incomparably weaker than the men": "We have no weapon with which to enforce our will" (*TG*, p. 13). By contrast, working-class women have direct power to "seriously" damage the war machine by laying down their tools: "if all the daughters of educated men were to down tools tomorrow, nothing essential either to the life or to the war-making of the community would be embarrassed" (*TG*, p. 13). Power, according to this logic, is a matter of weaponry—whether real or symbolic.[27] In the face of these realities, Woolf's words "falter" and "prayer peters out into three separate dots because of facts again" (*TG*, p. 91). She is silenced, and her text is littered with "dots, doubts and hesitations" (*TG*, p. 58).

Ellipsis opens onto an alternate reality visible in the "crudely coloured" photograph Woolf lays before her gentleman correspondent. It is a photograph, she writes, "of your world as it appears to us who see it from the threshold of the private house; through the shadow of the veil that St. Paul still lays on our eyes; from the bridge which connects the private house with the world of public life" (*TG*, p. 18).[28] Positioning herself on this bridge, denoted textually by ellipsis, Woolf encloses the next section of her argument in a loop. She responds to a second letter that has lain on her desk for three years "cheek by jowl" with the first letter. One expects her to lend enthusiastic support to its plea, which verifies the truth of her earlier argument, in response to the first letter, that women are educationally and economically deprived under patriarchy. It requests money for rebuilding a women's college that has fallen into disrepair because, as Woolf explains, it does not share full membership in the academic community (Cambridge University) where it is housed (*TG*, p. 30).

Woolf does not lend immediate support to the cause of women's education, however. Instead, she takes the position of the "outsider" (assuming the voice, if not the gender, of patriarchy) and composes a draft letter demanding that the honorary treasurer examine the premises of her logic. This rhetorical shift illustrates another meaning of ellipses, which can turn back on itself and reverse direction:

Your letter, Madam, has been waiting some time without an answer. But certain doubts and questions have arisen. May we put them to you, ignorantly as an *outsider* must, but frankly as an *outsider* should when asked to contribute money? [P. 31; emphasis added]

The first-person plural ("we") does not join woman-to-woman within its address. Rather, its rhetoric chastises ("how can you be so foolish?") and informs: "there is grave danger of war" (*TG*, p. 32). The letter serves Woolf's argument in two ways: enclosed within a long response to the first letter, it reveals the inherent ironies of asking *women's* advice on the prevention of war; it educates the male reader (the "Sir" to whom the comments to "Madam" are actually addressed) about the second-class status of women's colleges within universities (*TG*, pp. 30–31). The "we" encloses a double address, which recreates hierarchical gender divisions and the power structures of wealth. It assumes, that is, that the "giver of money" is "entitled to dictate terms" (*TG*, p. 31).

Woolf ultimately abandons her effort to subvert patriarchal logic and capitalism's vested interests by attaching conditions to the gift of the guinea. But not before she exposes the financial interests that structure education. She writes that capitalist energy feeds the wealth of Oxford and Cambridge, which use scientific research to stimulate the general economy (not least of all in the "invention of the implements of war"—*TG*, p. 32), investing in their most precious "product," their graduates, who then reinvest earned capital in the university through donations. Women's colleges have no equivalent means of gaining financial support, especially since they do not officially belong to the university. She resists concluding that women's colleges should follow the capitalist-patrician models of Oxford and Cambridge. To the contrary, Woolf encourages them to rebuild according to altogether new models of education—ones that will "produce the kind of society, the kind of people that will help to prevent war" (*TG*, p. 33). She proposes her own model, emphasizing that women's colleges should make virtues of their youth and poverty to overturn traditions. The curve of her logic now exceeds the terms of patriarchy altogether; hyperbole, not a mere deviation, it turns away altogether from the culturally imposed norm.

Woolf counsels that specialist-segregationist models of academic disciplines be replaced by ones that encourage cooperation rather than competition. She champions learning for its own sake and eschews "the arts of dominating other people . . . the art of ruling, of killing, of acquiring land and capital" (*TG*, p. 34; ellipsis mine). But her peroration halts in mid-sentence, in a silence marked by ellipsis, when she glimpses "the face on the other side of the page." The melancholy expression of the woman's face seems to say, "fire off your rhetoric, but we have to face realities": "students must be taught to earn their livings" (*TG*, p. 35). Woolf cannot disagree with this logic, since this is precisely the position she supports: "We have said that the only influence which the daughters of educated men can at present exert against war is the disinterested influence that they possess through earning their livings" (*TG*, p. 36). Her proposal, "at present," is entirely impracticable: in order to survive financially, the college cannot help but be co-opted by capitalist institutions. Discovering that her logic cannot untie the knot binding cultural values to capitalism, Woolf's argument turns back on the initiatory question of the first letter: "How in your opinion are we to prevent war?" She again consults biographies, endeavoring to understand how women are bound, consciously and unconsciously, to structures that oppress and endanger them.

Returning to August 1914, the eve of the previous war, Woolf observes how women were forced to collaborate with patriarchy, turning away from their own feminist agenda. Not having yet won the franchise or gained a measure of economic independence, without options for independence and self-support, women were forced to collaborate with the system that abused them. Complicit in their own oppression, they became accomplices in drawing brothers and husbands into the work of the war machine: they "used all their immense stores of charm, of sympathy, to persuade young men that to fight was heroic" (*TG*, p. 39).[29] In this scene, daughters of educated men are seen rushing forward to support the war effort. Woolf argues that generations of confinement to marriage and the private house "with its cruelty, its poverty, its hypocrisy, its immorality, its inanity" had filled women with immense loathing. They would take any route to escape its burden and "undertake any task however menial, exercise any fascination however fatal that enabled [them] to escape" (*TG*, p. 39). Such fascinations included the "menial" labor of hospital work, lorry driving, and field and munition factory labor that supported the Great War.

The degree of women's suffering was measured in their dedicated response to war's call: their desire for independence and fulfilling public work had been so shaped by the values of English society (in particular, the "education" of the private home, which taught self-sacrifice) that "consciously [they] desired 'our splendid Empire': unconsciously [they] desired our splendid war" (*TG*, p. 39). Woolf quotes Lady Lovelace, who commented on British colonialism in a phrase that both supported and challenged its agenda: " 'our splended Empire' " . . . 'the price of which,' she added, "is mainly paid by women' " (*TG*, p. 39). For Woolf, the lesson is obvious: women's desires are bent to capitalist and colonialist agendas by the economic necessity of women to marry. Addressing herself once again to the "Sir" who signed the first letter, Woolf writes: "If you want us to help you to prevent war the conclusion seems to be inevitable: we must help to rebuild the college which, imperfect as it may be, is the only alternative to the education of the private house" (p. 39). Thus at the close of chapter 1, she offers the first guinea, "rare" and "valuable," for the rebuilding of the women's college. The man's request for funds to prevent war must wait upon other concerns, in particular the plea for aid to poverty-stricken professional women. While the guinea to prevent war will be given freely at the close of chapter 3, Woolf's considered delay in bringing it forth mimes the patriarchy's slow response to women's concerns.

Woolf considered the second, middle portion of *Three Guineas* a "very difficult chapter," perhaps because it directly addresses the question of professions for women that had shaped her original conception of the work.[30] Initially, the essay's subject was to have been "the sexual life of women," a topic that appears at first glance unrelated to women's professional lives. In this second chapter Woolf addresses, however obliquely, the relation between the two topics. The narrative gestures of the chapter turn back to the overriding question of the first letter, reinscribing its power and urgency and the authority of the man who poses it. At the outset, Woolf cedes authority to the masculine perspective in order to reveal the misogyny that lurks behind its apparently benign "objectivity." She veils her perspectives behind a pose of naive literalism that reads his request letter by letter and dot by dot.

Resurrecting the initial letter from the stack of unanswered mail on her desk, Woolf puts its question of war and women before the "independent, the mature, those who are earning their livings in the professions" (*TG*, p. 40). She adopts the man's voice and erases her own gender by relying on the impersonal pronoun "one." This act of ventriloquism opens a series of dialogues embedded within quotation marks that distance Woolf from her reading audience, requiring that we keep careful track of the multilayered screens of her argument:

> "Here is a man," one has only to say, "whom we all have reason to respect; he tells us that war is possible; perhaps probable; he asks us, who can earn our livings, to help him in any way we can to prevent war." That surely will be enough without pointing to the photographs that are all this time piling up on the table—photographs of more dead bodies, of more ruined houses, to call forth an answer, and an answer that will give you, Sir, the very help that you require. But . . . it seems that there is some hesitation, some doubt— [*TG*, p. 40; ellipsis in original][31]

Hesitations and doubts are again signaled by ellipsis, and this invented conversation (or letter) breaks off to introduce yet a third letter lying beside the first one on the table. The new letter, "from another honorary treasurer," again asks for money—this time to relieve the poverty of professional women (*TG*, p. 41). Based on a real letter, received from the London and National Society for Women's Service (1938), this fictional appeal is desperate.[32] It acknowledges that its recipient may not herself be financially secure enough to give money: " 'Failing money,' she goes on, 'any gift will be acceptable—books, fruit or cast-off clothing that can be sold in a bazaar' " (*TG*, p. 41). The question behind this request is: why are professional women so poverty stricken that they must mount this kind of appeal, and what is its relation to impending war?

The narrative line of *Three Guineas*, determined by the initial letter from the man asking for women's advice on how to prevent war, has now been interrupted twice, each time by a request from women. The "overiding question" is thus doubly deferred, Woolf's attention always turning away from the predominant concern. Persistent, even irritating, these "feminine" interruptions redirect the narrative, displacing its energies. They illustrate repeated interventions of the semiotic into the symbolic, and they force Woolf to turn back on her own logic; each turn requires that she create a new voice or persona to carry the argument. Thus, before opening an investigation into poverty's causes occasioned by the third letter, Woolf creates yet another fictional respondent, who employs the rhetorical "we" in a draft letter very similar to the earlier response to the request for monies to rebuild the women's college. She drafts a letter that painstakingly rehearses arguments against the women's movement. The letter privileges voices that express deepseated misogyny, but its process of construction (to which we as readers are privy) develops as a dialogue between "Virginia Woolf," the narrator, and the "Sir" who signed his name to the letter of chapter 1. Implicitly, then, the attitudes and concerns of this unnamed "Sir" are juxtaposed (but also opposed) to those of other men. Men mirror and echo each other in this letter. Woolf also opens a space of difference among individual men, making distinctions among them, something the patriarchy refuses to women.

Miming the patriarchy's discourse, especially the dismissive irony with which it treats women's issues, this new (female) persona is notable for its agility in exposing women's faulty logic—that is, to find the elliptical deviation or falling short in the "feminine" argument. For example, the letter writer reads two meanings into her correspondent's poverty: first, "if she is as poor *as this letter indicates*, then the weapon of independent opinion upon which we have been counting to help you ["Sir," of the initial letter] to prevent war is not, to put it mildly, a very powerful weapon"; second, "if she is as poor *as she pretends to be*, then we can bargain with her, as we bargained with her sister at Cambridge, and exercise the right of potential givers to impose terms" (*TG*, p. 41; emphasis added). Poverty in the first instance is credited; poverty in the second instance is purported. Woolf's provisional response is ingratiating and insulting in its pretense to ignorance of the real situation:

Accept a thousand apologies, Madam, for keeping you waiting so long for an answer to your letter. The fact is, certain questions have arisen, to which we must ask you to reply before we send you a subscription. In the first place you are asking for money—money with which to pay your rent. But how can it be, how can it possibly be, my dear Madam, that you are so terribly poor? The professions have been open to the daughters of educated men for almost 20 years. Therefore, how can it be, that you, whom we take to be their representative, are standing, like your sister at Cambridge, hat in hand, pleading for money, or failing money, for fruit, books, or cast-off clothing to sell at a bazaar? How can it be, we repeat? [*TG*, p. 41]

The letter occupies more than two pages of Woolf's text, and its every rhetorical move distances the circumstances of the request from the potential gift giver.

Like the draft letter of chapter 1, this one is double voiced, directed toward both the honorary treasurer for professional women and to the male author of the initial letter. Assuming that this third letter has lain upon the writing table, like the others, for upwards of three years, the apology for "keeping you waiting so long" falls far short of politeness. It mimes cultivated (and conventional) gestures that have kept professional women waiting for full citizenship in society. The response repeats in their entirety the various requests of the letter to which it responds, questioning the premises of these requests and punctuating its discourse with rhetorical disbelief: "How can it be?" Finally, it joins in sisterhood the two female honorary treasurers who can only feebly echo the more pressing request of the grey-haired barrister. His values and concerns shape the provisional response to this third letter.

These values gain rhetorical power against the accusations of two men, C. E. M. Joad and H. G. Wells, whose quoted opinions on women consume fully 90 percent of the space in this letter. Speaking from their own professional perspectives (philosophy and literature, respectively) and from their writings, these men articulate more powerfully than the honorary treasurer all the reasons women in professions are poverty-stricken. Their words simultaneously expose their own misogynistic attitudes and lend authority to the woman writer's request. Woolf's argumentative technique situates men at the heart of her feminist critique, examining in excruciating detail the logic of their beliefs and attitudes, allowing their own words to damn them. She reveals the misogyny at the core of patriarchal culture.

Taking on the moral tone of male authority, Woolf chastises her correspondent. She writes that professional women have fallen short of society's expectations for them and have failed to take civic responsibilities seriously:

> You are drawing upon yourselves the censure and contempt of men of established reputation as philosophers and novelists—of men like Mr. Joad and Mr. Wells. Not only do they deny your poverty, but they accuse you of apathy and indifference. Let me draw your attention to the charges that they

bring against you. Listen, in the first place, to what Mr. C.E.M. Joad has to say of you. He says: "I doubt whether at any time during the last fifty years young women have been more politically apathetic, more socially indifferent than at the present time." That is how he begins. And he goes on to say, very rightly, that it is not his business to tell you what you ought to do; but he adds, very kindly, that he will give you an example of what you might do. You might imitate your sisters in America. You might found "a society for the advertisement of peace." [*TG*, p. 42]

The irony and anger of this address to sisterhood can hardly be missed, especially in the adverbial introjections "very rightly" and "very kindly," which read the tone of Joad's remarks from a presumably sympathetic viewpoint. His suggestions that British women "imitate" their American sisters in setting up a society for peace is intended to insult daughters of the British suffrage movement, women whose activism gave initial courage to their American sisters. Joad's published remarks dutifully record men's desire to set the agenda for women's political activism, to monitor their activities and behavior, and assume that it is both men's duty and right to point out women's failings.

The narrative voice of this chapter (the "I," who mimes the male voice) underwrites Joad's argument, underscoring his concerns and his rhetorical position:

"The vote is won," Mr. Joad continues, "but war is very far from being a thing of the past." *That I can corroborate myself*—witness this letter from a gentleman asking for help to prevent war, and there are certain photographs of dead bodies and ruined houses—but let Mr. Joad continue. "Is it unreasonable," he goes on, "to ask that contemporary women should be prepared to give as much energy and money, to suffer as much obloquy and insult in the cause of peace, as their mothers gave and suffered in the cause of equality?" And again, *I cannot help but echo*, is it unreasonable to ask women to go on, from generation to generation, suffering obloquy and insult from their brothers and then for their brothers? Is it not both perfectly reasonable and on the whole for their physical, moral and spiritual welfare? [Pp. 43–44; emphasis added] [33]

The narrative voice unwinds patriarchal logic by echoing its claims, repeating its gestures, recollecting the war photographs and returning to the concerns of the initial letter. But Joad's position that daughters of suffrage must suffer as much in the cause of peace as their mothers suffered in the cause of equality is echoed *with a difference*. His question is restated so that its rhetorical equation of generational suffering is repositioned along lines of gender, situating young women with respect to their brothers rather than their mothers. Whereas the generational movement from mother to daughter insured women's equality (with men), in brother-sister relations there has been no change from generation to generation.

Before all the changes implicit in this apparent restatement of Joad's question can register on the reader, the writer quickly returns Joad to his position of authority. She first employs the first-person plural pronoun ("us"), as if she were speaking on behalf of all women. She positions herself defensively in front of Joad's commentary, which is rendered through free indirect speech:

> But let us not interrupt Mr. Joad. "If it is, then the sooner they [women] give up the pretence of playing with public affairs and return to private life the better. If they cannot make a job of the House of Commons, let them at least make something of their own houses. If they cannot learn to save men from the destruction which incurable male mischievousness bids fair to bring upon them, let women at least learn to feed them, before they destroy themselves." [*TG*, p. 43]

Warning her sisters not to "interrupt" Mr. Joad, Woolf turns the tables on patriarchy's policing/silencing of women's speech. She silences her sisters' implicit objections to Joad's argument that suffrage brought no good either to British women or to the larger culture. Deferring, she cedes the platform to Joad so that he can further reveal the attitudes his rhetoric hopes to mask: his appeal for women's return to the private domain, to the kitchen, follows a litany of women's failures in public life. Women's public duties, Joad implies, were to save men from their own destructive tendencies. In this analysis, "incurable male mischievousness" (what Woolf, following Freud, elsewhere calls "infantile fixation") threatens to destroy civilization. For Joad, war making is a male enterprise, driven by "male mischievousness"—that is, by psychic necessity. War, and man's desire for it, is as apparently "incurable" as Woolf had first suspected. Hitler and Mussolini no longer seem frightening larger-than-life monsters on the horizon of civilization but as "mischievous" males who cannot help but play war games.[34]

H. G. Wells, however, takes a rather different position on the failures of the women's movement and the rise of totalitarianism:

"Mr. H. G. Wells says, 'There has been no perceptible woman's movement to resist the practical obliteration of their freedom by fascists and Nazis' " (p. 43). That is, he makes the women's movement responsible for organizing a viable anti-fascist political program. Wells returns the question of impending war and totalitarian threat to their gendered doubleness (like the barrister, he argues that war affects both men and women), but he appeals not for collaboration between the sexes in fighting totalitarianism and war (as does the barrister), but appeals to women's self-interest in collectively resisting fascist and Nazi efforts to obliterate women's freedom. Woolf mimes these male voices when she turns on the daughters of educated men:

> Rich, idle, greedy and lethargic as you are, how have you the effrontery to ask me to subscribe to a society which helps the daughters of educated men to make their livings in the professions? For as these gentlemen prove in spite of the vote and the *wealth which that vote must have brought with it*, you have not ended the war; in spite of the vote and the *power which that vote must have brought with it*, you have not resisted the practical obliteration of your freedom by Fascists or Nazis. What other conclusion then can one come to but that the whole of what was called "the woman's movement" has proved itself a failure; and the guinea which I am sending you herewith is to be devoted not to paying your rent but to burning your building. And when that is burnt, retire once more to the kitchen, Madam, and learn, if you can, to cook the dinner which you may not share. . . . [*TG*, pp. 43–44; ellipsis in original]

Against this recital of women's failures, Woolf's own voice, the voice of a socialist-feminist, falls into silence (. . .). Her mime cannot maintain itself any longer: whereas power and wealth, which men possess and women are denied, are required to bring an end to war or halt the rise of totalitarianism, *women* have failed suffrage, which men purchased for them by their own votes, thereby failing their country. Only the verb form (conditional past) reveals the anger and irony underwriting this draft letter to professional women. Rhetorically charged, the prose abruptly halts: "There, Sir, the letter stopped; for on the face at the other side of the letter—the face that a letter-writer always sees—was an expression of boredom was it, or was it of fatigue?" (*TG*, p. 44).

This rhetorical strategy, which counters words with images, requires commentary. The women authors of the second and third letters are effectively silenced by patriarchy, but their facial expressions ("melancholy" in one case, "fatigue" in the other) appear within the ellipses that close off Woolf's provisional letters of response (*TG*, pp. 35, 44). That is, these nonverbal modes of expression counter patriarchy's excess verbiage, which itself mimes cultural notions of women's excessive chatter. The images of melancholy and fatigue that appear to Woolf from the other side of the page reveal the visible effects of women's efforts to overturn the weight of cultural logic and escape the strictures of marriage and motherhood. The Joad-Wells commentaries expose a cultural logic that catches woman in a double bind: she is chastised for failing to save men from themselves *and* she is criticized for failing to recognize that this "incurable male mischievousness" has a vested interest in denying women freedom. The guinea enclosed with this letter, the second to be given, halts Woolf's internal dialogue, a silence marked here, as in the previous letter, by ellipsis (*TG*, p. 39).

THE RHETORIC OF SCENT

Then what a variety of smells interwoven in subtlest combination thrilled his nostrils; strong smells of earth, sweet smells of flowers; nameless smells of leaf and bramble; sour smells as they crossed the road; pungent smells as they entered bean-fields. But suddenly down the wind came tearing a smell sharper, stronger, more lacerating than any—a smell that ripped across his brain stirring a thousand instincts, releasing a million memories—the smell of hare, the smell of fox.

Virginia Woolf, Flush: A Biography

"Miss" transmits sex; and sex may carry with it an aroma. "Miss" may carry with it the swish of petticoats, the savour of scent or other odour perceptible to the nose on the further side of the partition and obnoxious to it. What charms and consoles in the private house may distract and exacerbate in the public house.

Three Guineas[35]

The defining property of leaks, according to the *American Heritage Dictionary*, is their capacity to escape "from normal or proper confinement." They share with odors the ability to defy efforts at containing them, escaping boundaries and overrunning categorial imperatives. Defined as "a flaw, crack, hole, or passage through which an escape occurs," a leak is also the "path followed by the escaping material." Before commenting on certain spatial and circulation properties shared by leaks, odors, and elliptical figures, I want to emphasize that by definition "information leaks" depend on secrecy. They obscure sources and confound facts. Woolf is led by her nose, then, when she searches out the facts and figures supporting her argument that women and children suffer under patriarchy, and that patriarchy and Fascism share important values and founding assumptions. The olfactory sense serves as more than a metaphor for her intuitive powers; it counters the dominant visual order of cognition that Woolf summons to her aid as she "draws pictures" for the patriarchy and shoves photographs under its nose in an effort to mirror back the effects of its greed, insensitivity, self-protectionism, and repressive social measures. Lest she be accused of relying on vague rumors or insubstantial evidence, however, her opinions are confirmed by a formidable array of evidence in footnotes that circle and entwine her argument, rendering it virtually impenetrable. Footnotes form a protective boundary that shelters and supports her text; they are a defensive ordering.[36]

Consulting *Whitaker's Almanac* regarding the economic status of professional women in Great Britain, Woolf discovers rank sex discrimination: among government officials, women's salaries are the lowest. She tries to root out the sources of this sex prejudice, following the odor of cigars and the scent of perfume down the corridors of Whitehall. Led by her nose to the smell of sex, she redirects her steps to the subject of *Three Guineas*, the "sexual life of women," which she "conceived" in her bath on a January morning in 1931. The link between sexual difference and women's salaries was already apparent in her working title for the project, "Professions for Women." More than irony, then, attaches to Woolf's discovery of the smell polluting Whitehall: "There! There can be no doubt of the odour now. The cat is out of the bag; and it is a Tom" (p. 52). Women pollute the sacred atmosphere of Whitehall not with perfume or their "sex" smell, but because they take jobs away from men. The odor of women's impropriety contaminates the work environment:

> You will agree that there is good reason to think that the word "Miss," however delicious its scent in the private house, has a certain odour attached to it in Whitehall which is disagreeable to the noses of the other side of the partition; and that it is likely that a name to which "Miss" is attached will,

because of this odour, circle in the lower spheres where the salaries are rather small rather than mount to the higher spheres where the salaries are substantial. As for "Mrs.," it is a contaminated word; an obscene word. The less said about the word the better. Such is the smell of it, so rank does it stink in the nostrils of Whitehall, that Whitehall excludes it entirely. In Whitehall, as in heaven, there is neither marrying nor giving in marriage. [*TG*, p. 52]

Public opinion urges that women return to their proper place, the home.[37] Keeping women within the confines of the "proper" is not easy, since "feminine instincts" always lead elsewhere—often to the sexually improper. The "feminine" shares an essential property with odors and leaks, whose nature it is to escape their proper and confined places. This is a particular danger in Whitehall—a sanctum of state secrets.

Attempting to discover "what flavour attaches itself to sex in a public office," Woolf turns away from her earlier reliance on the "facts" of women's lives to determine the "atmosphere that surrounds the word 'Miss' in Whitehall: "we are sniffing most delicately not facts but savours" (*TG*, pp. 50–51). She ponders whether women in government posts are poorly paid because "they have proved themselves untrustworthy; unsatisfactory" (*TG*, p. 48). In 1937, against the growing fear of war, the need for increased security measures, and continued public sentiment that women were depriving men of jobs, Mr. Baldwin, the prime minister, testified publicly to the trustworthiness of women in the Civil Services:

"Many of them," he said, "are in positions in the course of their daily work to amass secret information. Secret information has a way of *leaking* very often, as we politicians know to our cost. I have never known a case of such a *leakage* being due to a woman, and I have known cases of *leakage* coming from men who should have known a great deal better." [*TG*, p. 48; emphasis added]

Woolf comments with acerbity: "So [women] are not so loose-lipped and fond of gossip as the tradition would have it? A useful contribution in its way to psychology and a hint to novelists" (*TG*, p. 48).

Woolf is led by her nose to certain principles of chemistry and the chemical senses. She learns that the power of odor (or "atmosphere") rests in its impalpability (*TG*, p. 52). She also stumbles on basic properties of physics: "Atmosphere not only changes the sizes and shapes of things; it affects solid bodies, like salaries, which might have been thought impervious to atmosphere" (*TG*, p. 52). In Whitehall, women's "odour" circulates in the bowellike lower spheres, where salaries are small; the "higher spheres," where salaries are substantial, are protected from this noxious smell by means of sex discrimination. Woolf bumps up against the politics of "partitioning," the divisions of work spaces and labor according to sex difference. If natural and scientific law underwrite biological sex differences, economic and labor hierarchies are supported by civil and religious laws. Marriage, for example, is both a legal and religious union: "Husband and wife are not only one flesh; they are also one purse" (*TG*, p. 54). Patriarchal logic and social practice declare, therefore, that husbands—who have wives and children to support—be paid more than women. (Economic law is silent on the payment received by bachelors, but Woolf bypasses this oversight—*TG*, p. 55.) It is a personal affront to men's earning powers and a public affront to economic principles when married women earn salaries. This logic creates the "atmosphere" of Whitehall, where "Miss" stinks and "Mrs." is "an obscene word" (*TG*, p. 52). When married women take jobs outside the home, they are really earning two salaries: in the profession of marriage, "the wife's salary is half the husband's income" (*TG*, p. 54).

From the flesh-and-blood union of marriage, Woolf observes, wives receive only a "spiritual or nominal share" of their husband's income (*TG*, p. 57). Within marriage, she argues, "the person to whom the salary is actually paid is the person who has the actual right to decide how that salary shall be spent" (*TG*, p. 57). Married women, therefore, do not have equal access to the marital purse: their "half" of the income is spent for pleasures they do not share (clubs to which they are denied access, sports in which they cannot participate, etc.), while the monies to which they do have access are set aside for "household expenses." In reality, women find it difficult to maintain and support causes that their husbands do not also share: "if he is in favour of force, she too will be in favour of force" (*TG*, p. 58). The pressure for real social change must come from women who earn their own incomes. This argument returns Woolf to the letter on behalf of professional women and the question of how to prevent war: "But . . .—here again, in those dots, doubts and hesitations assert themselves" (*TG*, p. 58).

A few pages earlier in the text Woolf had anticipated this ellipsis, doubling back on her argument to repeat one of the opinions already quoted from the *Daily Telegraph* ("Homes are the real places of the women . . ."), placing beside it a quotation from Hitler. She reads the two against each other:

> "There are two worlds in the life of the nation, the world of men and the world of women. Nature has done well to entrust the man with the care of his family and the nation. The woman's world is her family, her husband, her children, and her home." One [opinion] is written in English, the other in German. But where is the difference? Are they not both saying the same thing? Are they not both voices of Dictators, whether they speak English or German, and are we not all agreed that the dictator when we meet him abroad is a very dangerous as well as very ugly animal? And here he is among us, raising his ugly head, spitting his poison, small still, curled up like a caterpillar on a leaf, but in the heart of England. [*TG*, p. 53]

According to Woolf, the attitudes expressed in the *Daily Telegraph* cradle "the egg of the very same worm that we know under other names in other countries" (p. 53). This "worm" is the enemy within, the facist "at home" in England: "there we have in embryo the creature, the Dictator as we call him when he is Italian or German, who believes that he has the right, whether given by God, Nature, sex or race is immaterial, to dictate to other human beings how they shall live; what they shall do" (*TG*, p. 53). Fascism is the offspring of patriarchy, she concludes, an "egg" waiting to be hatched. Woolf later comments that the scientific name for this "egg" is "infantile fixation" that she had "smelt in the atmosphere" in Whitehall (*TG*, p. 127). The voices of dictators, of course, recall Antigone, as does Woolf's insistence on the bond that ties political tyranny to domestic violence.

The claim that patriarchy spawns fascism marks the moment of rupture in *Three Guineas* when Woolf's "feminine instinct," feminist anger, and elliptical logic cross an invisible boundary into the irrational, or—to use Vita Sackville-West's term—"misleading argument." Sexual difference is no longer an impasse against which reason recoils or a stumbling block, a story that can only repeat itself. It becomes the ground of political change.

In this chapter, the story of women's oppression serves a heuristic function. By repeating the terms of that oppression and retracing "ancestral memory" (*TG*, p. 83), Woolf arrives at a different place. This new ground is not beyond the professions or outside the house. It is located, rather, at the meeting place of private and public, in the distinction "between the laws and the Law" (*TG*, p. 81).

Unfolding onto the logic of alterity, ellipsis allows Woolf to negotiate the dimension of this "in-between." The facts of married women's lives, she writes, "bring us back in a chastened mood and with rather altered views to our starting point" (*TG*, p. 57). She discards the initial letter of response to the honorary treasurer for professional women and begins again: "Your letter, Madam, has waited a long time for an answer, but we have been examining into certain charges made against you and making certain enquiries" (*TG*, p. 59). This revised letter takes up more than half the chapter, recounting in excruciating detail the history of women's struggle. Finally, it acquits professional women of the charges of idleness and obstinacy that the first draft letter had repeated: "As you know from your own experience, and there are facts to prove it, the daughters of educated men have always done their thinking from hand to mouth. . . . They have thought while they stirred the pot, while they rocked the cradle" (*TG*, p. 62). Woolf exchanges the language of the patriarchy for a language of liberation: "We have done with war! We have done with tyranny!" (*TG*, p. 83). She addresses her female correspondent directly, no longer speaking in an "aside" meant to be overheard by the patriarchy. Instead, her rhetorical strategy is to make patriarchy speak, and nearly two-thirds of this letter is direct quotation or restatement of educated male discourse. She thus reminds the reader that the history of actions is inseparable from the history of words.

Woolf offers the guinea, symbol of social and economic status, as a mnemonic. "Ancestral memory" presides over its powers, a call to remembrance of "the traditions and the education of the private house which have been in existence these 2,000 years" (*TG*, p. 83). Reminding women of the history of oppression—which extends beyond Antigone—the guinea binds them to the "four great teachers": poverty, chastity, derision and freedom from unreal loyalties (*TG*, p. 79). The gold guinea coin, no longer in circulation when Woolf wrote her text, tells a story of sexual difference inseparable from the history of writing and the inscription of coins with images and letters, a parable of the exchange of women among men. Coined in her word mint, Woolf's guinea holds powers that are rhetorical and symbolic rather than economic or literal: "We have no time to coin new words," she writes, "greatly though the language is in need of them" (*TG*, p. 78). The face of patriarchy is stamped upon her coin in the image of George III.[38] In ancient times, however, coins were associated with reproduction and proliferation, carrying images of women—goddesses and queens—whose representations marked the value of the coin. The coin *is* the female, according to Page duBois, "the thing that gives birth to the next generation—to the *tokos*, the interest, and the *tokos*, the offspring."[39] By the terms of her gift, Woolf's guinea crosses generations and social classes to reverse and rewrite the history of women as objects of exchange among men: "I give you this guinea with which to help the daughters of *uneducated* women to enter the professions" (p. 83, emphasis added). Economic and sexual circulation and exchange are replaced by an enfolding, renewing proliferation as the three guineas are transformed textually into ellipsis (. . .).

CHAPTER 6

Unveiling the Textual Subject:
Helen in Egypt and *Ulysses*

Melanctha tried a great many men, in these days before she was really
suited. It was almost a year that she wandered and then she met a young
mulatto.

Gertrude Stein, "Melanctha"

When I said that philosophy was the thesis of translatability, I meant it not
in the sense of translation as an active, poetic, productive, transformative
'hermeneia,' but rather in the sense of the transport of a univocal meaning,
or in any case of a controllable plurivocality, into another linguistic element.

Jacques Derrida, The Ear of the Other[1]

The crisis of subjectivity signalled by the effects of a textual "-fem-
inine" shifts ground in H.D.'s *Helen in Egypt* and Joyce's *Ulys-*
ses, crossing beyond grammatical-rhetorical boundaries. Manifest as a kind of wandering or infinite translatability, the crisis
proves to be as old as the West. Turning back to ancient stories
(the *Iliad* and *Odyssey*), H.D. and Joyce question cultural configurations of gendered identities. In their texts, the static image
of "woman-in-the-feminine," guarantor of man's fragile subjectivity, refuses to keep its place. The "-feminine" moves, per-
forms, and produces meaning across the vast spaces between
ancient and modern. Translating itself through radical textual dislocations and dislocations, the "-feminine" carries the text away.
But where? and to what purposes?

My interest is less in the act of translation (turning one language into another) than the *action* of translation, a transporting or carrying over from one place to another (from the Latin,
translatio). H.D. invites us to consider this sense of the word
when she writes: "*We all know the story of Helen of Troy but few*

*of us have followed her to Egypt. How did she get there? . . .
She [was] transposed or translated from Greece. . . ."*[2] *Helen
in Egypt* opens onto the problem of origins and authentic sources,
lines of inquiry and revisionary mythmaking. The answer to
its specific question—how Helen got from Greece to Egypt—
appears to rest with the lyric poet Stesichorus, who gives another
version of the legend in his *Pallinode*, a defense of Helen, or an
apology to her. Only a fifty-line fragment of this work has survived, but it is believed to reverse Stesichorus's earlier denounce-
ment of Helen, for which he was punished by blindness.[3] A post-
Homeric text, the *Pallinode* draws upon earlier, half-forgotten
pre-Homeric sources; it loops around the Homeric tradition and
obscures rather than clarifies questions of narrative origins. Like
the Homeric works, however, it contributes to a simplification of
Helen's character within oppositions (good/bad, truth/fiction) that
her displacement from Greece to Egypt further reinforces.[4] Still,
the question of *how* Helen got to Egypt, under whose aegis and
by what agency, hangs over the story, as does the problem of
textual relations between H.D.'s poem and other ancient texts,
especially the fragment of Stesichorus's *Pallinode*.

Horace Gregory argues that *Helen in Egypt* is not a "translation" of Stesichorus's text but a "re-creation in her own terms of
the Helen-Achilles myth."[5] That is, H.D.'s text is not a translation in the narrow "philosophical" sense Derrida refers to above,
"the transport of a univocal meaning." It is rather "an active,
poetic, productive, transformative *'hermeneia'* " (*EO*, p. 140).
Helen in Egypt revises traditional notions of translation, conceived of as a necessary but denegrated activity that transports
meaning from one language to another. Considered derivative,
translation is valued only to the degree that it produces accurately
(and impossibly) an *original* text. Opposing this Platonic ordering, H.D., Richard Aldington, and Ezra Pound took translation
in other directions. They became (in)famous for translations that
embroidered, extended, and "took liberties" with texts. When
H.D. in the early years of this century learned Greek in order to
read classical works, she tested the limits of her newfound abilities in translations that were forms of inspired praxis.[6]

Helen in Egypt deconstructs the hierarchical relation of original/
copy and dismantles the wall between poet and translator. Helen
too negotiates this impasse, imagined as the ramparts of Troy

where she (or her shadow sister) paces out the measure of her days. Trojans and Greeks alike try to read the message of her footsteps, the rhythm of her sandals on the stones. They are unable, finally, to determine whether there *is* a message to be deciphered and, if so, where to find it: in the direction of her walk? the speed of her footsteps? Meaning is lost on both sides: *"Greeks and Trojans alike fought for an illusion"* (*HE*, p. 1). Helen/*Helen* is produced as a text of radical undecidability, a psychic palimpsest constituted from the double action of forgetting and remembering. In Lacanian terms, Helen is a symptom, a textual effect (or metaphor) of an untranslated unconscious message.[7] Suffering from memory loss, an inability to say how she got "here," Helen is a symptom of subjectivity itself. Her translation from Greece to Egypt restages this drama, Otherwise: "Helen did not walk / upon the ramparts, / she whom you cursed / was but the phantom and the shadow thrown / of a reflection" (p. 5). This "reflection" mirrors the construction of the ego as an Other, an alien.

Before delineating more specifically the psycho-textual elements of Helen's figuration, I want to comment on the term palimpsest with reference both to psychic processes and the place Troy occupies in our cultural imagination. A palimpsest exposes remnants of previous writings ("memories") lost and regained through erasure ("forgetting"). The *failure* to expunge, erase, or repress textual/psychic imprints produces a richly discordant tapestry whose surface displays the effects of retrieval and loss—in psychic terms, the interaction of conscious and unconscious registers. It is a contested site where diverse, fragmented, and conflicting inscriptions coexist in an endless present. Simultaneously documenting and destroying its own history, the palimpsestic text provides a productive metaphor for psychic existence. Within the split of subjectivity (*je/moi*, I/me), its scribe/censor works with eraser in one hand and stylus in the other.[8]

For Western culture, Troy represents such a site or activity. Its story is grounded "in the bedrock of western culture" according to archeologist Michael Wood, yet excavations of the city reveal "the difficulty of distinguishing features of [its] different phases." No coherent picture emerges from its multiplicities and contradictions, and Wood concludes that "there is not . . . one single Troy."[9] Troy names a mystery of origins, especially for the birth of Western literature, which emerged from the ashes of its destruction. There are no documentary, written, or primary sources for the story of Troy, no way of confirming its prehistory except through Homer, whose accounts may not have been committed to writing until the seventh century B.C. (that is, just prior to Stesichorus). Production of historical chronologies in Greece resulted from the adoption of an alphabet in the eighth century (almost five hundred years after the sack of Troy in 1250 B.C.) and focused on the daunting task of situating legend, myth, and story with respect to an emerging concept of "history." Occupying a central place in our collective imagination, Troy reaches to us across this dim past through myth and poetry. Like H.D.'s Helen, we seek to position our own stories in relation to it, but historically Troy continues to elude us: did the Trojan War really take place? did it take place on the site we know today as Troy? what caused the conflict? who was Helen and why was her beauty so deadly?

Following H.D.'s lead, I place Troy within Freudian legend (as rewritten by Lacan, a modern Stesichorus), where it represents the "navel of the dream" of Western culture, a point of absolute incomprehensibility that belongs to a "domain of the unknown"— our cultural unconscious.[10] Helen appears as a symptom or message that we, no less than she, strive to decipher. She is represented in/as the hieroglyph, a radically Other symbolic mode whose structural meaning puzzles and confuses us. Confronting the Sphinx and its riddle ("the eternal *why*"—*HE*, p. 93), we encounter the unknowable. It is Egypt, then, that shows through the charred remains of Troy, site of the *failure* of the West to discover its origins, to uncover the beginnings of its own story.

The narrative perspective of *Helen in Egypt* is retrospective (the war is over), but the poem interweaves variations of the Helen myth through a "continuous present" (to use Gertrude Stein's phrase) so that past and present, here and there, cannot be clearly delineated. As the poem opens Helen stands in the Egyptian Amen-temple, a space outside of time. Never able fully to reconstruct her passage to this refuge, Helen offers oblique and fragmented recollections of Troy, visions perhaps gleaned from stories told *about* Troy, but her actual experience of Egypt during the war years remains a blank. Within the three sections of the poem, Helen is shifted from Egypt to Leuké and back to Egypt, these changes of scene perhaps representing other states of being (and other versions of the story) or her effort to recuperate the original loss, the gap in memory, that is Egypt. Since we (and she) never know how she is transported from one place to another, each change of location opens another hole within the narrative. At the center of this riddled text is Leuké, Thetis's *isle blanche*. Brought to the island at Thetis's call (made on behalf of her son: "Achilles waits," she says—p. 185), Helen enacts yet another rendition of the myth in which she marries Achilles and bears him a child, Euphorion. Admitting that while in Egypt she was in a "semi-trance state," she confesses that here, on Leuké, she "move[s] as one in a dream" (p. 109). These states may have been induced by the waters of Lethe, the river of forgetfulness through which souls pass from life to death (Paris claims that Helen died on the steps the night Troy burned—p. 141), or they may mark the passages between various versions of the story. On Leuké, Achilles and Helen are either ghosts or they have been reborn in another time and place—a dream world.

Dream and reality, remembrance and ecstatic trance overlap as Helen tries to make "sense" of her situation. She poses the questions familiar to any dreamer (where am I? what does this mean?), eventually intuiting that she herself is the dream's message—the writing, the wisdom of the Egyptian god, Thoth. Although the message is never fully recovered, the poem's veils, sails, scarves, spiral shells, songs, odors, poison potions, reels of yarn, doll figures, and icons, and the rhythm of sandals on stone are familiar to us as unconscious signifiers. These are the materials from which psychoanalysis and grammatology (re)construct psychosexual-textual myths. If the poem removes us from the familiar quadrants of time and space, it also eerily projects the insights of Lacan, Kristeva, and Derrida.

Like dreams, these textual symptoms point to repressed psychic material. They can be deciphered, but only by disintegrating the Imaginary unity that constitutes the *moi*, a terrifying enterprise for the subject, who rightly fears that disintegration of the ego means psychic death.[11] It is this dangerous journey, however, that *Helen in Egypt* undertakes, a journey that bears a remarkable resemblance to the analytic process Lacan calls *remémoration*. While Freud believed that symptoms were signs of neurosis that could be treated by bringing repressed material into consciousness, Lacan viewed symptoms as metaphors for the human condition. That is, they belong to the structure of subjectivity. In place of reminiscence, which focuses on the content of memories and in any case cannot reach the unconscious, Lacan hypothesized *remémoration*, a means of charting the subject's unconscious history as it is repeated in daily life. The symptom is a key element in this process, a "tracer" that the psychoanalyst follows in mapping the signifying field. Because the symptom comes from elsewhere (the unconscious, the axis of the Other's discourse of Desire), it produces discordance in the structure into which it emerges. Stated differently: the symptom does not appear in the same "language" as the signifying structure through which it reveals itself. Lacan describes the symptom as a hieroglyph that requires translation (or "transference," to use psychoanalytic terminology).[12]

To read Helen as a hieroglyph of the unconscious is to locate her within a specific discourse in which she is a discordant element. If *remémoration* stages a therapeutic breakdown of the ego, *Helen in Egypt* breaks down Helen's "perfection" as image and spectacle, the very model of Western representation. Aware that she represents "perfection" for the Greeks and Trojans who both curse and desire her, Helen does not herself, however, feel or experience this unity of form. Like all subjects, her wholeness and identity are always under attack by the semiotic. Various textual clues signal these challenges to her "perfection" or Imaginary wholeness: her limp, her unfastened sandal, her wounded feet, the rent in her veil as it catches on a fallen pilaster during the sack of Troy. Achilles, who tries to read her meaning from his position below Troy's wall, is particularly troubled by the symptoms of her failed perfection because they reflect a message from his own unconscious: he is mortal, he will die. The Achilles heel, mark of his vulnerability, complements (and translates as) her broken sandal, her limp. These part-objects betray the ideal of wholeness necessary to maintain images and symbols. They point us to the (m)Other world of fragments, inscriptions, and the "letters" that form the basis of a signifying system. We enter an in-between territory that does not recognize the either-or logic of consciousness.

Achilles' question, "Helena, which was the dream, / which was the veil of Cytheraea?" (*HE*, p. 36), situates itself between two psychic mysteries or scenes to be interpreted. Helen and H.D. together struggle with the question ("*Is the 'veil of Cytheraea' or Love, Death? Is the disguise of Death or the 'veil' of Death, Love?*"). They conclude that it is "too difficult a question to answer" (p. 45). If we locate the question within a psychoanalytic context, however, the dream figures the "Other" dimension that the veil of consciousness and rationality draws across our waking being. The dream/veil draws us to another place, another logic: "*She does understand. But there must be an intermediate dimension or plane*" (p. 45). Helen's question, "are we home-sick for what has been?" (p. 45), directs itself both to her past (reminiscence) and to the "intermediate" dimension in which *remémoration* takes place. The dream/veil reveals the conjunction and overlap of these dimensions, the interplay of textual fields through which the subject is articulated. To locate herself as a point of connection between these registers, Helen cannot rely only on memory (which functions "in time" and is therefore conscious); she must connect to "timeless time," the territory of the unconscious. This route goes by way of the (m)Other, and Egypt and Leuké are mapped as maternal realms.

The encounter between Helen and Achilles on Leuké, which takes place at the exact center of the poem, collapses chronological time. Projected forward into a future in which they are parents rather than children, they are also returned to childhood. However, they follow quite different psychological routes to these states or conditions. Whereas Helen's is a process of *remémoration*, Achilles is caught in a form of psychic regression. She follows a "Lacanian" path, while Achilles reaches a "Freudian" impasse that she helps him negotiate.

Helen finds her way back to Theseus, the legendary hero-king of Athens who stole her from Sparta when she was a child (p. 147). This initial abduction produced trauma, separation from her family, and the necessary rescue by her brothers, the Dioscuri. While accounts of the abduction vary, in the most sinister version of the story (not related by H.D.), Theseus impregnates her, and she delivers a baby. At the mythic-psychic level, Theseus's actions render Helen vulnerable: the second abduction (by Paris) is related to the first, and the two events are inscribed in relation to each other within the unconscious. Taken together, they repeat the structure of primary and secondary repression out

of which the division between unconscious and conscious is created. That is, Helen's subjectivity is structured in/as abduction.[13]

Within H.D.'s poem, Theseus is a figure of intellectual, or
"Greek," thought: he represents the primacy of consciousness in
Western culture. Trying to help Helen *"reconcile Trojan and
Greek"* (p. 159), he warns that *"Greek creative . . . thought
must not be entangled in the labyrinth or dissolved or washed
away by 'the ancient Nile' "* (p. 169). That is, Egypt—the
(m)Other territory—must be repressed, and he recalls Helen
"from the dream, 'the opiate of non-remembrance' " occasioned
by her sojourn in Egypt (p. 169). Theseus, of course, has a certain (unconscious) investment in maintaining Helen's perfection,
keeping her centered within the symbolic and consciousness. He
encourages her to stay in present time and resist the pull toward
transcendental time or infinity. H.D. also casts him as a figure of
Freud, and he stages a scene of analysis in which Helen appears
as "Psyche," a revenant from Egypt. Drawing her couch near to
the brazier where he wraps her in "soft woven wool" (p. 170),
he tells her of "his own primeval terror," the fear of the Minotaur
against whose danger he protected himself with "strands of
hemp-like wool" stuffed into his wallet (p. 167). Tying knots in
the wool, he created a chain (an Ariadne's thread) to assure his
escape from the labyrinth; one of these knots he names "Aethra,"
his mother.[14]

Although this story recollects the protective, pre-Oedipal mother,
it does so only to illustrate the dangers of being "drawn back . . .
to the past" (p. 168). Theseus dismisses the monster as a "hallucination of infancy," a childish fear that adult intellect puts
aside. He argues for the primacy of the symbolic, "the delight
of the intellect," which is founded on a certain "forgetting"
(p. 168). The story ends with a question that both is and is not
rhetorical: "but what is thought/ to forgetting?" (p. 168), that
is, what is the conscious to the unconscious, the intellect to in-
tuition? Theseus's story turns back on him to pose the question of subjectivity as *loss*: at what price does one enjoy "the
delight of the intellect" or enter the symbolic? This question
drives Achilles' anger and haunts Helen.

Like all the stories in H.D.'s text, Theseus's tale and Helen's
overlap. His is a cautionary account, however. He "forgets" the

knotted strands of wool and the woman's name he gave to each (p. 167). Helen, by contrast, tries to learn the structure of her psychic "knot" despite the discouragement and risks the task entails: "why do I lie here and wonder, / and try to unravel the tangle / that no man can ever un-knot?" (p. 298). Indeed, "man" may never be able to untangle the knot (sexual difference is at work). The textual-textile structure of the psychic symptom that Lacan repeatedly emphasized can be imagined by reference to the domestic art of weaving, which produces its text on a loom, and to music, which in ancient times produced its text on the lyre, a stringed instrument. In H.D.'s text (and to a lesser degree in Joyce's *Ulysses*), the loom and lyre become metaphors for the process of *remémoration*. They produce textual effects that reveal unconscious structures.

To understand how the unconscious works in these modern texts, we need to look again at the Homeric tradition, where the complexities of Helen's character and her ambiguous status as signifier for the Trojan War undergo a sharp change from the *Iliad* to the *Odyssey*. In relation to Penelope's patience and fidelity, Helen is viewed as fickle and untrustworthy, a sexual wanderer and deceiver. She is marginalized in the later text when Penelope displaces her as weaver. Whereas the *Iliad* weaves Helen into a text not of her own making, a tapestry of others' stories about her, in the *Odyssey* Penelope employs the loom to figure and de-figure her own meaning as the desired other, object of the suitors' attention and focus of Odysseus' dream of return.[15] She holds her place as Queen of Ithaca and wife of the absent Odysseus by knotting and unknotting the threads of her text: she makes a "liar" of her loom. It awaits Joyce, however, to imagine Penelope as singer with connections to the East, the Gibralter of Molly Bloom's childhood. Molly's lyric soprano seduces Blazes Boylan (a modern-day Paris), and she is also a weaver/storyteller whose monologue spins a complex narrative of sexual difference.

But the relation of psychic and textual structures, or the place of ancient stories with respect to modern literature, is not found (only) in thematic correspondences. It is also registered in rhythm, meter, and alliteration, elements of the oral tradition that must be "translated" into the graphic codes that organize texts. H.D.'s poem opens onto this Other, forgotten register. Organized into strophes, its action is strophic, turning from side to side, like the chorus in Greek drama. Its rhetorical questions constantly shift the direction of address and mime the action of apostrophe, which turns aside and away. Apostrophes punctuate the text as Helen and Achilles are caught up in Other's Desire: "O careless, unspeakable mother, / O Thetis" (pp. 253–54). Pronouns shift, referents lose their grammatical grounding, and homophonies echo across the page. These poetic effects are of special interest to the psychoanalyst, who hears in them the work of *remémoration*. When Helen asks, "Was Troy lost for a kiss / or a run of notes on a lyre? / was the lyre-frame stronger / than the bowman's arc, / the chord tauter?" (p. 230), the analyst hears (and the attentive grammatologist sees) at least two plays on words in her questions: "lyre" and "liar"; "tauter" and "taught her." The lyre sings lies, the loom weaves fictions, but the "lies" and "fictions" structure a truth. The question is, what is the structure of this truth?

The "truth" of *remémoration* does not follow the circuit of the Freudian *fort/da*. Indeed, the success of *fort/da* risks foreclosure of *remémoration* because it attempts to "master" trauma by repeating the loss as gain or pleasure. *Remémoration* does not promise (or provide) a simulacrum of restitution; rather it maps the structure of trauma repressed in the unconscious. We can read the differences between these psychic models in two powerful scenes from *Helen in Egypt*. In the first, Helen returns to Sparta following her "analysis" with Theseus to discover (not recover) her losses: "She had lost her childhood or her child" (p. 227). Although we are told that all oppositions are now reconciled "in Theseus," it was his actions that occasioned her loss of childhood. Helen later loses her own child, Hermione, when she abdicates her marital and maternal responsibilities to the abduction/ elopement with Paris. Hermione, her daughter by Menelaus, figures both forms of loss:

> I had all that, everything,
> my Lord's devotion, my child
> prattling of a bird-nest,
>
> playing with my work-basket;
> the reels rolled to the floor
> and she did not stoop to pick up

the scattered spools but stared
with wide eyes in a white face,
at a stranger—and stared at her mother,

a stranger—that was all,
I placed my foot on the last step
of the marble water-stair

and never looked back;
how could I remember all that?
Zeus, our-father was merciful. [P. 228]

This drama recollects familiar psycho-textual elements: the bird-nest (a woven object), the work-basket with its sewing/weaving materials, the scattered spools of thread, the child's staring regard, the (m)Other-stranger disappearing into nowhere.

In a richly nuanced reading, Deborah Kelly Kloepfer focuses this scene in relation to two others. The first, which provides the interpretive paradigm, recalls Freud's grandson as he rolled the thread and reel underneath the bedskirts in an effort to master the loss of his absent mother. The other finds Achilles in Chiron's cave cradling a doll he has fashioned, the "Thetis-eidolon," which he worships. Kloepfer's double reading establishes an equivalence of sorts between the spool and the doll; for her, the child's psychic investment is in the object. In contrast, I want to stress the motion of the *fort/da*: the child reinvests his pain with pleasure by *reenacting* the mother's leavetaking and return rather than by *replacing* her with an eidolon, emblem of loss.[16] Hermione refuses either to create a doll or to retrace the *fort/da* action. Instead, she mirrors loss (of self) by returning the mother's gaze. She repeats the act that "freezes" Helen as image: the mother disappears. The daughter's gaze duplicates another— Helen's glance—which has the opposite effect: it releases Achilles into the process of *remémoration* (p. 62.) Hermione's gaze, however, draws our attention to what Kloepfer calls the "daughter *text*," which fills the hole left by the disappearing mother (*UM*, p. 166). For H.D., daughter of Helen Doolittle, the "daughter text" is her own writing. For Hermione, the text is a blank—she herself disappears from the poem.

Here we can remark on a crucial difference between *remémoration* and the Freudian paradigm. The *fort/da* movement con-

structs a text, but one that sews over (and knots up) a hole in the
Real rather than retracing the structure of the symptom that
comes to fill the hole. That is, the *fort/da* is itself a symptom of
trauma. This is what Helen learns through *remémoration*, a process that *Helen in Egypt* reconstructs. Following the circuit to her
childhood, to her abduction and loss of the (m)Other, Helen
comes upon the child who has been eclipsed: herself, her daughter. The scene flashes into the present moment; the unconscious
spills across the boundary into consciousness—like the overturned basket. Helen cannot yet consciously know the meaning of this, but she has retraced one level of the symptomatic
structure.

The companion scene to this one occurs in the third and final
section of the poem, the Eidolon, where we meet Achilles as
a child. He has been sent by his mother to the cave of the centaur Chiron, who must teach him to "learn to rule a kingdom"
(p. 287). The cave represents the seat of symbolic law and the
entrance to subjectivity. Like all subjects, Achilles is caught
within an oppositional structure; he must choose between a
masculine or feminine subject position. In the myth, his fate is
doubly plotted: he may choose to live a long but unremarkable
life as ruler of his mother's island-kingdom, envisioned in H.D.'s
poem as a pre-Oedipal space, or he can take up arms and die
young but gloriously in battle. Thetis tries various means to repress the "masculine" side of the prophecy. A goddess, she intervenes against the symbolic law that demands recognition of
mortality as the price for subjecthood. As we will see, her efforts
fail, and Achilles hates her for failing to protect him.

Not yet ready to leave his mother, the young Achilles fashions
a doll in her likeness, which he hides from the centaur (p. 284).
He believes the doll is magic and can grant his wishes. He builds
an altar to this goddess and worships her in secret (p. 284). The
eidolon is a fetish, a totem of the world he has lost, and the
centaur, who guards the law and serves the Name of the Father,
must not learn of this ritual mother-worship. Later, Thetis intervenes again in her son's fate, hiding him in Scyro and "entreating
the king to instruct him, / as the Centaur Chiron had done, / in
the laws and the arts of peace" (p. 286). (These scenes of instruc-
tion complement Helen's double abduction and serve the same
psychological purpose: they structure the double repression nec-

essary for subjectivity.) This time, however, Achilles answers "the lure of war" (p. 286), apparently accepting his glorious fate, and "forgets" his various vows of allegiance to mother and family. He heads for Troy, hurtling toward death in a ship whose prow is adorned with the figurehead of Thetis (pp. 244–45). As Kloepfer comments, the forgotten "eidolon and the [ship's] hull become indistinguishable from each other and from the mother" (*UM*, p. 163). Thetis's future power in Achilles' life is due to his having forgotten her. Psychically, it translates as the death-dealing (and death-seeking) power of his inexplicable rage.

Achilles successfully enters the symbolic the moment he forgets his mother, and his story repeats the movement of memory and repression. He creates the doll to "repair a loss and a failure," as Kloepfer suggests (*UM*, p. 163), but he later loses the eidolon. That is, the loss is twice inscribed in the unconscious. As Helen seeks to recall Egypt, Achilles searches for his lost talisman: "he only remembered it, / remembered and wanted it back, / when it was gone" (p. 283). Too late he discovers that Thetis cannot fulfill her promise to guarantee his immortality; she has "forgotten" to dip his heel in the river Styx, but by then he has also misplaced the magic doll that grants all his wishes. Helen rightly suspects that the loss of this little "nothing" is the source of his terrifying anger (p. 282).

It is the (m)Other rather than the mother that the subject necessarily represses. Repression creates a *text* of Desire that metaphor and metonymy distribute along the signifying chain, one woman substituting for another.[17] Achilles' desire, for example, is represented as anger and fear of Helen *in place of the mother* who failed him. Unaware of his desire to reconnect with the (m)Other (to experience a *jouissance* that can only be found beyond the "Name of the Father"), Achilles attacks Helen when they meet on the beach. He asks if she is "a vulture, a hieroglyph, / the sign of the name of a goddess" (p. 16). He has repressed the goddess's name, the Name of the Mother (which is always lost): "he could name Helena / but the other he could not name" (p. 277). Helen tries to direct Achilles along the path of *remémoration* by which he will learn the structure of (m)Other's Desire encoded as a hieroglyph. She has learned that the (m)Other's powers, the magic and sorcery that Achilles tries to channel into the eidolon, can "only be defined by the most abstruse hieroglyphics or the most simple memories" (p. 297).[18]

As symptom, Helen points to the structure of (m)Other's Desire, which Theseus, Paris, and Achilles misread as their own desire for (but also hatred of) the all-powerful, protective mother of infancy. The pre-Oedipal mother represents for the child a false shield against injury, illness, and death. The price of subjectivity is the recognition and acceptance of mortality—in short, the realization that the mother cannot protect her child from death. For this, Helen is cursed by Trojans and Greeks; this is an illusion for which they fight. Helen is a catalyst for their encounters with the (m)Other who is mistaken for the real mother: Theseus is led back to the Minotaur's maze (pp. 167–68); Paris asks Helen to "take the place of his mother, Hecuba, the Trojan Queen, who had left him 'like Oedipus to die' " (p. 216); Achilles is directed along the path of unconscious substitutionary processes: "Was not his own mother more desirable than the 'wooden doll' he had made to represent her?" (p. 295).

Helen too is led back to "the million personal things, / things remembered, forgotten, /remembered again, assembled / and re-assembled in different order / as thoughts and emotions" (p. 289). She learns a "different order," that is, she learns "order *as* thoughts and emotions." In Lacanian terms, Helen experiences the *jouissance* of the symptom, and recognizes the relation of "*La Mort, L'Amour*," whose meanings are linked homophonically in H.D.'s text. Death and love, represented by Achilles and Helen, are joined in a "miraculous" double birth. Euphorion, the product of this union, is "not one child but two": Achilles, "the child in Chiron's cave," and Helen, the "frail maiden" stolen by Theseus (p. 288). The parents encounter again their own lost selves. Helen remembers Hermione, "a child that stared," then immediately denies this identification ("the child's name is Hermione, / it is not Hermione"—p. 290). The child is Helen, whose abduction is reinscribed in the daughter text as abandonment.[19]

At the crossroads of these temporal spaces, where repression is doubly registered, stands the (m)Other, the screen-text of subjectivity. In H.D.'s mythic fabrication, Helen refigures this tapestry, *Helen in Egypt* forecasting a psychoanalytic moment that H.D., analysand of Freud, could only have dreamed. H.D. rejects Freud's notion of the unconscious as a collection of unverbalized "thing-presentations" not amenable to analytic transference and substitutes instead the ideo-phono-grammic materials of the Lacanian unconscious. She has glimpsed the fundamental relation of psychosexuality and language: subjects speak (across) the failure of the psychic law to maintain sexual difference; symptoms speak (through) repression. The language of the poem repeats the flow and drift of psychoanalysis, and through its shifts and reversals Helen is "translated" from image to action, from noun to verb. Two scenes illustrate how this transference takes place.

Drawn to Theseus's fire and wrapped like a mummy in the woven wool cloth, Helen turns her gaze inward. She tries to read her relation to the women whose names Theseus recites— Chryseis, Deidamia, Briseis, Polyxena, women sacrificed to the Trojan War or exchanged as tokens among men. Earlier, on a different plane of existence, Helen had stood before the temple wall trying to read her relation to its hieratic symbols. The flight of a bird (the hieroglyphic figure of Isis, the Egyptian Thetis) helped her to recognize herself as "a living hieroglyph." It is the bird's movement that occasions this insight: "when the bird swooped past, / that first evening, / I seemed to know the writing" (p. 23). The later scene recognizes another kind of writing; internal, it comes not in speech or words, but as breath. It produces a dialogue between Helen and Helena: "do you see the cloth move, or the folds, to my breathing? / . . . do you hear me? do I whisper? / there is a voice within me, / listen—let it speak for me" (pp. 174–75). This is the voice of the Other, who is figured in the poem as a sister, Helen's twin and phantom. Her own mother, Leda, is markedly absent from H.D.'s script, which figures Otherness within the terms of sisterhood.[20] The intake of breath, the folded, moving cloth, and the whisper all suggest the (m)Other's presence, however: a word that is not yet a word breathes across the void of the Real, and the analyst and poet listen to an Other who can be heard but not seen.

⁂

TRANSLATING THE (M)OTHER

How did she know the word, / the one word that would turn and bind / and blind him to any other?

[HE, p. 277]

Textualizing the Feminine

Tell me the word, mother, if you know now. The word known to all men.
[U, 15.4192–93]

We have been told that the "ultimate experience, *La Mort, L'Amour*," carries a price tag. "*Is the price too great?*" Helen asks (*HE*, p. 288). If the love-death knot that binds Helen and Achilles represents the experience of human subjectivity, then the price of love is death: "so the dart of Love / is the dart of Death, / and the secret is no secret" (p. 303). Not only physical death, mortality, but the "death" or loss of childhood signified by Helen's first abduction, Hermione's abandonment, Theseus's encounter with the Minotaur, and Achilles' experiences in the centaur's cave. Theseus's story foreshadows Helen's question: "but what is thought / to forgetting?" (p. 168).

In psychological terms, then, the initial losses that structure the later acceptance of one's own mortality involve the renunciation of childhood, "the numberless / tender kisses, the soft caresses, / given and received" (p. 289). H.D. represents the process of engendering subjectivity as a boundary crossing—in literary terms, the shift from the lyric to epic genre: the story "was epic, heroic and it was far / from a basket a child upset / and the spools that rolled to the floor" (p. 289). Helen acknowledges that this threshold inscribes the mark of sexual difference: "I see the pitiful heap of little things, / the mountain of monstrous gear, / then both vanish, there is nothing" (pp. 301–2). "Little things" is H.D.'s shorthand for the material realm of mother and child; it contrasts with the "mountain of monstrous gear," the accoutrements of the Symbolic that signals the adult male world of war. Lyric is little, childish, and feminine; epic is big, frightening, and masculine. Helen has traditionally held a place in both worlds, the domestic enclosure and the arena of war, and H.D.'s poem acknowledges this by endowing Helen with a double voice, one lyric, the other heroic.[21] In the heroic mode, she takes her place within the epic tradition, the woman fought over by men ("do I love War? / is this Helena?"—p. 177). Her lyric voice, "*a song rather than a challenge*," invokes mother figures, Isis-Thetis, and "*takes us back to Egypt but in a Greek mode*" (p. 178). The lyric mode conveys meaning apart from the content of its story: "*the rhythms must speak for themselves and the alliterations . . . take many shapes*" (p. 178).

178

Joyce's writings both repeat and reverse traditional distinctions between lyric and epic: in *Ulysses*, for example, heroism moves from the battlefield to the home front, where heroes are defined by humanity rather than hubris. Nonetheless, Leopold Bloom, a modern Odysseus, ventures out into the world, while Molly, his impatient Penelope, remains within the domestic enclosure. Like H.D., Joyce tried to untangle the love-death knot of human subjectivity in both his life and writings, but he avoided any direct engagement with psychoanalysis. While H.D. had a personal interest in Freud's work, Joyce feared and rejected analysis. Lacan, however, recognized Joyce's texts as forms of analysis created without the experience of psychoanalysis, but "not without Freud": "*James Joyce, il n'aime pas la psychanalyse. Pourquoi?*" he asked.

Lacan's answer to this question is perhaps less insightful than one would expect. He reasoned that Joyce's Catholicism (he, like Lacan, never fully abandoned Catholicism) closed out the possibilities for analysis, which "might have lured him with an unlikely outcome." [22] The outcome Joyce may have feared was probably less the loss of Catholicism than the loss of his art. Nonetheless, psychoanalysis is at work in Joyce's art, especially in the later works. From the close of "Nausicaa," when night falls in *Ulysses*, through the night world of *Finnegans Wake*, Joyce explores human subjectivity not only as subject matter of his writing but also within the terms of Lacanian analysis. Anticipating Lacan's claims that the unconscious is structured like a language, Joyce translated and textualized this Other language. In the darkness of his own blinded night world, he opened himself to the madness that he feared, creating texts that shielded him from the abyss of psychosis. [23] In the process, Joyce invented an as yet undefined genre of literature, nameable only as the *Wake*, and silently abandoned (or significantly revised) his early aesthetic theories written in the name of Stephen Dedalus.

Stephen's aesthetic "theory" defines literary genres from a neo-Aristotelian, post-Aquinian perspective. Literary art divides itself into three forms, and these are hierarchically arranged from lowest to highest: lyric, epic, dramatic. [24] Briefly sketched, art is beauty, and beauty is form; the progression of genres eventually refines the artist (or his "image") out of the work of art (pp. 214–15). [25] By the terms of this theory, *A Portrait of the*

Artist as a Young Man, where Stephen first presents his ideas, is lyrical: "the artist presents his image in immediate relation to himself" (p. 214). The image of the artist, however, undergoes change as Stephen moves from childhood to young adulthood. By the close of the novel, Stephen as literary character has been refined out of existence; he exists only as text, entries in a diary. The narrative perspective, which maintained close proximity to him at the beginning of *A Portrait*, has slowly distanced itself from him. At the close of the novel, the artist's "immediate relation to himself" has already been significantly mediated, and Stephen's focus is fixed not on himself but on a larger canvas. He looks away from Ireland toward continental Europe and France: "Welcome, O Life!" (p. 252). When he appears in *Ulysses*, a latter-day epic, Stephen the proto-artist is presented in "mediate relation to himself and to others" (p. 214). What is lost in this translation from one place to another, from one genre to another?

Keeping in mind the meaning of translation as transference or transport that effects a "carrying over" or "carrying away," I want to track Stephen's journey from Dublin to Paris in reference both to epic / lyric literary genres and the psychosexual process by which humans enter into gendered subjectivity. The 3 April diary entry of *A Portrait* reports: "Told him [Davin] the shortest way to Tara was *via* Holyhead." This statement is laconic (or "Lacanic") not only by the brevity of the diary form but also because the route between Tara and Holyhead figures a psychic loop or hole within the spatial-temporal quadrants of the Real. In *Ulysses* Stephen translates this figure into the mythic terms of fatherhood and sonship:

> Fabulous artificer. The hawklike man. You flew. Whereto? Newhaven-Dieppe, steerage passenger. Paris and back. Lapwing. Icarus. *Pater, ait.* Seabedabbled, fallen, weltering. Lapwing you are. Lapwing be.[26]

Stephen is not transported from Tara, the seat of the High Kings of ancient Ireland, by the wax wings of Icarus, his mythic counterpart. He travels by more mundane conveyance—the night boat—to Holyhead, a place that (despite its name, which carries with it the tradition of druidical nature worship) is not the seat of a king or bishop but a port, a place of commerce. That is, Stephen's journey hooks him up to the Symbolic circuit of exchange, which demands his exodus (or exile) from the (m)Otherland.

In the *Portrait* notation, Stephen is "outward bound," readying himself for artistic exile. In *Ulysses* he has made his return, the reversed trajectory of the flight—Paris, Dieppe, Newhaven, London, Holyhead, Dublin—bringing him back to the father who is not at all the mythic hawklike Daedalus. Even in *Portrait*, Stephen's laconic notations refer inexactly to the science of cartology, which requires precision. Rather, they are speculations on destiny and destination that a father's message will circumvent. Reduced to telegraphese, the message reads: "—Nother dying come home father" (3.199).[27] Earlier editions of *Ulysses* transcribed the "sense" of the message ("—Mother dying come home father") by erasing its orthographic "curiosity" (3.198). While "nother" may be read in reference to the numerous, recent losses within the Dedalus family (i.e., as "another" death), "nother" for "mother" also opens the message to a negative otherness ("not other," "no other"). It is not possible to interpret the sense of this message without exposing its otherness as a textual resistance to the action of translation, a "carrying over" of the topic, topos or place.[28]

The telegram message transports Stephen, not figuratively but literally, from Paris to Dublin. Wearing his "Latin quarter hat," he carries Paris with him on his return, just as he had hoped to "transport" Tara (a place like Troy, now available only in myth) to Holyhead and beyond when he boarded the night boat. This was to have been a journey of epic artistic achievement. The 26 April diary entry records his intentions; it is perhaps the most famous sentence in all of Joyce's writing: "I go to encounter for the millionth time the reality of experience and to forge in the smithy of my soul the uncreated conscience of my race" (*AP*, pp. 252–53).

Stephen's precipitous return brings with it a crisis of identity and of purpose. He suffers much in the (re)translation, forced to hide behind rhetorical posturings, accused by Buck Mulligan of bringing back with him "Paris fads" (1.342), hiding his guilt for his mother's death behind the pose of official mourning: "He kills his mother but he can't wear grey trousers" (1.122). Stephen's identity crisis is situated not in the "legal fiction" of paternity (9.844) but in the loss of the mother—the "nother" or "not other" or "no other" of the telegram. This link to origins takes us, circuitously, through the French verb for "translate," *traduire*, which shares a common Latin root with the English word traduce (Mulligan's "slander"), obsolete meanings of which are "to produce as offspring, or in the way of generation; to propogate"; or "to pass on to offspring or to posterity; to transmit, especially by generation" (*OED*). That is, this "nother/mother" raises the question of causation, and from the posthumous world she returns to haunt her son.

In the "Proteus" chapter of *Ulysses*, Stephen imagines the umbilical cord, a "strandentwining cable of all flesh" (3.37), as a telephone line. He rings up Edenville to speak with his first mother, Eve, the woman with no navel. He need not telephone or telegraph his own mother, however. She has already appeared to him in a dream. As he recalls it in "Telemachus," her "wasted body" is veiled by "loose graveclothes" that give off "an odour of wax and rosewood," and her "secret words" are "mute" (1.271–72). She emerges from a fold in her son's memory, caught between two versions of herself. She appears first as a young woman of "phantasmal mirth," who locked her past secrets in a drawer: "old featherfans, tasselled dancecards, powdered with musk, a gaud of amber beads" (1.255–56). In a second vision, she is the prematurely aged woman ravaged by cancer, the phantom with "glazing eyes" who comes to "shake and bend" her son's soul, her breath smelling of "wetted ashes" (1.273). The first figure represents (m)Other's Desire, which exceeds the bonds and boundaries of motherhood; the second is a betrayer who comes to claim his soul in the name of Irish Catholicism: "Repent! O, the fire of hell!" (15.4212).

It is this second figure that is reincarnated in "Circe." A ghoul, she announces herself under her "maiden" name: "I was once the beautiful May Goulding," she tells her son (15.4173). (Twice in *Ulysses* she is described as a "ghoul," which carries homophonically a trace of her "other" name, *Goul*ding—1.278, 15.4200.) Divested of her former beauty, this death figure supplants in Stephen's memory the younger woman of his early childhood, a woman whose presence stirs in him conflicted feelings of mother love and incestuous desire. Both versions of May Dedalus are endowed with a palpable materiality that Stephen responds to through all five senses: he sees "her shapely fingernails" (1.268) and the "*subtle smile of death's madness*" (15.4176), hears the sounds of her impending death, the "hoarse loud breath rattling" (1.275), feels the touch of her breath (1.271), tastes the "cored apple, filled with brown sugar" that roasts for her on the hob (1.267–68).

The olfactory, however, is Stephen's most acute sense (a trait he shares with Leopold Bloom), and the odors of wax, rosewood, wetted ashes, and the "muskperfumed" scent of the locked drawer powerfully evoke the (m)Other world of his childhood. As I have already observed, infants are born with a highly developed sense of smell (that later fades, surpassed by other senses, particularly seeing and hearing). Within days the newborn infant can distinguish its mother by the smells of her breast milk, skin, and hair. It is through the olfactory mechanism, we recall, that young Stephen first learned of sexual difference: "His mother had a nicer smell than his father"; recognition of the father requires the "higher" faculty of vision ("his father looked at him through a glass: he had a hairy face"—*AP*, p. 7).[29]

When May Dedalus first appears to her son in "Telemachus," her spirit moves over the surface of the sea, a "great sweet mother" (1.77, 80). This maternal space of memory and desire, awash in amniotic fluid, harbors mysteries of origins and endings for Stephen. He is in awe of its hidden powers: suffering from hydrophobia, he admits that he swims poorly, fears death by drowning, and has not bathed in eight months (17.238–39). The sea (as) mother, source of all life, also represents for him a womb of death: his nearsightedness foreshortens the visual field, and the sea contracts into the china bowl of green vomit, his mother's "bowl of bitter waters" (1.249). While *Helen in Egypt* provides no scene to parallel the encounters between May Dedalus and her son (Achilles and Thetis do not meet face to face), mother and son are linked to each other through their association with the sea. A sea goddess, Thetis can, like Proteus, assume many shapes, and she often shows herself as sea waves or foam, as a mermaid, or through the metonym of the "sail fluttering" (*HE*, p. 163). Achilles' love of the sea connotes his relation to this ancient, primordial mother: Thetis's body is imaged as the hollow ship's hull that carries him to Troy.

Ulysses and *Helen in Egypt* offer traditional (even classic) rep-

resentations of the mother as sea (*mer/mère*).[30] Of greater importance to the textual thematics of these two works, however, is
their representation of the maternal as a text of loss or absence.
Mothers are dead, have disappeared, or are otherwise disengaged
with their children's lives. Sexual difference structures one set
of these nonrelations (sons experience the maternal text differently from daughters), and the interplay of generations structures
another (mothers are also represented as daughters). Briefly,
Stephen, like Achilles, tries to decipher the text of maternal absence (this interpretive translation becomes a new text); Molly,
like Helen, tries to construct a text of her own subjectivity out of
the absent maternal that leaves her vulnerable to men. Molly's
mother, Lunita Laredo ("whoever she was"—18.847), disappeared early from her daughter's life, leaving a legacy of maternal loss and traces of physical resemblance. Molly cannot recall
her mother and has apparently never seen a photograph of her.
Confirmation of familial likeness, then, must come from her father, Major Tweedy: "Ive my mothers eyes and figure he always
said" (18.890–91). The father's word, if it can be trusted, as-
sures that the legacy from mother to daughter is beauty, the quin-
tessential ingredient of "woman-in-the-feminine." The relation
between mothers and daughters is defined, then, either by a
daughter's text in lieu of the mother (Helen, Molly) or by an
absent or minimalized daughter text (Hemione, Milly Bloom).

H.D. and Joyce focus most directly on how sons create *a text
of the mother* out of her absence. Sons want to fill the hole that
maternal absence creates in the Real with a word, a name. When
Stephen prepares at the close of *Portrait* to leave his mother
country, his own mother provides a text for him: "She prays now,
she says, that I may learn in my own life and away from home
and friends what the heart is and what it feels" (*AP*, p. 252).
Stephen is forced by the event of his mother's death to read this
text back home, in Ireland, where the lesson his heart learns
is maternal loss. In Lacanian terms, Stephen experiences a tear
in the Real that he tries to repair by re-creating his mother in
memory. He makes a text of her:

> Stephen, an elbow rested on the jagged granite, leaned his palm against his
> brow and *gazed at the fraying edge of his shiny black coatsleeve*. Pain, that
> was not yet the pain of love, *fretted* his heart. Silently, in a dream she had

come to him after death, her wasted body within its loose brown graveclothes giving off an odour of wax and rosewood, her breath, that had bent upon him, mute, reproachful, a faint òdour of wetted ashes. *Across the threadbare cuffedge* he saw the sea hailed as a great sweet mother by the wellfed voice beside him. [1.100–107; emphasis added]

These verbal resonances of "frayed" and "fretted" repeat the textual figure of loom and lyre already observed in *Helen in Egypt*. Both words mean to produce a hole by rubbing or chafing, but while fraying unravels the weave of fabric, fretting produces sound on a stringed instrument; both words refer to anxiety (frayed nerves, a baby's fretting). The rich sensory associations of this passage play on all these meanings. Stephen sees the sea foam as "twining stresses" and hears "a hand plucking the harpstrings, merging their twining chords" (1.245–46). Fretting his heart with a pain "that was not yet the pain of love" (1.102), the mother's loss pulls the heartstrings so that, when plucked, they produce sound. Stephen recalls his mother's request that he sing Fergus's song from *The Countess Cathleen*. The song opens on a rhetorical question drawn from the heroic/epic mode: "Who will go with Fergus now, / And pierce the deep wood's woven shade." [31]

The textile references so significant to this scene are drawn even more explicitly in "Circe," when May Dedalus appears dressed "*in leper grey*" wearing a "*wreath of faded orange-blossoms and a torn bridal veil*" (15.4157–58). The torn bridal veil, which represents the bride's passage from virginity to marital sexuality, has its counterpart in Helen's rent veil, metonym of her failed perfection. The ripped veil and penetrated female body are "reading" effects, the result of man's effort to fathom woman's mystery (see *Finnegans Wake*, where the professor, an autocrat at the breakfast table, mutilates the letter by puncturing it with his fork).[32] Fergus, who "rules the shadow of the wood" in Yeats's poem quoted above, would master the body of nature, the "deep wood's woven shade." "Piercing" it, he would make it signify the power of his own being.

The veil is not only a vestment, it also signifies the hymen that conceals and protects the female sexual organs. It hints at a "truth" hidden behind and within surfaces. The veil/hymen constitutes (and complicates) the classic vision of "woman-in-the-

185

feminine," and it invites penetration. Rachel Blau DuPlessis has analyzed with great care how *Helen in Egypt* both represents and refuses woman as veiled spectacle. She describes this veiling-unveiling of the sexual-textual body as the process of scrimming (from *scrim*, a word of obscure origin to denote a thin canvas that admits light, from which comes *scrimer*, someone who fences) and scriving (from *scrive*, the tool used to cut numerals or letters into wood). Scrive, meaning the instrument, evolved etymologically to mean the person who writes—scribe, scrivener, and in French *écrivain*. As Derrida explains, the word for style, quintessence of "woman-in-the-feminine," derives from stylus, a writing instrument.[33] Style and stylus, scrim and scrive, write on and in each other, inscribing an undecidable limit of textuality.

Helen has traditionally figured this undecidable limit for all women. Patriarchy tries to contain her between oppositions (goddess / whore), but in H.D.'s poem, Helen as icon and text is also plural and palimpsestic. She destabilizes reading/writing and subject/object positions, as DuPlessis explains: 'The poem allows icon to become critic, yet remain icon; object to become subject, yet remain object; interpeted [*sic*] to become interpreter, yet remain interpreted" (*HD*, p. 109). This is true for May Dedalus as well, whose appearances are structured as double readings: her "glazing eyes" silently read Stephen as he tries to fathom her. Indeed, he demands that she pass on to him a textual sign, a word. He rejects the word she gives him ("repent"), but stands transfixed as "*her toothless mouth utter[s] a silent word*" (15.4161). This tableau opens itself to a number of readings, but May Dedalus's message, delivered across death's divide, is that subjectivity and mortality are indivisible: "All must go through it, Stephen. . . . You too. Time will come" (15.4182–83).

Stephen turns away from her testimony, just as he refused Mulligan's clinical description of her as "*beastly dead*" (1.198): "They say I killed you, mother. He offended your memory. Cancer did it, not I. Destiny" (15.4186–87). This (self) justification only confirms the accuracy of his mother's knowledge (and Mulligan's): death is inevitable. Whereas for Mulligan, physician of the Real, death is the destiny of all animals, for May Dedalus, death marks a passage (a veil of sleep or dream) to the other world promised by Catholic faith. Her statement is carefully worded: "All must go through it, Stephen." For Stephen, death is yet another text that demands interpretation. Because her religious text cannot help him to understand the meaning of death, he calls for another word: "Tell me the word, mother, if you know now. The word known to all men" (15.4192–93). She refuses this request and responds with a series of rhetorical questions that reinforce guilt: "Who saved you the night you jumped into the train at Dalkey with Paddy Lee? Who had pity for you when you were sad among the strangers?" (15.4195–96).

According to the new "Critical and Synoptic Edition" of *Ulysses*, the word Stephen wants, and the *"silent word"* his mother's "toothless mouth" probably utters in "Circe" (15.4161), is "love." Recovered by the editorial process, the word "love" is supplied by Stephen himself in the library scene as he muses about his theory of the ghost in *Hamlet*: "Do you know what you are talking about? Love, yes. Word known to all men. *Amor vero aliquid alicui bonum vult unde et ea quae concupiscimus"* (9.429–30). The Latin phrase that provides the context for the word conjoins two phrases from Aquinas's *Summa contra gentiles* that distinguish between love as the genuine wish for another's good and selfish pleasure or concupiscence (p. xi). How is it possible that in daylight hours Stephen's conscious mind discovers the word he so desires but at midnight, in the Circean nightmare, his unconscious mind represses Desire? Editorial desires appear to have outrun principles of psychoanalytic theory in this instance, and "love" is contextualized within the paternal rather than the maternal.[34]

Although the discussion of familial relations in Shakespeare's life and art that occurs in "Scylla and Charybdis" provides a general context in which "love" might illuminate textual relationships, Stephen's argument focuses on fathers, sons, and grandsons. His general topic is paternity in relation to patriarchy. As Richard Ellmann's analysis suggests, Stephen's internal dialogue about "love" seems to echo May Dedalus's hope, expressed at the close of *Portrait*, that her son may learn "away from home and friends what the heart is and what it feels" (*AP*, p. 252).[35] When he is called home from Paris to her deathbed, he has not yet learned what the heart feels; his mother takes as evidence of this his refusal to kneel down and pray at her bedside. It is her very death that forces him to confront the loss of precisely the person who (it is culturally agreed) is responsible for teaching the heart's lessons: the mother. Where there was once mother love, there is now absence through death.

The word "love" is never spoken, either by Stephen or by his mother: it is "thought" (9.429) or, possibly, "mouthed" (15.4161). In *Ulysses* this word is a phantom; in front of it, readers confront issues similar to those faced by the Trojans and Greeks who tried to interpret Helen. To them, she stood for self-ish desire, the kind of false "love" that Aquinas distinguished from "genuine love" (*amor vero*) in his *Summa*. She represented a dangerous, self-seeking desire that trespasses all boundaries—national, familial, sexual, social, and marital.

Where there has not been an adequate word to describe this condition, we have written the name "Helen," a name that un-veils woman as a spectacle of sexual desire. H.D.'s Helen resists this textual inscription; she withdraws from the scene of battle over the meaning of her body. Helen becomes a phantom, an illusion created by men. Greeks and Trojans fight for this illusion, fight over Helen's image, fight *in* her name. Outside of time, and in a domestic space far from battle, she gives another name to Achilles. She names his mother, and in that name he comes to know what the heart is and feels:

> but there is one secret,
> unpronounceable name,
> a whisper, a breath,
>
> two syllables, yes, like the Isis-name,
> but broken, not quite the same,
> breathed differently;
>
> or spoken as only one could speak,
> stretched on a pallet,
> numb with memory. . . . [*HE*, p. 279]

The name "Thetis" is not spoken by Helen; it never appears in this section of the poem. A goddess's name, it is an "unpro-nounceable" name-of-the-mother. It names "love," not the law of "Yahweh," the ineffable Name-of-the-Father. In the first-draft version of the Eidolon, the name is not even a name: it is "not even a whisper,/ a breath only may summon her." [36]

A whisper, a breath, the possibility of a name. *Helen in Egypt* and *Ulysses* thematize the desire to name and the resistance to naming, thereby crossing one boundary between lyric ("O care-less, unspeakable mother, / O Thetis"—*HE*, pp. 253–54) and epic ("Stately, plump Buck Mulligan came from the stairhead"—*U*, 1.1). At the moment the Name-of-the-Father secures the Symbolic order is the name-of-the-mother lost in a sigh, a whisper, a cry, an apostrophic "O"? Or is her name inscribed in a different order? H.D. and Joyce bypass these questions, even as their texts call for a word, a name to fill the void in subjectivity that the mother's absence hollows out. Moving within and against the Symbolic, the nameless, unspeakable (m)Other breathes, rippling the veil of representation. When this veil is violently torn away (and there are many social forms of this unveiling), there is nothing to be seen. Only psychotic hallucination can fix the gaze on a subject that has already disappeared. May Dedalus fixes her smouldering eyes on Stephen (15.4212), Hermione stares "with wide eyes in a white face, / at a stranger—and stared at her mother, / a stranger" (p. 228). In the absence of subjectivity, there is only space: "I hear their voices, / there is no veil between us, / only space and leisure" (*HE*, p. 2).

Last Words/Lost Words

So that gesture, not music, not odour, would be a universal language, the gift of tongues rendering visible not the lay sense but the first entelechy, the structural rhythm.

Ulysses

What I am saying to you is that if this heterogeneous body, this risky text provide meaning, identity, and jouissance, they do so in a completely different way than a "Name-of-the-Father." Not that they do not operate under the shield of a tyrannical, despotic Name-of-the-Father; I understand that, and we could engage in endless forensic contests. But it is only a question of power; the important thing to see is what exceeds it.

Julia Kristeva, "The Novel as Polylogue" [1]

This book opened with Jacqueline Rose's reminder that "psychoanalysis describes the psychic law to which we are subject, but only in terms of its *failing*." It closes with Julia Kristeva's admonition to to see what "exceeds" the "despotic Name-of-the-Father." The structural relations—psychic, grammatic—between these failures and excesses are of increasing interest to contemporary feminist studies. What structures, for example, woman as image and spectacle, focus of the masculine gaze? Rose and Kristeva underscore the power and limitations of the visual field which, in Rose's view, "maintain[s] a particular and oppressive mode of sexual recognition." I have tried to account for the tenacious grip of this form of sexual recognition and to catalog textual forms that simultaneously support and exceed it. I have focused relentlessly upon the textual, upon the representational veil that the Symbolic weaves to hide its fictions and fears. But all the while my analysis has been haunted by another question: if there is no escaping the Symbolic, in which our systems of representation function, is there hope of transforming it?

Epilogue

Feminists dream, as Rose reports, of a "wholly other psychic and representational domain," which would not force us into the nightmare of psychosis or a plunge into the Real.[2] If psychosis or death is the only exit from the Symbolic and the "tyrannical 'Name-of-the-Father,' " then what options do we have? Are we, like Paris (the failed and feminized suitor of Helen), to live on our "slice of Wall, / while the Towers f[a]ll" (*HE*, p. 128)? To put it otherwise, how can we transform social institutions while remaining within the "shield" (as Kristeva puts it) of the Symbolic enclosure?

It seems to me that *Ulysses* and *Helen in Egypt* shed light on this question. These texts illustrate that Symbolic constructs, letters and names, strive to represent the Real, but they fail utterly to do so: signifiers rush to fill the vacuum created by death (May Dedalus's absence) or destruction (the disappearance of Troy). How is this so? We might say that the absolute disjunction between the Real and the Symbolic is expressed in the difference between a hieroglyph and an alphabetic symbol. While alphabet letters can be substituted for each other, (hesit*e*ncy," "hesit*a*ncy"; "differ*e*nce," différ*a*nce"), hieroglyphs are not interchangeable: they do not participate in the substitutionary logic of the Symbolic.[3] Although the hieroglyph can be transported from one discourse to another (unconscious/conscious), one hieroglyph cannot be substituted for another. Moreover, hieroglyphic script exists only as inscription; as text it is "unspeakable."

Helen exists in this dimension, as an inscription to be read. While her meaning has been read by Western culture as a metonymic for the exchange of women among men (she is handed from Tyndareus, her stepfather, to Theseus, to Menelaus, to Paris, to Achilles and beyond), Helen-as-hieroglyph cannot be substituted or exchanged. She signifies, that is, to the degree that she represents the *failure* of signification. Something else altogether is at work when May Dedalus appears to her son in the "Circe" chapter. She presents herself not as hieroglyph but hallucination, and while she is a "symptom," she comes from a very different place than Helen does. Her death creates for Stephen a hole in the Real (her absence is absolute, she cannot be resurrected), but her reappearance in "Circe" signals a hole in Stephen's Symbolic. He hallucinates his mother because what has been foreclosed to him in the Symbolic returns in the Real. This is psychosis, which Lacan defines as a "disease in language," a failure of the Name-of-the-Father to join signifier and signified. It refuses absolutely the Other.[4]

Psychosis repudiates the symbolic threat of castration represented by the phallus (i.e., mortality). Michael Walsh explains that the psychotic pursues

> a reinvention or reimagination of this signifier ("Name-of-the-Father") in such a way that it does not partake of the other. With Lacan, we can say that the psychotic forecloses on the Other with a capital O, "the absolute Other" (*Psychoses*, 62), the Other as horizon of discourse, the Other which is Otherness as such, above and beyond both other people and the "internal" other which is the moi. In other words, we might say the psychotic is someone who seeks to imitate or institute a Symbolic of his or her own device; that such an aspiration is quixotic, hopeless, may only serve to redouble the subject's determination. ["Reading the Real," p. 78]

From what materials, then, does the psychotic structure her or his language? Presumably from the semiotic matter and "letters" of the (m)Other world, the very same materials that enrich poetry. Walsh comments that the psychotic text is marked by a "simultaneous grandeur and poverty" (p. 78). I would underscore the grandeur of the psychotic enterprise, which dreams in a global Imaginary, in contrast to the poverty of its language, which circulates among fragmented part-objects, unable to connect with or resonate within intercultural and interlocking Symbolic structures. A "swarm of images" (signifiers of the Imaginary) comes to fill the hole in the Symbolic, an overabundance of signifiers that cannot signify because there is nothing (no Other) to anchor them. Psychotic language, then, cannot be confused with poetic language or "literary" language (however experimental): it is a pathetic simulacrum of art.

Far from being a disease of the hopelessly alienated, however, paranoid psychosis according to Lacan *is* the personality. In "*Le Sinthome*," a neologism that homophonically refers to Joyce as both "symptom" and "holy man," Lacan defines psychosis as the condition of personality, "the armature of the personality."[5] There is, of course, a clinical difference between "personality" and psychosis: whereas the ego erects itself against the other (its own, alien, reflection), psychosis constructs itself as a defense against Otherness. That is, psychosis is blinded to "otherness" (which operates by substitutionary logic) because it has repudiated absolute Otherness. Walsh comments that, as a culture, we repress (our fear of) psychosis; and because we refuse to recognize it, we mirror its refusal to recognize the Name-of-the-Father necessary for subjectivity.

The Name-of-the-Father draws a veil over the Absolute Otherness of death. Confronted with the death of the subject, the Symbolic tries desperately to recuperate the Real, to signify it. (Remember Stephen Dedalus, who tries to make a text of his dead mother.) Struggling to represent what is not amenable to representation, the Symbolic attempts to ward off the inevitable: it covers the Real with a veil, a web of language, which it calls "reality." As subjects, we cover over death with *words*, we fill the void that death opens in the Real with *words*, we try to comprehend psychosis with *words*. But we fail, and most of all when we enlist the Imaginary to fill the hole in the Real with redeeming *images*. It is no surprise, then, that the (m)Other screens the fall into psychosis; "she" is a limit text, a fragile barrier, and also a talisman, an idol or eidolon against death.

To this way of thinking, Helen is the symptom of an impending psychosis of civilizations that refuse to acknowledge death. She serves to screen this knowledge, and long after the goal of the war (to recapture her, to secure her place) has failed to support the meaning she is supposed to represent. Accurately reading the Trojan War as the Real, Mihoko Suzuki argues that the war becomes its own goal: the more the dead are piled up, the longer the war perpetuates itself.[6] Those who fight in Helen's name cannot recognize her as symptom.

By contrast, May Dedalus's appearance in "Circe" is not symptomatic of psychosis, but rather its cultural effect. Because of fatigue, guilt, or alcohol, Stephen experiences a fall into psychosis. His mother's ghost marks the return in the Real (from outside himself) of what has been excluded from the Symbolic. But in the horror show parody of "Circe," the mother's ghost is not "Real" (the hallucination is a fiction). Indeed, her appearance refutes the Real by urging Stephen to repent and bridge the gap between the Symbolic and Real. Her Catholicism is based in the belief that the Real can be negotiated if one's investment in the Symbolic is strong enough: God, the ultimate Name-of-the-Father, can turn death into eternal life. Against his mother's pleas to the Sacred Heart of Jesus to "save him from hell," Stephen lifts his ashplant (a veiled phallus) and smashes the chandelier, bringing about the ruin of space and time (15.4243–45). In one stroke, he crashes through the Imaginary (the (m)Other) and—momentarily—shatters the Symbolic (Catholicism). His is a psychotic repudiation of the Symbolic and a failure of the Imaginary, at once.[7] While he damages the Real (breaking the chandelier and tearing his coat), he does not destroy it. He discovers in comic fashion what the psychotic discovers in the tragic mode: the Real exists absolutely beyond the boundaries of the Symbolic and Imaginary.

What has all this to say to (or about) feminism? Certainly not that feminism is a form of psychosis or that "woman's language" (as *écriture féminine* or *parler femme*) is a regression to infantilism. The dream of a "wholly other psychic and representational domain" carries the risk of psychosis, a retreat to the Imaginary, only when it constitutes an absolute repudiation of the Symbolic—that is, a refusal to recognize (as Achilles did not) mortality. There is a space within the Lacanian structure (itself a symbolic representation) where the Imaginary and Symbolic overlap: here, it seems to me, feminisms can dream/think. This is also a dangerous space, and the dangers must be recognized: this is where the Symbolic has lodged its dream of a totalizing structure, which goes by the name of patriarchy.

In this space, we must keep our wits about us. We cannot afford to confuse the Symbolic terrain of representation with the Real, the intractable and substantial world that resists or exceeds interpretation. This is to say that we should distinguish the Symbolic phallus from a Real penis, precisely because the Symbolic constantly tries to *represent* the Real. And we need to know how it is that the phallus fails to veil Absolute Otherness (death) and then searches for another veil ("woman-in-the-feminine") with which to cover (up) its failures.

If on one side, it is vitally important to distinguish the Symbolic from the Real, it is also imperative to differentiate the Symbolic from the Imaginary—particularly because the Symbolic and Imaginary can overlap. The Symbolic would be a totalizing discourse and would have us (all subjects, women and men) believe that its constructions are the final word, the absolute meaning. It would not have us know that patriarchy is a Symbolic invention or that patriarchy's failures can be (and are being) exposed from *within the Symbolic*, which is the only place from which patriarchy can be named.

It is crucially important, I believe, to see the Symbolic for what it is, a screen that both reflects our mortality, our inability to establish mind over matter, and shields us against a dreadful Real that we cannot comprehend, even (or especially) when we pass into its domain through death. The Absolute Other is neither the Phallus nor its Imaginary reflection, "woman-in-the-feminine" in her pseudo-plenitude or phallic *jouissance*. It is death, which any real transformation of the Symbolic must (inevitably and impossibly) take into its account. The failure of the Symbolic to encompass the Real, to account for it in any way other than by falling back against its intractability, is a "truth" the Symbolic hides from itself by the Imaginary fictions it constructs. Perhaps this is why discussions of Lacanian psychoanalytic theories so often shuttle between binary sets—Symbolic/Imaginary, conscious/unconscious—as though the Real does not exist, or exists only as the construct ("reality") that we invent to take its place. Focusing relentlessly on the "speaking subject," we lose consciousness of the ways we as subjects are also "spoken" by the social systems and language functions into which we are born and through which our individual subjectivities are constituted. We forget that the Real effects the irreconcilable split between the speaking and spoken subject, the split in subjectivity reflected in the dialogical symbolic structures that would "articulate" it.[8] We speak, and are spoken, because the Real does not (speak).

Daily life constantly reminds us that gendered subjectivity is a fragile construction, a gossamer web that weaves and reweaves itself. We live with the (often painful) awareness that subjectivity is demanding and requires constant negotiation against heavy odds. We are surprised and frustrated at the gaps between what we *want* to say and what we *can* say, at the grandeur of our desires and the poverty of our accomplishments. Realizing that subjectivity is not a given, that it is (re)constructed day by day and minute by minute, we can glimpse the (failed) designs of systems that would totally deny our subjectivity. This is not cold comfort in a world where "woman-in-the-feminine" is the sign both of maternal destiny (reproduction) and dark fate (death): Holy Mother and *femme fatale*. How the "-feminine" fails to hold this structure in place, how it escapes the binary terms of its construction, gives us pause—which is just enough time to re-consider the consequences of taking gender for granted or of granting patriarchy the right to its totalizing schemes. Taking a deep breath, we begin to act, to move.

Notes

Introduction

1. For a stimulating discussion of the feminine in relation to a number of other primary concerns relevant to my study, see Spivak with Rooney, "In a Word, *Interview*," pp. 124–56 (hereafter referred to as "Interview"). At one point in the interview, Spivak says, "All we really want to claim is that there is no feminine essence" (p. 141). Granting that, I want to graph some intersections of feminine/essence within bodies of literature, not forgetting—as Rooney reminds us—that "the body is of course essentialism's great text: to read in its form the essence of Woman is certainly one of phallocentrism's strategies: to insist that the body too is materially woven into social (con)texts is anti-essentialism's reply" (p. 125).

2. Derrida, "Freud and the Scene of Writing," pp. 196–231 (hereafter referred to as *SW*); "To Speculate—on 'Freud' " and "Le facteur de la vérité," *The Post Card*, pp. 257–496. Bass retains the French title for the second essay, but I will refer to it throughout my text as "The Purveyor of Truth," the translation provided by Willis Domingo et al., *Yale French Studies* 52, 1976. (*The Post Card* hereafter referred to as *PC*.)

3. Derrida, *Spurs: Nietzsche's Styles*; *Glas*.

4. Elliot, *From Mastery to Analysis: Theories of Gender in Psychoanalytic Feminism*, examines the reasons for feminism's conflicted relation with Kristeva.

5. See Friedman, "Who Buried H.D.? A Poet, Her Critics, and Her Place in the Literary Tradition."

6. Derrida, *PC*, p. 4.

7. Excepting Irigaray and Wittig, whose work is not discussed at length here, the theorists I include have worked extensively on James Joyce's writings. Devoting a year of his *école freudienne* seminar to Joyce's writings, Lacan's work with *Finnegans Wake* led to his theory of the "symptom," the fourth term that traverses the triad of Real, Symbolic, and Imaginary, which he announced in 1975. During the past twenty years, Kristeva and Derrida have written about *Ulysses* and *Finnegans Wake*, recently participating in conferences on Joyce's works, including the 1984 biannual symposium of the James Joyce International

Foundation in Frankfurt, West Germany. In 1972 Cixous's *doctorat d'état* on Joyce was published in English as *The Exile of James Joyce*. Her writing practices, which like Derrida's confound the borders between theoretical and fictional forms, are often described as "Joycean."

8. Stein, *How to Write*, p. 14. Dydo, "Gertrude Stein: Composition as Meditation," p. 56.

9. I have written about this elsewhere, in particular the problem of the term "Modernism," as separate from, say, "modernity" as French writers use this term. Todorov's comments are helpful, especially his assertions that "Modernism is not opposed to classicism, but to realism or symbolism—to artistic movements of the nineteenth century that were no less 'modern.' . . Its manifestations are varied, but several features frequently recur: abstraction, or a renunciation of any representation of the concrete forms of the world, hence an intention to be universal; a systematic character, in which the work is a product of a conscious and rational system." See "Postmodernism, a Primer," p. 34. This emphasis on the work as a "product of a conscious and rational system" is important to my argument that Modernism denies the work of the unconscious, even as it (unconsciously) replicates its effects. See Benstock, *Women of the Left Bank: Paris, 1900–1940*, pp. 25–30, "Expatriate Modernism: Writing on the Cultural Rim," and "Beyond the Reaches of Feminist Criticism: A Letter From Paris."

10. Friedman, *Psyche Reborn: The Emergence of H.D.*, p. 98.

11. Ellmann, *James Joyce*, p. 702.

12. For analysis of Stein's critics, see *Women of the Left Bank*, pp. 151–69.

13. See Bridgman, *Gertrude Stein in Pieces*; Simon, *The Biography of Alice B. Toklas*; Fifer, "Is Flesh Advisable? The Interior Theater of Gertrude Stein"; Stimpson, "The Mind, the Body, and Gertrude Stein," and "The Somagrams of Gertrude Stein."

14. See Stimpson, "Gertrude Stein and the Transposition of Gender"; also Wittig's discussion of gender as a grammatical category in "The Mark of Gender."

15. Jardine, "Gynesis," p. 56.

16. Elaine Showalter, "Towards a Feminist Poetics," p. 35.

17. See Ruddick, *Reading Gertrude Stein: Body, Text, Gnosis* (hereafter called *Reading Gertrude Stein*); and DeKoven, "Gertrude Stein and the Modernist Canon."

18. Although they came to understand psychosexuality and textual orders in different ways, two of these writers were directly influenced by Freud's work. H.D. was his analysand for a short period in the 1930s; the Hogarth Press published Freud's complete works, and Virginia Woolf read them in translation.

19. Jardine, "Gynesis," p. 62.

20. Ruddick investigates Stein's "body language" and the burial of "common" sense in *Reading Gertrude Stein*.

21. Stein, *How to Write*, p. 121.

22. Ibid., p. 116. To the ear rather than the eye, a "noun" can be "our by our," a reinforcement of a particular kind of Steinian coupling in which a gay couple (Gertrude and Alice) mime—with specific differences—the dominant heterosexual model of the couple/copula unit.

23. Ibid., p. 157.
24. See Ruddick, *Reading Gertrude Stein*, esp. chap. 2.
25. Stein, *How to Write*, p. 277. This line echoes distantly the words of English mystic Juliana of Norwich, an early literary foremother. In "Little Gidding," T. S. Eliot employs more directly her phrase, "All shall be well": "All shall be well, and / All manner of thing shall be well." The Steinian version moves the notion of "wellness" from the religious to the philosophic realm, interrogating the relation of ear to eye. While Stein is not usually thought to share with Modernist colleagues like Eliot the penchant for highly allusive texts, this aspect of her work needs far greater attention than it has so far received. See T. S. Eliot, *Collected Poems 1909–1962*, p. 206.
26. See Kristeva, *Revolution and Poetic Language*, (hereafter referred to as *R*), and *Desire in Language* (hereafter referred to as *D*).

Chapter 1

1. Rose, *Sexuality in the Field of Vision*, p. 232 (hereafter referred to as *Sexuality*).
2. See Rabine's astute analysis of woman as visible object for male desire in "A Woman's Two Bodies: The Ambiguities of Fashion."
3. Rose, *Sexuality*, p. 232, emphasis added. Derrida discusses how laws of language and grammar command their own violation in *PC*, p. 59.
4. Whereas it was once thought that "images evoked pictures" and that literary/cinematic imagery was figured solely through the visual, "today it is agreed that images involve any sensations (including those of heat and pressure as well as those of eye, ear, etc.) and that the literal sensory objects in the work . . . are images." See Barnet et al., *A Dictionary of Literary, Dramatic, and Cinematic Terms*, p. 61. In written texts, "imagery" also signifies figurative language, especially metaphors and similes. See Abrams, *A Glossary of Literary Terms*, p. 44.
5. Langbauer suggests that recent theories of "Woman" have emphasized its subversive possibilities (usually termed "the feminine") and overlooked how these constructions support phallic/patriarchal orders. See *Women and Romance: The Consolations of Gender in the English Novel*.
6. Jardine, *Gynesis: Configurations of Woman and Modernity*, p. 101. Responding to Jardine's argument, Willis comments: "One way to avoid reducing real women's experience to the sign 'woman,' and to avoid reducing woman as sign to a signifier only of 'difference,' is to consider 'Woman' and 'women' as historical, as always produced in and operating within social formations." See "Feminism's Interrupted Genealogies," p. 32. Willis's point is well taken, but my interest is in how the sign "woman" is produced and how it has come to register "only difference."
7. Rose, *Sexuality*, p. 19.
8. Derrida, "Confrontation, 'Les Fantômes de la psychanalyse,' "*Geopsychanalyse* 'and the rest of the world,' " pp. 327–52, and "*Du Tout*," pp. 497–521.
9. In *PC*, Derrida proposes the postal relay as a metaphor of the " 'ego' and

of fantasy," a form of the *fort/da* in which the subject (sender and receiver, the one who leaves and the one who remains) occupies both positions simultaneously (p. 199). Commenting on this "definition" by way of Spivak's essay, "Love Me, Love My Ombre, Elle," Rose rejects the psychoanalytic grounds of the model, stating that it might lead back to "uniqueness" or essentialism of the subject that deconstruction tries to unsettle. She claims, erroneously I think, that Derrida identifies woman with the "underside of truth," where "it cannot be *analysed* at the point of its psychic effectivity for subjects" (*Sexuality*, pp. 21–22, fn. 38). For a useful commentary on the constitutive elements of feminine subjectivity and Derrida's work, see Spivak, "Interview," pp. 127–28. Rose mistakes Derrida's critique for his beliefs, since deconstruction begins as a gesture of repetition. Psychoanalytic critiques of deconstruction consistently overlook the psychic exigency, as well as the strategic necessity, of this step. That is, deconstruction begins by repeating the violation of the structure it dismantles in order to illustrate that the violation is inherent within the law of structure. Spivak also comments on the "failure" of Derrida's efforts to deconstruct and displace gender categories in "Displacement and the Discourse of Woman." See also *In Other Worlds: Essays in Cultural Politics*, esp. chaps. 5, 9.

10. Johnson, *The Critical Difference*. Rose calls on feminism not to overlook the unconscious in its analysis of sexual difference and feminine sexuality (*Sexuality*, p. 101).

11. Mitchell, "Introduction I," *Feminine Sexuality: Jacques Lacan and the École Freudienne*, p. 6 (hereafter referred to as *Feminine Sexuality*).

12. Lacan, "The Agency of the Letter in the Unconscious," *Ecrits: A Selection* (hereafter referred to as *ES*). This is the "speaking subject" that Kristeva refers to as the *sujet-en-proces*, i.e., the subject-in-process or "on trial." See chap. 2.

13. Derrida, "Law of Genre," p. 202. In French, "genre" encompasses "gender." See chap. 4, where I discuss their etymological links.

14. Rose, *Sexuality*, pp. 20–21.

15. See Ulmer, *Applied Grammatology*, pp. 10–12. Derrida comments in *Positions* that he wants to "fracture the closure that shelters the question of writing (in general, and notably philosophical and literary writing) from psychoanalysis, but equally the closure that *so frequently blinds psychoanalytic discourse to a certain structure of the textual scene*" (p. 84, emphasis added).

16. Lacan, "The Signification of the Phallus," in *ES*, p. 285.

17. Ragland-Sullivan, *Jacques Lacan and the Philosophy of Psychoanalysis*, comments that Lacan criticized "traditional philosophy for never having fully understood that meaning only exists at all because it can refer to perceptions already structured (ordered) in a realm of repressed (unconscious) representations (references)" (p. xvi) (hereafter referred to as *Jacques Lacan*). Derrida examines this process through Freud's metaphor of writing in "Note on the Mystic Writing-Pad" in "Freud and the Scene of Writing," discussed below.

18. In 1953 Lacan proposed three orders that structure subjectivity: the Symbolic (discursive order of culture and language), Imaginary (*imago*, perception, relationship interaction), and Real (concrete, material world of objects and experiences), to which he later added a fourth, the Symptom (metaphor for an

untranslated unconscious message). Lacan was always interested in the role of discourse in psychoanalytic analysis, and he was influenced by Saussure's *Cours de la linguistique générale*, by Levi-Strauss's work in structuralist anthropology, and also by the surrealists. For a critique of Lacan's relation to Freud and the influence of surrealism (rather than Saussure) on Lacan's theories of language, see Macey, *Lacan in Contexts*. See Lacan, "Le Symbolique, l'Imaginaire et le Réel." For explanations of the orders, see Wilden, *Speech and Language in Psychoanalysis*, and Ellie Ragland-Sullivan, who comments that "Lacan increasingly stressed that the Real order stands behind and outside the Imaginary and Symbolic. The latter exist, in part, as efforts to account for the Real that shapes them, and on which they, in turn, put their stamp: the Imaginary by identificatory, fusional logic; the Symbolic by a differential logic which names, codifies, and legalizes" (*Jacques Lacan*, pp. 130–31).

19. The term "masquerade" is taken from Riviere, "Womanliness as Mascarade." Rose comments that for Riviere "masquerade" "indicated a failed femininity" (Mitchell and Rose, *Feminine Sexuality*, p. 43). Lacan, "Guiding Remarks for a Congress on Feminine Sexuality," p. 90 (hereafter referred to as "Guiding Remarks"). For an extended discussion of these issues, see André, *Que veut une femme?*

20. See "The Phallic Phase and the Subjective Import of the Castration Complex" (anonymous), in Mitchell and Rose, *Feminine Sexuality*, p. 113, and Rose's comments, p. 42. Lacan, "Guiding Remarks," p. 90.

21. Beauvoir, *The Second Sex*.

22. Lacan, "Introduction of the Big Other," in *The Seminar of Jacques Lacan, Book II* (hereafter referred to as *Seminar II*). The diagram reproduced below is found on p. 243:

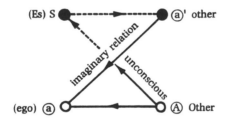

Man endows woman with the phallus through Imaginary constructs, one of which is woman-in-the-feminine; he adores the "phallus" in her, a worship produced from the repressed phallic mother of the unconscious. That is, the social-cultural burden of representing the phallic is transferred from the man to the woman. It is for this reason that woman's *jouissance* is marked by ○, the point where the representation (masquerade) of the phallic reveals the fraudulent nature of the phallic. Her *jouissance* is a default of the cultural masquerade, the point of collapse for woman-in-the-feminine.

23. Ragland-Sullivan, *Jacques Lacan*, p. 16, emphasis added.

24. This relation structures a double signification: empowerment ("phallic mother") and lack, or submission to the phallus. It operates for infants of both

sexes, and it functions in the development of heterosexuality and homosexuality. See Lacan, "The Signification of the Phallus," *ES*, pp. 290–91, for comments on the phallic structuring of homosexuality.

25. Lacan, *Le Séminaire de Jacques Lacan*, Livre XX, p. 46 (hereafter referred to as *Séminaire XX*).

26. Lacan, "Desire, Life and Death," *Seminar II*, p. 223. Desire is constitutive of the subject, who is a "speaking subject" precisely because she or he seeks wholeness and completion that subjectivity by definition can never provide. Language use is an effort to make up the lack, as are attachments to objects and people. See also Lacan, "Subversion of the Subject and Dialectic of Desire," in *ES*, pp. 312–13, and Ragland-Sullivan, *Jacques Lacan*, who refers to Lacan's emphasis in *Séminaire XX* on *la dite maternelle* or *lalangue* (the mother tongue) "as the source of Desire, linked to Being and to need. Behind all quests and meaningful choices, as well as behind the motivation to speak and relate to others, is the question 'Who am I?' " (p. 83).

27. Lacan, *Séminaire XXI*. Quoted in Mitchell and Rose, "Introduction II," *Feminine Sexuality*, p. 47.

28. Lacan, "The Agency of the Letter," *ES*, p. 172.

29. Lacan, *Seminar II*, p. 224.

30. See Lacan, "The Mirror Stage as Formative of the Function of the I as Revealed in Psychoanalytic Experience," *ES*, pp. 1–7; also the bibliographical note, p. xiii, which describes the development of Lacan's theory of the mirror stage between 1936 and 1949. See Lacan, *The Seminars of Jacques Lacan Book I*, pp. 146–47 (hereafter referred to as *Seminar I*).

31. Lacan, "The Agency of the Letter," *ES*, pp. 147–48, and Ragland-Sullivan, *Jacques Lacan*, pp. 18–20.

32. Lacan, "The Mirror Stage," in *ES*, p. 4. Liedloff describes the misery of the newborn's dependent condition, emphasizing the need for warmth and touch that initiates Desire, in *The Continuum Concept*.

33. Lacan, "Aggressivity in Psychoanalysis," in *ES*, pp. 11–12. See Ragland-Sullivan's résumé of primary infant experience, *Jacques Lacan*, pp. 18–19.

34. Montrelay, "The Story of Louise," comments: "hearing is very close to the eye, which is seen by the child as an eye-ear, an open hole" (pp. 82–83). This "confusion," which is retained in the unconscious and operates within Kristeva's semiotic, has its origin in the Real.

35. Ragland-Sullivan, *Jacques Lacan*, p. 20. See Leclaire, *Psychanalyser*, esp. chap. 3.

36. Lacan, "The Mirror Stage," in *ES*, p. 4; and Lacan, *The Four Fundamental Concepts*, p. 83 (hereafter referred to as *Concepts*).

37. Ragland-Sullivan, *Jacques Lacan*, p. 27, emphasis added. The discord that the mirror stage falsely represents as unity is, in part, a visual trick: the infant's visual capacities are far more developed than its muscular coordination. Freud placed enormous emphasis on the visual in constructing penis envy and fear of castration, while Lacan stresses its role in mis-representation.

38. Lacan, "The Mirror Stage," in *ES*, p. 2.

39. Lacan, *Concepts*, p. 161. Ragland-Sullivan, *Jacques Lacan*, pp. 82–83, 106. In "Seminar of 21 January 1975," reprinted in Mitchell and Rose, *Femi-

nine Sexuality, Lacan remarks that "there is nothing in the unconscious which accords with the body" (p. 165). Rose comments that "the unconscious severs the subject from any unmediated relation to the body as such" (p. 55).

40. Lacan, "The Agency of the Letter," *ES*, pp. 150–53. See Mitchell and Rose, *Feminine Sexuality*, pp. 55–56.

41. Mitchell and Rose, "Introduction II," *Feminine Sexuality*, p. 51. Jacques Lacan, *Séminaire XX*, p. 33. As Rose uses the term, "Woman" is not fully compatible with my construction, "woman-in-the-feminine." Lacan explains that "Woman" is excluded within the categories of language (see below); the fantasy figure erected in place of this (non)-category is "woman-in-the-feminine." Women develop different relations within gendered sexuality, however, not all taking "woman-in-the-feminine" as the sign of "Woman." It is precisely this measure of difference within Woman and between women that my construction, "the feminine," invokes. Consequently, "woman-in-the-feminine" is also not equivalent to Derrida's category, "Woman," discussed below.

42. Derrida, "The Law of Genre," p. 203.

43. Rose articulates feminist discontent in *Sexuality*, p. 21. Derrida calls attention to the limits of psychoanalysis on the grounds of its desire to render a full account of Desire, the element of psychodynamics that always exceeds its own Demand. This Desire inhabits the discipline of philosophy as well, which admits no "outside," taking its own limit as its object of investigation. (Much of Derrida's work has addressed the question of the "limits" of philosophy.) Ulmer comments that philosophy "appropriates the concept of limit and believes that it can dominate its own margin and think its other" (*Applied Grammatology*, pp. 30–31). In psychoanalytic terms, Desire is what remains after the analysis (of the dream, for instance); the idea that everything can by fully analyzed belongs to the Lacanian Imaginary. See James Glogowski's comments on Desire and the dream in Ragland-Sullivan, *Jacques Lacan*, pp. 117 and 325, fn. 51. Spivak, following Derrida, refers to what remains after analysis (any analysis) as *ce qui reste*. Around questions of the "feminine" and subjectivity, *ce qui reste* constitutes what is often (and confusingly) referred to as "essence." Arguing for "essence as *ce qui reste*," Spivak refers to "irreducible specificities" that are "minimalizable" and also "cross-hatched." She comments on her analytic methods: "I find, in that kind of a work which is not against essentialism but which completely pluralizes the grid, it is my task as a reader, as it is with deconstruction, to read it and run with it and go somewhere else. It is my task as a reader to see where in that grid there are the spaces where, in fact, *woman oozes away*" ("Interview," p. 145, emphasis added).

44. Derrida, "Law of Genre," p. 206.

45. Ibid.

46. This occurs when pre-mirror stage letters, early identifications and sensory experiences, undergo primary repression during the mirror stage. See Lacan, "The Mirror Stage," *ES*, and *Concepts*, pp. 206–8.

47. See Mitchell and Rose, "Introduction II," *Feminine Sexuality*, p. 42. Lacan, "The Agency of the Letter," *ES*, p. 155.

48. Rose, "Introduction II," *Feminine Sexuality*, p. 47. In *Sexuality*, Rose comments that "psychoanalysis becomes one of the few places in our culture

where it is recognised as more than a fact of individual pathology that most women do not painlessly slip into their roles as women, if indeed they do at all" (p. 91).

49. Lacan, "God and the *Jouissance* of The Woman," in *Feminine Sexuality*, Mitchell and Rose, eds., pp. 152, 147. As the editors explain, these two essays are central chapters of Lacan's *Séminaire XX* (1972–73), pp. 61–82. The year is important: it followed close on the feminist debate initiated by the events of May 1968; the seminar devoted to feminine sexuality preceded the seminar devoted to Joyce's writings (hereafter referred to as *JL*). See Mitchell and Rose, "Introduction II," *Feminine Sexuality*, p. 51.

50. "The Phallic Phase," *Feminine Sexuality*, emphasizes the import of phallic libido for sexuality and, therefore, for subjectivity: "There is only one libido, meaning that there is no psychic representative of the opposition masculine-feminine. The essence of castration and the link of sexuality to the unconscious both reside in this factor—that sexual difference *is refused to knowledge* [*savoir*], since it indicates the point where the subject of the unconscious subsists by being the subject of non-knowledge" (p. 120, emphasis added). That is, what of *jouissance* lends itself to symbolization is *male jouissance*, and it is here that woman must represent it as woman-in-the-feminine. According to Lacan, "*signifiance* lies in *jouissance, jouissance* of the body" (*JL*, p. 142). Rose, "Introduction II," *Feminine Sexuality*, explains that "the concept of *jouissance* (what escapes in sexuality) and the concept of *signifiance* (what shifts within language) are inseparable" (p. 52). See also Macey's rereading of *jouissance* in relation to *la femme, Lacan in Contexts*, chap. 6. He asserts that Lacan's theories can make no positive contributions to feminist thought or studies of gender and subjectivity because they are based on "virulently sexist discourse" (book jacket cover). Although he provides a helpful history of the shifts in Lacan's thinking on subjectivity and the evolution of his terminology (phallus/penis, *la femme, jouissance*), Macey ends up able only to repeat the familiar charges of essentialist sexism against Lacan. I find that his analysis is based on shaky understandings of the psychosexual and cultural problematics of the feminine within Freudian-Lacanian discourse.

51. In Lacan's diagram, the O is joined to *The*, the non-category, Woman. In relation to the male subject (*S*), this is where meaning fails. The symbol for female is lost in primary repression. See Kristeva's analysis of primary repression in chap. 2.

52. Jacques-Alain Miller, "Another Lacan," quoted in Ragland-Sullivan, *Jacques Lacan*, p. 297. Lacan writes: "Freud argues that there is no libido other than the masculine. Meaning what? other than that a whole field, which is hardly negligible, is thereby ignored. This is the field of all those beings who take on the status of the woman—if, indeed, this being takes on anything whatsoever of her fate" (*JL*, p. 151). Note that one need not be female to "take on" the status of woman.

53. *La femme* structures an ambiguity that Lacan does not play with here. It signifies both "woman" and "wife," and the difference in meaning can only (but sometimes not always) be determined by context. Lacan claims human subjectivity signifies in relation to a phallic order of meaning in which The woman does not exist, which is not to say that women do not exist.

54. Lacan, *Seminar II*, p. 254.

55. Lacan, *Concepts*, pp. 53–54.

56. Lacan argues that the *jouissance* of the woman is of an entirely different order, what escapes the phallic dialectic to which she is subjected. That is, men know nothing of it: "short of castration, that is, short of something which says no to the phallic function, man has no chance of enjoying the body of the woman, in other words, of making love" (*JL*, p. 143). In *Applied Grammatology*, Ulmer comments that Lacan's notion of *jouissance* follows "Freud's lead (the conjunction of science and pleasure in the formulation of the Pleasure Principle)" (p. 200).

57. Lacan, *Séminaire XX*, p. 127. For *"jouis-sens"* see Ulmer, *Applied Grammatology*, p. 201, and Lacan, *Télévision*, pp. 19–21. Lacan outlines four levels of "sense": sense, nonsense, common sense, and *jouis*-sense.

58. See Lacan, *ES*, pp. 150–52, especially the anecdote about the train/chain of signification, and Mitchell and Rose, *Feminine Sexuality*, pp. 42–43, esp. fn. 7.

59. These efforts characterize much of Derrida's recent writing, e.g., *Feu la cendre*. For Rose's and Spivak's questions about his methods, see Rose, *Sexuality*, p. 21, and fn. 18.

60. See Derrida, *Speech and Phenomena and Other Essays on Husserl's Theory of Signs*, pp. 67–68.

61. Freud, "Note on the Mystic Writing-Pad," p. 232 (hereafter referred to as "Mystic").

62. Lacan, "The Function and Field of Speech and Language in Psychoanalysis," *ES*, pp. 49–50. The mystic pad does not fully account for conscious-unconscious structures, and the double-sided structure is too simple. There is a "third layer," which is not a layer at all. Kristeva calls this the "thetic" (see chap. 2). In *Concepts*, Lacan describes the primordial unconscious through a variety of metaphors: it is formed as a spiderweb or fishnet, knotted in places of trauma, or operating like a bladder, its opening-closing movements producing discontinuity, pp. 133–50. See also Ragland Sullivan, *Jacques Lacan*, p. 102.

63. Mitchell and Rose, "Introduction II," *Feminine Sexuality*, p. 32.

64. Ibid., p. 51, and "Phallic Phase," *Feminine Sexuality*, p. 151.

65. See the cover of *Séminaire XX* for the representation of St. Teresa, and Ulmer's comments on Lacan's use of the photograph, *Applied Grammatology*, pp. 194–97. Freud's choice of the "mystic" writing pad is fortuitous, a structure of mystery, mystification, mysticism.

66. Mitchell and Rose, "Introduction II," *Feminine Sexuality*, p. 51. See Macey's commentary, *Lacan in Contexts*, pp. 200–210.

Chapter 2

1. Kristeva, "Woman Can Never Be Defined," p. 137. Moi, *Sexual/Textual Politics*, p. 165.

2. Kristeva, "Ellipsis on Dread and the Specular Seduction." Quoted in Rose, *Sexuality*, p. 141.

3. Quoted in *The Kristeva Reader*, p. 12.

4. See Silverman, *The Accoustic Mirror*, for a discussion of feminine sexuality in relation to image and sound, and Hirsch's comments on the gaze in *Modernism Revised*.

5. See Irigaray, *Speculum of the Other Woman*, esp. the opening section, "The Blind Spot of an Old Dream of Symmetry," pp. 25–33, 46–54, and *This Sex Which Is Not One* (hereafter referred to as *Sex*), esp. "Psychoanalytic Theory: Another Look," pp. 34–76. Hirsch reviews the charges of essentialism against Irigaray's work. My resistance to Irigaray's analysis is threefold: (1) she does not clearly distinguish differences between Freud's story of sexual difference and Lacan's (Lacan functions as a silent Other within *Speculum*); (2) her critique of the gaze seems to presume a gendered subject prior to creation of the symbolic; (3) she collapses Lacan's distinctions between "real" mothers and fathers and the social constructs of "feminine" and "masculine." For example, she reads the child's relation to the mother as always already inscribed as a relation to lack. This analysis overlooks the phallic mother (or, in Kristeva's terms, "Master-mother") that powerfully embodies the mother's own relation to the phallus (represented by the child, not the father), a relation that threatens to suffocate the infant. Irigaray writes: "it is *in the mother* that castration must, first and foremost, be located by the child, if he is to exit from the imaginary orbit of maternal desire and be *returned* [my emphasis] to the father, that is, to the possessor of the phallic emblem that makes the mother desire him and prefer him to the child" (*Sex*, p. 61). Silverman, *The Acoustic Mirror*, reading Kristeva, also elides the distinctions between the phallic "Master-mother" and the Freudian notion of the mother who embodies lack (a version of motherhood that Lacan does not theorize), pp. 112–26. Confusions such as these often arise in trying to articulate another psychoanalytic model (Lacan's or Kristeva's, e.g.) with Freud's narrative of the Oedipal complex. At other times, the *process* of engendering sexual difference is elided with the *experience* of sexual difference. See, for example, Silverman's analysis of the *chora*: she suggests that, in order for the child to enter into language (presumably the realm of the father), the mother herself must be put into the choric enclosure, thereby "stripping her of all linguistic abilities" (*The Acoustic Mirror*, p. 105). Although patriarchy devalues language it codes "feminine," it does not (and cannot) deny women linguistic abilities. Rather, society denies women power, including the power to make their own speech be perceived as powerful. The Name of the Father, which represents the symbolic function of fatherhood (not to be confused with real fathers), is a societal injunction lodged in the paternal/patriarchal b(i)ases of society. Either males or females may enforce such an injunction, or represent it, depending upon whether they take up a position as "woman" or "man." The "third term" that intervenes between mother and child need not necessarily be a male. It need not even be a person; as Kristeva argues, the third term can be a social or economic function—the necessity of work, for example.

6. See Roudiez's glossary of Kristevan terminology in Kristeva, *Desire in Language*, pp. 13–20, and Kristeva's résumé of the semiotic process in "On Melancholic Imaginary."

7. Kristeva's references to species memory and bio-energetic neuron maps

separates her from Lacan, who theorizes letters, or signifying marks, in relation to differentiation of body parts but avoids her specification of drives in relation to the body. The relation of word to flesh is the aspect of Kristeva's theory least amenable to summary.

8. Lacan, *Concepts*, p. 205. Rose comments that "there is a parallel here with the subject's submission to language, just as there is an analogy between the endless circulation of the drive and the structure of meaning itself ('a topological unity of the gaps in play')." See Rose, *Sexuality*, p. 58; Rose quotes from Lacan's *Concepts*, p. 121. Neither Lacan nor Kristeva posits this presymbolic spatiality in terms of subject-object distancing that comes into play after the mirror stage.

9. See Kristeva's comments on the semiotic *chora* and the ordering of the drives: "Although our theoretical description of the *chora* is itself part of the discourse of representation that offers it as evidence, the *chora*, as rupture and articulations (rhythm), precedes evidence, verisimilitude, spatiality, and temporality. Our discourse—all discourse—moves with and against the *chora* in the sense that it simultaneously depends upon and refuses it. Although the *chora* can be designated and regulated, it can never be definitively posited: as a result, one can situate the *chora* and, if necessary, lend it a topology, but one can never give it axiomatic form. . . . Neither model nor copy, the *chora* precedes and underlies figuration and thus specularization, and is analogous only to vocal or kinetic rhythm" (*R*, p. 26). See Moi's comments on the *chora* and the drives in *Kristeva Reader*, pp. 94–96, and Silverman's critique of it, pp. 99–132, which retraces Kristeva's confusing (and often contradictory) conceptions of the *chora*. Note that choric effects are registered in *all* speaking subjects, female and male.

10. Kristeva believes that all enunciation is thetic, whether or not it is yet formulated in sentences. Thus the thetic posits itself long before the child commands language (just as Lacan's "letters" are in place before the child can speak words or sentences). Secondary repression, however, secures the thetic; it is the psychic equivalent of the "guardrails of grammar" that guide speaking and writing (*Revolution and Poetic Language* hereafter referred to as *R*, p. 209). Grammar positions reveal the relational status of subjectivity with reference to others (but also to the Other): "I" (*je*, a correlative of spoken language, which shifts against Imaginary representations of the subject as object of the gaze, is semiotically inflected and follows the "know-how" of *lalangue*; it is the enunciative position of least stability, since it de-centers the transcendental ego and registers these destabilizing effects), "me" (*moi*, a coefficient of corporal experience), and the third-person pronouns (he, she, it). Subjectivity divides between *je*, the speaking subject within language, and *moi*, which objectifies—and is objectified by—people and things.

11. Rose, *Sexuality*, p. 144. For analysis of Lacan's description of primary and secondary repressions, see *Seminar II*, p. 105, and Ragland-Sullivan, *Jacques Lacan*, p. 114. See Grosz, *Jacques Lacan*, p. 154.

12. Kristeva seeks confirmation for this in Lacan's work. See *R*, p. 244, fn. 56, where she quotes from "The Subversion of the Subject," *ES*, p. 301.

13. Lacan, *Concepts*, pp. 205, 218–19. Freud was led to the conclusion, pre-

sented in *Beyond the Pleasure Principle*, that the ultimate goal of Desire is death, a sealing of the scission in which subjectivity is created. See Ragland-Sullivan, *Jacques Lacan*, pp. 113–16; Moi, *Sexual/Textual Politics*, pp. 99–101.

14. Kristeva is quoting from Lacan's seminar, 1969–70. See *R*, p. 251, fn. 111.

15. Derrida discusses "originary repetition," which shares with Kristeva's semiotic the ability to reactivate drive residues. He follows Freud, however, in describing the condition by which traces (formed by psychic breaching) in the unconscious text come into consciousness. He writes that the unconscious text "is already a weave of pure traces, differences in which meaning and force are united—a text nowhere present, consisting of archives which are always already transcriptions. Originary prints." When the unconscious is translated into conscious discourse, it is not a "transcription because there is no text *present elsewhere* to be transposed or transported" (*Writing and Difference*, p. 211). Note that Derrida specifies more particularly than either Lacan or Kristeva the role of writing as textuality in the unconscious/conscious. See Kristeva's comments on grammatology in *R*, pp. 140–46, where her critique of Derrida on psychoanalytic grounds seems to misconstrue the implications of *différance*. See also Ulmer, *Applied Grammatology*, pp. 75–81.

16. Kristeva also posits a boundary function, or "regulation," for the *chora*: "a nonexpressive totality formed by the drives and their stases in a motility that is as full of movement as it is regulated" (*R*, p. 25). Thetic positing, however, is something quite different—porous yet resistant, it is a text. It is different too from Lacan's metaphors of the unconscious as fishnet or bladder.

17. Negativity in Kristeva's vocabulary is associated with the process of "charges and stases," the place where the subject's unity fails. It is already present in the semiotic *chora* and is linked to the death drive that structures all drives. See *R*, pp. 28, 119.

18. Ragland-Sullivan, *Jacques Lacan*, p. 20, and Lacan's "Seminar of 21 January 1975."

19. Kristeva notes that the oral and anal drives are "oriented and structured around the mother's body" (*R*, p. 27). The modalities she describes are textually reproduced in *Finnegans Wake*, where the daughter's sexualized language explores orality as a swallowing up and spitting out of meaning while the twin brothers plot ways to establish meaning through the overthrow of the father, making "names" for themselves in the place of the paternal metaphor. The characterization of Issy, the daughter in *Finnegans Wake*, works the often indistinguishable boundaries between schizophrenia and poetic language.

20. Oralization cuts up and reorganizes the narrative or syntactic line. It works something like Derrida's end of "linear writing." See *Of Grammatology*, p. 86.

21. Cixous, "The Laugh of the Medusa," p. 285. Kristeva, *Desire in Language*, p. 238.

22. Rose, *Sexuality*, p. 151, and on psychic resistance to identity, p. 91.

23. Kristeva is speaking of a cultural fantasy not of her own making as she reviews feminist attitudes toward the feminine: "The first feminist generation rejected, through the 'woman-as-object,' the narcissistic wound constituted by maternal sexuality, and countered it with the image of the virile activist who

was less a libertine than a monitor; the second advocated a *centripetal, mitigated, soothed feminine sexuality*, before unearthing, quite recently, under the guise of romances among women, sadomasochistic havoc." See *Tales of Love*, p. 374, emphasis added. Kristeva, like Derrida and Lacan, is often accused of believing in, even representing, that which she critiques.

24. Ragland-Sullivan comments that "the bedrock text of 'self' rests in the Imaginary identification with the mother, the "site" of the primordial discourse of the unconscious," (*Jacques Lacan*, p. 30).

25. Kristeva, *Desire in Language*, p. 191. In *Tales of Love*, she argues that the pre-Oedipal father (i.e., Other's Desire within the mother) intervenes at the fourth month of the child's life to effectuate the first, preliminary split within the voice of primary narcissism (p. 34); and Moi, *Kristeva Reader*, p. 12.

26. See Alice Miller, *Thou Shalt Not Be Aware*; and Abraham and Torok, *L'Écorce et le noyau*.

27. Moi, *Sexual/Textual Politics*, p. 154.

28. See Silverman's comments on Kristeva's "Stabat Mater" *The Acoustic Mirror*, pp. 114–15), and her references to Kristeva's "*choric* fantasy" (p. 117). Any knowledge of or speculation about the *chora* and semiotic can come only from the perspective of the symbolic, where the semiotic produces its effects, which are themselves mediations and not the elements per se of primary repression that they represent. We must constantly remind ourselves that subjectivity is necessarily retrospective, always *après-coup.*

29. Schor interprets Kristeva to mean that "the feminine does not enjoy a privileged relationship with the semiotic" except in "nonartistic, nontextual forms: for Kristeva, pregnancy and childbirth have been historically in our culture, the female equivalent of avant-garde art." See *Breaking the Chain*, p. 155. I believe Kristeva refers to the social-cultural injunction that pregnancy represent for woman what avant-garde art represents for man, e.g., evidence of creativity. Whether Kristeva herself believes that only men can produce poetic language or make avant-garde art is another question, one that Kristeva's literary analisis keeps shadowed (on this see Silverman, *The Acoustic Mirror*, p. 113). See also Stanton's comments in "Difference on Trial," especially in her discussion of the artist/child's metaphorical incest with the mother through "semiotic," poetic language. She argues that the semiotic structure privileges the male at the expense of the female. Her remarks present two problems: first, they imply a gendered semiotic; second, they suggest that the semioticization of the symbolic constitutes a "return of the repressed" (p. 166). Kristeva states repeatedly that the semiotic is constituted from residues of unbound energy (i.e., motor discharges) and sensory inscriptions. Stanton's comments about Kristeva's notions of textuality are better applied to Cixous and Irigaray, as her own analysis suggests. For Kristeva's comments on incest, see *Desire in Language*, p. 136. See Rose, *Sexuality*, p. 145 on gendering signification of body *après-coup*, i.e., after the break (effected by primary/secondary repression) that creates the symbolic.

30. Schor, *Breaking the Chain*, p. 156. Silverman writes: "What I am in effect suggesting is that accession to language marks not only the eclipse of the real, and the child's division from the mother, but the inception of the Oedipus complex for both boy and girl" (*The Acoustic Mirror*, p. 122). These comments

posit the infant's unmediated access to a (Lacanian) Real Mother's body prior to subjectivity. The infant at no time (even in the womb) has unmediated access either to the mother's body or its own. The rudimentary system of "letters" that Lacan theorizes mediates the infant's experiences of the mother's body and are part of a double-bottomed structure on which subjectivity erects itself.

31. Stanton's claim that "the delineation of the subversive semiotic apparatus relies on a series of traditional images" is based on a belief that the body imprints language. Those "images," which are not limited to the visual order, are indeed imparted from the outside and inscribed within the infant, but the imprinting process is a form of mediation that brings with it social-cultural values. See Lacan, *Concepts*, p. 147.

32. Again, there are problems with Freud's imagery and metaphors of sight. Kristeva's language is not free from such difficulties, especially as she formulates the *chora*. See Silverman's comments on container/contained, interiority and the claustral, *The Acoustic Mirror*, pp. 76, 79, and 102–9.

33. See Derrida's discussion of prosthetic devices in *PC* and his discussion of Freud's writing machine in "Freud and the Scene of Writing."

34. *Enceinte* as an enclosure comes from the Latin *incingere*, but its adjectival form comes from *incincta*, which means "unbelted." *Ceinture* derives from Latin *cinctura*. The binding-unbinding opposition and transposition works nicely in this form of *lalangue*. See Silverman, *The Acoustic Mirror*, pp. 107–8.

35. Lacan offers examples of *lalangue* in *JL*, *Feminine Sexuality*, p. 155. This same passage is discussed by Ulmer, *Applied Grammatology*, p. 205. Derrida analyzes a complex textualization of unheard diacritical marks that change word meanings in *Feu la cendre*. These are significantly different textualizations than those announced by the semiotic (sound/rhythm) or the symbolic (gaze/image). Instead, they constantly cross over the boundary between vision and hearing.

36. Kristeva, "Stabat Mater," p. 249 (hereafter referred to as *SM*). Ulmer comments that linguistics must exclude homophonic linkages in order to establish itself as a science. See *Applied Grammatology*, p. 204. Derrida discusses the place of pure idiom of dream language in "Freud and the Scene of Writing," pp. 212–13.

37. Herr, "Fathers, Daughters, Anxiety, and Fiction," p. 175. Herr provides important readings of Joyce's representations of father-daughter anxieties, especially in *Finnegans Wake*.

Chapter 3

1. Johnson, *A World of Difference*, p. 185. My essay examines three functions of the apostrophe, as defined by the *O.E.D.*: (1) A figure of speech in which a writer suddenly stops in his discourse and turns to address pointedly some person or thing, present or absent; an exclamatory address. Modern use has extended the apostrophe to the *absent* or *dead*, but it is by no means con-

fined to these, as is sometimes erroneously stated. (2) Omission of one or more letters of a word (*don't*). (3) A sign of the modern English genitive or possessive case (*woman's*).

2. John Milton, *Paradise Lost*, Book 9, li. 1067–68.

3. Culler, *The Pursuit of Signs*, p. 136.

4. See Sollers, "*Comme si le vieil Homère*," pp. 73–74: "Joyce? It is sufficient to hear his voice. More precisely, his recording of a fragment of *Finnegans Wake*. . . . Unreadable, this book? Untranslatable? Listen, listen. Immediately, from the depths of the night, rises this strangely assured, even emphatic voice, cunning, hardened by hundreds and hundreds of troubles, but always melodious; this voice, blindly firm, separating the branches and the blinds of sleep; it is as if Homer, an old man, but one always young, comes toward us through the weave of a thousand adventures, a thousand stories, a thousand and one languages encountered in his underwater wanderings, syllables respond and illumine each other, vivified by a new breath" (my translation). Heath opposes this popular assumption. See "Ambiviolences: Notes for Reading Joyce," and Simkins, "The Agency of the Title: *Finnegans Wake*."

5. All references to *Finnegans Wake* are to the Viking Press edition (New York, 1947), included parenthetically by page and line number.

6. See Mink, *A Finnegans Wake Gazeteer*, p. 198. The grammatical structure of this phrase is apostrophic: it suppresses the noun subject of the apostrophe (church) and reverses its popular name, "Adam and Eve's Church." Rather than a general reference to our mythic first parents, "Eve and Adam's" designates the Church of St. Francis of Assisi located at a bend in the Liffey River on Merchant's Quay. Its name derives from a tavern, situated in a lane of the same name behind the church, that the Franciscans rented as a secret chapel during the British repression of Catholicism. By reversing the names Joyce is able to include his fictional name from *Portrait* and *Ulysses*, also the name of his grandson Stephen: "pa*st Eve an*d Adam's." Bernard Benstock sees the names of five Joyce family members appear on the first page of the text. That is, *Finnegans Wake* opens in an apostrophe to the Joyces, past and future.

7. For an extended analysis of the effects of this circularity, see Aubert, "riverrun." Aubert suggests that "riverrun" is unreadable because it is *undifferentiated*: "Reading is obstructed by lack of difference" (p. 69). Further, "riverrun" is "unhearable," not corresponding "to any vocable which the ear can honestly claim to recognize," and a common reading—"River, run!"— inserts a "pause, a silence," by resituating the comma that follows "riverrun." The comma that might confer meaning is absent. This reading makes "riverrun" both an apostrophe and a directive that owes its sense to an (unmarked) silence.

The *Wake* inscribes silence dozens of times. A structuring feature, it dramatically stops the storytelling, which must recommence again, on four occasions (hundreds of other "pauses" are embedded elsewhere in the text). These "silences" are not ascribed to any voice that calls them into being. Rather, silences are marked by forms of inscription that must be read but cannot be heard: "(Silent.)"—14.6; "silence:"—98.2; "(Silents)"—234.31; "SILENCE"—501.08.

8. Felman, "Turning the Screw of Interpretation," pp. 121–22, discusses similar effects in Henry James's *The Turn of the Screw*.

9. See Bishop, *Joyce's Book of the Dark*, p. 4. Bishop discusses the realm of dreamless sleep as "blank memory": "if we think of sleep (as opposed to 'dreams') as that part of the night which cannot be remembered, this would mean finding a way of 'reveiling' (220.33 [note the occluding 'veil']) an interval of life inherently barred from 'mummery' (535.30 ['memory'])" (p. 7).

10. Postcards and brief letters are incorporated as part of the footnotes to chapter 10 (the Lessons chapter), composed by Issy as countertexts to the chapter itself. The first duplicates and anticipates the letter to her mirror double: "Well, Maggy, I got your castoff devils all right and fits lovely. And am vaguely graceful. Maggy thinks" (273, fn. 6). The second, a footnote to Shaun's question, "And how zare you, waggy" ("And how are you/how dare you Maggy?"— 280.14) is actually a postcard: "Dear old Erosmas. Very glad you are going to Penmark. Write to the corner. Grunny Grant" (301, fn. 5). The addressee and subject are HCE ("Erosmas") and the play on the two kinds of intercourse— sexual and epistolary—is available in "Penmark." The message contains all the crucial elements of the contract that binds father and daughter, aspects of incest/ inscription that will be exposed in their letters.

11. See Derrida, "Two Words for Joyce." "He war" is a version of YAH- WEH, where HE WAR "exchanges the final R and the central H in the anagram's throat" (p. 154, and below, fn. 22). Derrida writes: "he declared war in lan- guage and on language and by language, which gave languages, that's the truth of Babel when YAHWE pronounced its vocable, difficult to say if it was a name" (p. 146). To translate "He War" or YHWH "into the system of a single language . . . is to erase the event of the mark" (p. 155). The apostrophe also marks this erasure—Y'HW'H, the supplied vowels are "a" and "e," as in He War and Earwicker. YAHWEH, HE WAR, declares war on individual language and on translation, as does *Finnegans Wake*: "And how war your maggies? Answer: They war loving" (142.30–31). See also *PC*, pp. 141–42.

12. The *Wake* includes many letters and fragments of missives that mutually support and contradict each other. Issy's letter duplicates in some interesting ways ALP's manifesto, a defense of the father against his accusers (pp. 119– 23), and also the Maggy letter dug up by Belinda of the Dorans on the midden heap (111.5–24). ALP's closing letter (pp. 615–19), however, appears to in- corporate all versions of the dream story, including each letter and anonymous message. See Devlin, *Wandering and Return in Finnegans Wake*. Following Freud through Lacan, Devlin reads the *Wake* as an uncanny text whose *unheim- lich* "is that which was once written, the literary fictions of Joyce's earlier artis- tic phases, ostensibly finished and put aside" ("Preface"). In chapter 5 of *Wan- dering and Return*, Devlin analyzes Joyce's fictions from the perspective of the Lacanian gaze, focusing especially on Joyce's depiction of men looking at or imagining a female I/eye. Chapter 6 addresses issues surrounding female voice. Although we diverge on certain matters, I am indebted to Devlin's careful analysis.

13. These dimly remembered scenes are constructed through the primary sense of sight and sound, present in the *Wake* text as both dreamwork and film montage. Earwicker is "framed" by the scene of indiscretion in the park, and

Issy is one of his observers; his sin is having observed two young girls micturating. Although *Finnegans Wake* is generally considered to be linguistically a far more experimental text than *Ulysses*, its sensory apparatus is more restricted, confined to "seeing-through-the-ears" rather than deconstructing sensory orders. The *Wake* is the more traditionally Freudian of the two texts; *Ulysses* operates according to a more Lacanian scheme of unconscious desires.

14. I use Ragland-Sullivan's definitions of Lacanian terminology outlined in *Jacques Lacan*. Thus, "(m)Other" is a formulation "meant to express the idea that the human subject first becomes aware of itself by identification with a person [object], usually the mother" (p. 16). The "Other," or "Other(A)" in Lacanian terms, "refers to the Symbolic other, or to the real father, i.e., the secondary unconscious created by subjugation to the social order of symbols, rules, and language. In a broader sense the Other(A) infers familial prehistory, as well as the social order of language, myths, and conventions" (p. 16). Issy's psychic structure incorporates both forms of Other.

15. Personality splintering (or "multiples") is a common effect of severe child sexual abuse. See Miller, *For Your Own Good*, pp. 107–41, and Bass and Davis, *The Courage to Heal*, pp. 208–10, 423–24, 44–49.

16. Prince, *The Dissociation of a Personality*.

17. Derrida examines this tension between the written and spoken in "*Ulysses* gramophone: Hear say yes in Joyce." See also Derrida, *Feu la cendre*, which presents a "tangle of voices" whose gender and number are indeterminate. Derrida plays with the accent grave, the unheard adverbial marker that both is and is not present in the phrase "feu la cendre." He describes its effects as a "vibration of grammar in (of) the voice" (p. 7, translation mine). Like apostrophe, *Feu la cendre* makes "a call to the voice" (p. 8); it is a *mise en voix*—a "voicing." The *voix* can be heard through several variant spellings—*voie* (way), *vois* (to see)—perhaps invoking the expression, *mise en scene*, to stage: tensions between ear and eye are dramatized. Like *Finnegans Wake*, Derrida's text problematizes translation, calling out for it (e.g., the ` of *la*) and resisting it.

18. See Culler, *The Pursuit of Signs*, pp. 148–49.

19. Culler outlines several levels of the "I-Thou" structure of apostrophe: the constitution of the object ("thou") as another subject "with whom the poetic subject might hope to strike up a harmonious relationship" (p. 143); the O of apostrophe as trope that might parody apostrophic procedures, so that the O is an "invocation of invocation" (p. 144); the apostrophic fiction implicit when the poet addresses Earth: "things of earth function as *thous* when addressed" (pp. 145–46); the call to O, which "seems to establish relations between the self and the other can in fact be read as an act of radical interiorization and solipsism" (p. 146). Culler reads apostrophe "as sign of a fiction which knows its own fictive nature . . . to stress its optative character, its impossible imperatives: commands which in their explicit impossibility figure events in and of fiction" (p. 146).

20. There are seven sigla for the Doodles Family (299, fn. 4). Of these, I emphasize only the   for Earwicker and the   for Anna Livia. Shem's sign provides an association with Cain, and Shaun's   repeats part of the form for the mother. Issy's sign as Isolde   is a mirror image of the alphabetic symbol

213

earlier used to designate Tristan . In a letter to Harriet Shaw Weaver on 24 March 1924, Joyce wrote out a more inclusive set of signs than the set of seven, among them the capital S (for Snake) and P (for Saint Patrick). My own interest has to do with alphabetic symbols that are associated (through a movement of disassociation) with the family characters: E, O, A, L, P, S. For information on the use of sigla, see McHugh, *The Sigla of Finnegans Wake*, pp. 8, 133.

21. The *Wake* makes various references to incriminating documents, the most important of which are the two that founded the Irish Free State in 1921 ("ducomans nonbar one"—358.30; "deckhuman amber too"—619.19). See Garvin, *James Joyce's Disunited Kingdom*, p. 141.

22. I am indebted to Professors Augustine Martin and Terence Dolan, University College, Dublin, for this reference.

23. See Crystal, *The Cambridge Encyclopedia of Language*, p. 202; and the exhibition catalog, *Period Styles: A History of Punctuation*, pp. 6–8. I cannot address here various issues in the movement from oral to written cultures, nor do I mean to suggest that the boundary between the two is clearly marked and strictly drawn. Indeed, this border area is of great interest. In his critique of the Saussurian "ethnocentrism privileging the model of phonetic writing" and of the "epigenetist" concept of writing held by Lévi-Strauss, Derrida points to the implicit failure of the effort radically to distinguish language from writing: "This [distinction] allows [Lévi-Strauss] to consider the passage from speech to writing as a *leap*, as the instantaneous crossing of a line of discontinuity: passage from a fully oral language, pure of all writing—*pure*, innocent—to a language appending to itself its graphic 'representation' as an accessory signifier of a new type, opening a technique of oppression." See Derrida, *Of Grammatology*, p. 120. Writing that extends beyond this "usual" or "narrow sense" of writing is already present "in the difference or the arche-writing that opens speech itself" (*Grammatology*, p. 128). This movement of "e" to "a" in *différance* is seen but not heard (written differently but spoken as though it were the same), a movement already apparent in YHWH, which carries the trace of this "arche-writing," a trace that leads us toward apostrophe as grammatical marking and the mark of the lyric genre.

24. Derrida, "Two Words for Joyce," p. 155.

25. See Derrida, *The Ear of the Other*, for discussion of what might be termed "ototextuality."

26. Stein, "Yet Dish," p. 55.

27. Bernard Benstock provides a close reading of the l, p, s letters in *Joyce-again's Wake*, pp. 148–55.

28. According to Bernard Benstock, "*P-q* becomes a leitmotif . . . not just by dint of incorporation into proper names of the two seductresses or the single Prankquean figure ["Peena and Queena"—377.18; "prunktqueen"—250.29, among others], but in the very flow of language" (pp. 153–54). The letters "p-q" serve several functions. They signify the mirror opposites through which the daughter is read (pepette, Coquette—239.33); the Prankqueen, a female marauder and counterpart to both Earwicker (as Scandinavian invader) and Anna Livia (especially as water and river, urination and vaginal liquids); and the brothers, who are both twins and opposites, who do battle with each other

for possession of the mother and combine forces to overthrow the father. The shapes of these letters suggest the form of spermatazoa that disperse and swim against the current. Their multiple numbers are opposed to the singular ovum.

29. For a discussion of the "arrival" or possible "non-arrival" of the letter, see Muller and Richardson, *The Purloined Poe*. This text includes Lacan, "Seminar on 'The Purloined Letter' "; Derrida, "The Purveyor of Truth"; and Johnson, "The Frame of Reference."

30. In the "Seminar on 'The Purloined Letter,' " Lacan argues that the letter is "like an immense female body, stretch[ed] out across the Minister's office," and that its hiding place "between the cheeks of the fireplace" (p. 48) is well known to those, like Inspector Dupin, who can read the map of sexual difference.

31. See Ragland-Sullivan's comments on Desire and its relation to dreaming in *Jacques Lacan*, p. 117, and in chapter 1 of my text.

Chapter 4

1. Nicholas Breton quoted in Robert Adams Day, *Told in Letters*. Barreno, Teresa Horta, and Costa, *The Three Marias*, p. 1.

2. Derrida, *PC*, p. 3. Because Derrida plays with gender markings in certain French words and makes anagrams of others ("*déjà*" for the initials J.D.), I sometimes refer to the French text, *La Carte Postale*. I alternate between the intimate French address, *toi, mon amour*, and its English translation, "you, my love," which cannot mark gender or distinguish the French pronominal forms. "Envois" refers to the collection of dispatches under the law of epistolary genres; *envois* refers to individual dispatches. See *PC*, "Translator's Introduction," pp. ix–xxx, for glossary.

3. See Kamuf's comments on genre/gender and "The Law of Genre" in "Hawthorne's Genres: The Letter of the Law *Appliquée*," p. 71.

4. Kauffman, *Discourses of Desire*, p. 85. Important questions remain concerning the "authenticity" of the Heloise and Abelard letters amid speculation that Heloise may not have written any of them, that her letters were penned in her name by Abelard. The legitimacy of *The Portuguese Letters* is in question, some critics claiming that they were written by the nun and others that the Frenchman Guilleragues wrote them as a literary hoax. See Kauffman, pp. 18–19, esp. fnn. 2, 3, and pp. 85–87, and Day, *Told in Letters*, p. 38.

5. See Altman, *Epistolarity*, pp. 114–15, fn. 17.

6. Kauffman, *Discourses of Desire*, p. 120. Derrida's formulation "under erasure," what is both deleted and retained, has philosophic and psychoanalytic analogues. See "Translator's Preface," Derrida, *Of Grammatology*, pp. xiv–xv.

7. Derrida, "The Law of Genre," p. 225. Nancy K. Miller, " 'I's' in Drag," p. 49.

8. Derrida, "The Law of Genre," p. 221.

9. Ibid., p. 202. Reading *PC* in a restricted way, forcing it inside the boundaries of epistolary form, I want to be clear about my uses of Derrida's discussion of "the law of genre." He writes that "the law [of genre] is in the

feminine. She is not a woman (it is only a figure, a 'silhouette,' and not a representative of the law) but she, *la loi*, is in the feminine, declined in the feminine; but not only as a grammatical gender/genre in my language. . . . No, she is described as a 'female element,' which does not signify a female person" (p. 225). The relationship of "feminine" to "female element" is the central problematic here.

10. There are significant differences between women's situations in England and France in the eighteenth century that result in rather different fictional representations of women. My comments on women readers and writers are more pertinent to England than to France. In both countries, however, the epistolary tradition specifically courted women, and in both countries these fictions appropriated female creativity. Moreover, the heroine's fate was similarly prescribed in fictions that relied on epistolary forms and in those that did not. In *The Heroine's Text* Nancy K. Miller observes: "In one way or another, the novel has always been associated with women. The eighteenth-century novel, it seems reasonable to say, indeed, it has been said, would never have happened without a certain collective 'obsessing' about an idea called 'woman,' and without a female reading public" (p. ix). See also Nancy K. Miller, "Female Sexuality and Narrative Structure in *La Nouvelle Heloise* and *Les Liaisons dangereuses*," p. 609, and "The Exquisite Cadavers," p. 37.

11. For background information on the beginnings of epistolary fiction in English I have relied on four traditional studies: Allen, *The English Novel*; Day, *Told in Letters*; Singer, *The Epistolary Novel*; and Watt, *The Rise of the Novel*. Among the four, only Day examines the relation of letter writing to epistolary fiction in the years just preceding the birth of the epistolary novel; he is also the only one to emphasize the importance of the letter form for French fiction. A fifth study, Altman's *Epistolarity*, examines the dynamics of epistolary fiction, especially its relation to theater and drama. Her analysis broadens the concept of "epistolarity" to include narratives that do not rely solely on letter exchanges. Four other studies explore the connection between women and writing in epistolary fiction. Among them, Perry's *Women, Letters, and the Novel* catalogs the functions letters served in alleviating the isolations of early eighteenth-century women: letters provided an outlet for creativity and offered a means for women to compose images of themselves in a society in which they were denied creative or intellectual outlets for their energies, where they remained passive and mute, sexually repressed, and intellectually constrained (see in particular pp. x–xi). The remaining studies, none of which concentrates solely on epistolary discourse, apply contemporary critical theory to fictions that purport to inscribe woman's experience. See Nancy K. Miller, *The Heroine's Text*; Kamuf, *Fictions of Feminine Desire*, which studies narratives that "stage the confrontation of a specific and active woman's desire with a social or symbolic order that represents no place for such a desire" (pp. xviii–xix); and Kauffman's *Discourses of Desire*, which plots the relation of letters to literature and "the transgressions of genre" (p. 18).

12. Quoted in Perry, *Women, Letters, and the Novel*, p. 128.

13. Kauffman, *Discourses of Desire*, p. 105.

14. Altman, *Epistolarity*, p. 128.

15. Kauffman, *Discourses of Desire*, p. 102.

16. See Derrida, "Freud's Legacy" and "Paralysis" in *PC*, pp. 292–386, and Spivak, "Love Me, Love My Ombre, Elle" (hereafter called "Love Me"). For Derrida's possible reenactment of *fort/da*, see Ulmer, "The Post-Age," p. 43.

17. Spivak, "Love Me," p. 30.

18. Derrida comments on repetition, supplementation and hollowing out of the *fort/da* structure in "Freud's Legacy," pp. 313–14, 351–53.

19. Bleier, *Science and Gender*, states that "the kingpin in the patriarchal formations that serve to oppress women is sexuality and the heterosexual structuring of consciousness of *institutions*" (p. 164, emphasis added). Underlying the creation and operation of social institutions is the founding assumption of patriarchal social structures, "that men own and have the right to control the bodies, labor, and minds of women" (p. 164).

20. Kamuf, *Fictions of Feminine Desire*, p. xvii.

21. Nancy K. Miller, " 'I's' in Drag," p. 39.

22. Nancy K. Miller, "Female Sexuality," p. 609.

23. Nancy K. Miller analyzes the problem of authorship in *The Portuguese Letters*. She pursues a "riddle": "why were these letters written by a man as a woman to himself and then thought to be written by a woman?" (" 'I's' in Drag," p. 48). Pondering the kinds of "secondary gains [that] accrue to a male writer who supplies first-person feminine fictions," Miller suggests, following the work of Kristeva, that "female drag allows the male 'I' not so much to please the Other—by subscribing or capitulating to women's 'taste'—as to become the Other, what Kristeva calls in *Le Texte du roman* the pseudo-Other, the better to be admired by and for himself" (" 'I's' in Drag," p. 49 and fn. 7). The pseudo-Other constructs a complex route by which the heterosexual underwrites the homosocial (and also homophobic) in these fictions. See Kamuf, "Writing as a Woman"; and Kauffman, *Discourses of Desire*, chaps. 2 and 3. Sedgwick reads the social, legal, and erotic dynamics of homosocial bonding among men in *Between Men*.

24. Kauffman, *Discourses of Desire*, pp. 18, 168–69.

25. Ibid., p. 68.

26. Epistolary fiction figures woman's body as a letter or cipher whose central blank space is the place of writing and sexual encounter with the pen(is). Gubar examines this classic figuration of woman in " 'The Blank Page' and the Issues of Female Creativity"; see also Castle, *Clarissa's Ciphers*; and Kauffman, *Discourses of Desire*, pp. 140–41, 221–22.

27. In certain epistolary fictions, rape is not merely a trope of interpretation but a violent appropriation of the heroine's subjectivity. See Castle, *Clarissa's Ciphers*; and Warner, "Reading Rape," pp. 12–32. Warner examines Castle's portrayal of Clarissa's "powerlessness. . . . Her linguistic oppression [that] is linked to other sorts of oppression: economic, social, psychological" (*Clarissa's Ciphers*, p. 116). See Eagleton, *The Rape of Clarissa*.

28. I borrow Derrida's notion of the crypt. See Johnson, "Fors." See Kauffman on epistolary crypts (*Discourses of Desire*, p. 155). See my chap. 1 for the relation of scopic economy to the field of vision.

29. Lacan, "Seminar on 'The Purloined Letter,' " p. 53.

30. Derrida, "The Purveyor of Truth," in *PC*, p. 201.

31. Derrida, "The Law of Genre," p. 206. Johnson, *The Critical Difference*, p. 124.

32. Nancy K. Miller, "'I's' in Drag," p. 55.

33. Barthes, *A Lover's Discourse*, pp. 13–14, emphasis in original. Barthes capitalizes "Woman" to emphasize its cultural and mythic dimensions.

34. Nancy K. Miller, "'I's' in Drag," p. 57.

35. Barthes, *A Lover's Discourse*, p. 13.

36. Ibid.

37. Spivak opens questions of the "feminine operation" in Derrida's deconstructive project within the Woman/woman split (i.e., Woman generalized as a category; woman specified in a narrow sense), shadow figures ("ombre/elle"), and displacement. "Love Me, Love My Ombre, Elle" gives a succinct review of Derrida's project and the work of the "feminine" in *PC*. See also "Displacement and the Discourse of Woman." For Spivak, Derrida's deconstruction of Western metaphysics fails to displace the binary oppositions of masculine/feminine as a grammatological writing project. Spivak follows a different logic from the Lacanian critique (see comments of Rose and Ragland-Sullivan in chap. 1) but arrives (almost) at the same place. Repeating the argument Derrida set forth in *Spurs: Nietzsche's Styles*, "Woman is the name of the absolute limit of undecidability" ("Love Me," p. 24), Spivak passes too quickly by the internal cleft of subjectivity which makes of the false grammatical categories "he" and "she" a "s/he." She bypasses the psychogrammatical structures at work in textualizing woman's materiality.

38. Derrida plays with textual spacing, grammar, punctuation, the image of photographic negatives or indentations of bas-relief to suggest what is usually overlooked by analyses of writing. See *Glas*.

39. The postcard that represents this "apocalyptic revelation" of Socrates and Plato in a reversal of their traditional roles was discovered in the Bodleian Library, Oxford, as the frontispiece of *Prognostica Socratis basilei*, an English fortune-telling book of the thirteenth century, the work of Matthew Paris. That it tells a "fortune" which is the inverse of our historical understanding is important to Derrida's discussions of generational relationships: of dissemination through paternity and patriarchy, of relations between fathers and sons, and of the binary oppositions (and doubles) implicit to the dialogue of twins. Thus, Socrates and Plato are variously represented (and "representation" is one of the topics under philosophic discussion) as father and son to each other, but also as homosexuals.

40. See Derrida, "The Heritage of the Pharmakon," which proposes a familial relation between Socrates and Plato, between speech and writing, that is further examined under the representation of the postcard.

41. Derrida, *Dissemination*, p. 146.

42. Elshtain, "Feminist Discourse and Its Discontents," p. 606.

43. Langbauer comments that feminist criticism is too quick to read the subversive in women's writing, thus overlooking how the category Woman unavoidably collaborates with and supports systems of its representation. See *Women and Romance*.

44. From the woman's perspective, the love letter is a form of death warrant,

where woman "kills" her desire by scripting it to meet and match man's desire. As Mme de Merteuil in *Les Liaisons dangereuses* teaches her pupils, the love letter can either portray or mask the desire of the "I" who writes; and, she would add, it is dangerous to "portray" this desire (see Altman, *Epistolarity*, pp. 185 ff.). Clarissa Harlowe writes out her will, which becomes a posthumous weapon against Lovelace. The will already predicates (and predicts) her own death, which has inscribed itself in virtually every letter she has written. As Kauffman observes, "Clarissa's will is thus less a protest against the death sentence that has been imposed upon her, than a response to it. In each line of her will she is literally composing a death sentence of indeterminate length, since she cannot know when she will die" (*Discourses of Desire*, p. 146).

45. Reference to the "erotic *dos*" on which Plato directs Socrates's writing brings to mind the famous letter (no. 48) of *Les Liaisons dangereuses* in which Valmont uses the courtesan's back as his desk, bringing himself to sexual orgasm as he writes a letter (which becomes her death sentence) to the angelic Tourvel. All writing is, of course, orgasmic: it bursts, spills, overruns its boundaries, and "disseminates." Autoeroticism that uses an imagined woman to effect a "lovemaking" with the same, or self, is also implied by this erotic positioning. The "event" in amorous epistolary discourse is writing, always an opening of the circuit of desire (Altman, *Epistolarity*, p. 128). The "destination" of the letter is figured in the opening, and retracing, of the circuit of "sameness" that violently erases differences.

46. Johnson, *The Critical Difference*, p. 145. Johnson, and also Nancy K. Miller in "'I's' in Drag," discuss the difficulty of distinguishing the narcissistic message from the message dictated by the Other. The inability to "tell" the difference is examined by *The Post Card*, which confounds the problem further (as does epistolary fiction) by making gender difference mask the homoerotic as well as the autoerotic. Ultimately in "Envois" one cannot distinguish the lover from oneself, the Other from the one who dictates the messages of desire.

47. In French the verb *apostropher* can mean "to speak brusquely or brutally to someone." The effect is carried by "tone," as Derrida states. No such meaning inheres in the English "to apostrophize," where the word carries only the mark of genre: to apostrophize something or someone.

48. Perry, *Women, Letters, and the Novel*, pp. 138–39.

49. Rousseau, *Julie, ou la nouvelle Héloïse*, p. x, translation mine.

50. Rousseau, *Julie*, p. 9, translation mine.

51. See Spivak's comments on the measured textual spaces in "Love Me," p. 29. In his comments on "Envois," Derrida writes: "As for the 52 signs, the 52 mute spaces, in question is a cipher that I had wanted to be symbolic and secret—in a word a clever cryptogram, that is, a very naive one, that had cost me long calculations" (*PC*, p. 5). He claims to have forgotten "the rule as well as the elements of such a calculation, as if I had thrown them into the fire" (p. 5). The blank spaces mark the effects of a consuming fire in which the writer tried to destroy the letters. Altman notes that in epistolary discourse the letter exchange is a death-defying duel where "after the holocaust survivors inherit the correspondence; as soon as all the secret weapons have been confiscated, the collection is complete, as is the novel" (p. 154). See Kauffman's comments

on ciphers, especially with reference to Rousseau's *Émile* (*Discourses of Desire*, pp. 222–23.

52. To address and post letters is to invoke "destination." "Envois" plays on the verb to post ("to put, to place") and on the genre of its noun forms, following Littré, who writes: "Le poste ne diffère de la poste que par le genre" (quoted in "Envois," p. 54). On the back cover of the text "J.D." addresses a postcard, which encompasses *The Post Card*, to the reader. He comments that from "its lack or excess of address," the love letter lends itself to a certain risk, to falling into anyone's hands. Kauffman examines the word *adresser* in *The Portuguese Letters*, remarking that the various meanings of the word (*l'adresse* as skill and dexterity, and in *The Portuguese Letters*, sexual expertise; finesse and delicacy of spirit; the address of a letter) are all at work in epistolary discourse (*Discourses of Desire*, p. 111). *L'adresse* is also an "appeal to the lover" that links the artifice of letters and love. Artifice always displays itself as an effect of the asymmetricality of relations, either by lack (*faute*) or excess. "*Je vous adresse . . .*" inaugurates a discourse of desire.

53. Spivak, "Love Me," p. 31.

54. Derrida, *Writing and Difference*, p. 226. Barthes, *A Lover's Discourse*, p. 132.

55. Derrida, *Of Grammatology*, p. 143.

56. Rousseau, *Confessions*, p. 114.

57. de Man, *Allegories of Reading*, p. 214.

58. Ibid., p. 213.

59. See Derrida, *Feu la cendre*, for a discussion of writing's holocaustal effects.

60. Spivak ponders whether "Bettina" refers to Bettina von Arnim, "whose childhood letters to Goethe, collected and published by herself in maturity as *Briefwechsel mit einem Kinde*, are of course always carefully cross-indexed to Goethe, the overshadowing receiver" ("Love Me," p. 27, fn. 13).

61. Ulmer, "The Post-Age," p. 3.

62. Radice, *Letters of Heloise and Abelard*, p. 113.

63. Epistolary fiction repeats Lacan's Imaginary structure. See "The Mirror Stage as Formative of the Function of the I." See also Spivak, "Love Me," pp. 19–20; Barthes, *A Lover's Discourse*, pp. 132–33.

64. Lacan, *Écrits*, pp. 128–29. Freud's statement, *Wo Es war, soll Ich werden*, translates as "Where id was, there ego shall be."

65. Derrida, *Dissemination*, pp. 209–15, emphasis in original.

66. Derrida, *Writing and Difference*, p. 226.

67. Derrida, "Law of Genre," pp. 224–25.

68. Kristeva, *Desire in Language*, p. 237; Derrida, *Spurs*, p. 55.

69. In *Spurs* Derrida speaks of the "feminine operation" within Nietzsche's writing and observes: "Because woman is (her own) writing, style must return to her" (p. 57).

70. Day, *Told in Letters*, p. 5, emphasis added.

71. Derrida, "The Law of Genre," p. 22.

72. For an extended discussion of the doubled affirmative and another tracing of the postal trajectory, see Derrida, "*Ulysses* Gramophone," pp. 27–76.

Chapter 5

1. Woolf, *Three Guineas*, p. 122, brackets and quotation marks in original text (hereafter referred to as *TG*). Sophocles, *Antigone*, pp. 700–41, lines 1344–48, ellipsis in text. All citations are by line number.

2. In Woolf's fiction, criticism, and autobiographical writings, fathers figure the Law: they design, implement, and enforce it; in short, they represent it. This "law," to which Woolf makes only elliptical reference in *Three Guineas*, encompasses the theoretical and practical components of The Law of the Phallus as the Law of Genre, outlined in chap. 1 of my text.

3. Woolf, *A Room of One's Own*, p. 15, ellipsis in original (hereafter referred to as *Room*).

4. It is not entirely clear to what aspect of Freud's work the term "infantile fixation" applies. Woolf adopts this construction, which is probably of her own making, as a shorthand for the emphasis in Freudian theory on the child's insatiable demands, its narcissistic placement at the center of (an Imaginary) universe. That is, Woolf uses the term to suggest adult regression toward an earlier stage, prior to the moment when the infant is brought into socialization under the Law. From her perspective, the Law authorizes, even encourages, men to follow their pre-Oedipal urges. A strain of "essentialism" runs through Woolf's argument (apparent in Freud as well) that allows her to sometimes too quickly conflate "male" and "masculine."

5. Woolf was powerfully influenced by Freud's writings, which she read from the early 1920s through the 1930s, when the Hogarth Press began publishing the complete edition of Freud's works. See *The Diary of Virginia Woolf*, vols. 1, 2, and 5 passim for references to Woolf's knowledge of Freud. See also DeSalvo, *Virginia Woolf*, pp. 126–31.

6. DuBois, "Antigone and the Feminist Critic," p. 373, ellipsis mine (hereafter referred to as "Antigone").

7. DuBois retells the legend in "Antigone," p. 374, and in *Sowing the Body*, pp. 55–56. She draws our attention to an important exchange in *Antigone* around the metaphor of woman as agricultural field. When Ismene asks whether Creon would really kill his own son's bride, he responds, "Absolutely: there are other fields for him to plow" (lines 642–43).

8. Lacan's rereading of Freud, which tried to account for the language laws of psychic structures, drew heavily on Jakobson's linguistic theories. Precisely because metonymy and metaphor belong to the Symbolic order of language and culture (including myth), they cannot fully account for language ordering in the unconscious (they say nothing about *lalangue*, for instance). Without pressing the analogy too far, or trying to literalize it, one might see Antigone as a figure of the semiotic process: she resists the repressive necessity of the Symbolic, her discourse irrupting into and unsettling its governing (and unstable) order. That is, Antigone can be seen to disrupt the oppositional structure of metonymy-metaphor by exceeding the symbolic limits it would set on her language and behavior.

9. Freud, "Some Psychical Consequences of the Anatomical Distinction

between the Sexes," vol. 19, pp. 257–58. Quoted in duBois, "Antigone," p. 371, 372, emphasis added.

10. Marcus has written on this and other topics important to my discussion of *Three Guineas*. In particular, her discussion of prolepsis in Woolf's writing, which shares properties with ellipsis, is of interest. See her *Art and Anger*, "Sapphistry." For the compositional process of Woolf's text, see Silver, "*Three Guineas* Before and After," pp. 254–76.

11. Nor does Woolf, like some of her Modernist contemporaries (including Freud), see Greek culture as the "unconscious" of modernity, a roughhewn and less refined culture than our own.

12. Women must fall into line, come to order under the "head" or leader. See Cixous, "Castration or Decapitation," pp. 36–55.

13. In *Gynesis*, Jardine writes: "It is upon this process that I am insisting in this study: the transformation of woman and the feminine into *verbs* at the interior of those narratives that are today experiencing a crisis in legitimation" (p. 25, emphasis in original). Traditionally signified as passive and receptive, associated from ancient times with vessels, containers, sacred spaces—objects both of speculation and fear—woman now signifies activity and movement, adopting not only linguistic subject positions (first-person pronouns, subject nouns), she translates herself into action—performing, doing, functioning. The interiority which woman has always inhabited (the private space of home and hearth) is now transformed to an exteriority (the public world of action and deed). Woolf's argument recognizes this shift in cultural inscriptions of women.

14. See Kamuf, *Signature Pieces*, p. viii. Hanging was the preferred means of killing women (particularly virgins) in the ancient world. Eva Cantarella speculates that this means of murder symbolically separated women from their ancient associations with the earth and fertility (in death, they hung like dead fruits from trees). In precivic society the primary organizational model was by age and sex; the basis of later city organization was the differentiation between free and slave. The male/female distinction was "the first cornerstone" of social organization in Greece, and women were subjected to socially approved misogyny and frequently victims of rape, to escape which they often hanged themselves. See "Dangling Virgins: Myth, Ritual, and the Place of Women in Ancient Greece," in Suleiman, *The Female Body in Western Culture*, pp. 57–67.

15. Changed attitudes to male homosexuality figure importantly here. Male bonding in Greece was privileged for military reasons. Creon forbids the burial of Polyneices' body because he turned against the state (he is a traitor), having killed his loyal brother, Eteocles. Antigone crosses into this territory of fraternal battles and state loyalties, entering a homosocial conflict. Modern totalitarian states, and fascism in particular, also foster homosocial bonding among men whose virility was tested, as it was in Greece, through sports activities and the ability to control women, whose duty was to produce (male) children for the military. Male homosexuality is forbidden within modernity because it is not (re)productive and, further, because it is associated with women's weakness.

16. Showalter, "Feminist Criticism in the Wilderness," pp. 179–206. Showalter draws on Ardener's "Belief and the Problem of Women," p. 3. Note, however, that colonization (in the sociohistorical model) or total repression (in

the psychoanalytic model) of this zone always fails; it is this failure that modernity recognizes as its crisis, which is why it codes as "feminine" the space over which its narratives have lost control (Jardine, *Gynesis*, p. 25). This is a site where the Law of the Phallus fails; it is a space of silence, absence, and (internal) exclusion; the place where truth eludes its determined seeker, a place of wrong turning, of deviation from the straight and narrow path of phallologic, a moment when one is forced to turn back. Virginia Woolf often finds herself here, in a place of catastrophe. She marks its textual un(re)markableness by ellipsis.

17. But it was on just these grounds that her argument met resistance. For Woolf's contemporaries the elliptical structure of *Three Guineas* fell short of reader expectations. Its reasoning was marked by gaps and twists of logic; repetitions defeated the forward movement of its analysis; fictional pretexts overlapped confusingly. The textual spaces created by these holes, gaps, knots, and imbrications suggested to Woolf's readers the places where her narrative had lost control of itself. In short, the argument seemed merely to repeat a feminine—that is, hysterical—rhetoric. More radically than *A Room of One's Own*, *Three Guineas* confounds fact and fiction, crosses genre barriers, creates a multi-voiced structure that reorganizes the imaginative and intellectual space between reader and text. The defense network of its footnotes marks off a new textual space. This protective barrier, erected by Woolf in an effort to shore up her argument and ward off accusations of eccentricity and excess, establishes a *dialegesthai*, or dialogue, between fictional forms and scholarly methods. See fn. 26 below.

18. Marcus, *Virginia Woolf and the Languages of Patriarchy*; p. 187; *The Diary of Virginia Woolf*, vol. 4, p. 6.

19. The transformation of the seed to a language code are suggested in Gimbutas's description of ancient sculptures: "The dot, representing seed, and the lozenge, symbolizing the sown field, appear on sculptures of an enthroned pregnant goddess and are also incised or painted on totally schematized figurings. A lozenge with a dot or dash in its centre or in the corners must have been the symbolic invocation to secure fertility." See *The Goddesses and Gods of Old Europe, 6500–3500 B.C.*, p. 205.

20. Dayan analyzes the more common usage of the dash as a mark of punctuation in "The Analytic of the Dash," p. 437.

21. *The Diary of Virginia Woolf*, vol. 5, pp. 101, 112.

22. *The Letters of Vita Sackville-West to Virginia Woolf*, pp. 412–13.

23. *The Letters of Virginia Woolf*, vol. 6, pp. 242–43, emphasis in original.

24. The accusation has recently been repeated by Meisel, *The Absent Father*. See McGee's response, "Woolf's Other." Vita turns Virginia into an Orlando figure, a Renaissance gentleman who duels to defend his honor. Vita also crosses class boundaries when she proposes "fisticuffs," the peasantry's preferred form of fighting. These references to altercations between men inadvertently point to the crux of Virginia's argument: that violence is bred by the smallest unit of social structures and begins in the family. This thesis, which Vita and others close to her (including Leonard Woolf) found exaggerated, has been confirmed by contemporary research. See Alice Miller, *For Your Own*

Good, which examines the rise of Nazism within the terms of a socially sanctioned ideology of family violence toward women and children. See esp. section 1, "Poisonous Pedagogy."

25. For convenience, I refer to the woman writer as "Virginia Woolf," enclosing that name in invisible quotation marks to signal all the strategies by which Virginia Woolf fictionalizes the author function of this text. The name is hidden within the elliptical structure of the text—a signature that repeatedly opens (on) the question of signature.

26. Quentin Bell speaks for many of Woolf's contemporaries when he objects to the priorities she establishes: "Virginia did not preach in vain. A great many women wrote to express their enthusiastic approval; but her close friends were silent, or if not silent, critical. Vita did not like it, and Maynard Keynes was both angry and contemptuous; its was, he declared, a silly argument and not very well written. What really seemed wrong with the book—and I am speaking here of my own reactions at the time—was the attempt to involve *a discussion of women's rights with the far more agonising and immediate question of what we were to do in order to meet the ever-growing menace of Fascism and war. The connection between the two questions seemed tenuous and the positive suggestions wholly inadequate.*" Bell, *Virginia Woolf: A Biography*, vol. 2, pp. 204–205, emphasis added. Like Vita Sackville-West, Bell wholly missed the point of Virginia's logic.

27. In a footnote, Woolf remarks that through human reproduction women supply "cannon fodder" for the war effort. Helena Normanton encouraged women to refuse to bear children—advice offered "in very similar circumstances over two thousand years ago by Lysistrata." Woolf notes that during the 1930s the birth rate in the educated classes was falling and wonders whether educated women are using this means of "indirect influence" (*TG*, p. 147, fn. 10).

28. This "photograph," like the pictures from the Spanish Civil War to which Woolf makes reference later, do not exist in the text. She tries to dramatize women's poverty and the cruelty of war through visual images of the effects they produce. The first edition of *Three Guineas*, however, did include a set of twenty-two photographs of men dressed in representative robes and uniforms of their professions—law, religion, military, government, royalty, etc.

29. See Marcus, "Corpus/Corps/Corpse," pp. 241–93, and Culleton, "Gender-Charged Munitions," pp. 23–32.

30. See 28 June 1938 entry, *Diary*, vol. 5: p. 100.

31. The war photographs to which she makes reference here and elsewhere were available daily in the press during the months she was writing *Three Guineas*. Indeed, her nephew Julian Bell's death in the war in Spain (1937) may have spurred her to write it. Woolf mourned his loss deeply, horrified by the violence in Spain and outraged at the spread of fascism across Europe.

32. Woolf quotes in part the appeal, extracted from "a letter received from the London and National Society for Women's Service," 1938: "This letter is to ask you to set aside for us garments for which you have no further use. . . . Stockings, of every sort, no matter how worn, are also acceptable. . . . The committee find that by offering these clothes at bargain prices . . . they are

performing a really useful service to women whose professions require that they should have presentable day and evening dresses which they can ill afford to buy" (*TG*, p. 159, fn. 1, ellipsis in original).

33. Woolf's use of the fluid feminine first-person "I" here and in the earlier *Room* deserves an essay of its own. In both texts, she moves in and out of pronominal identifiers, as though to indicate how fragile subjectivity always is and against what odds it is constructed. Here the "I" mirrors the patriarchy. As in the photographs of the Spanish Civil War atrocities, one cannot clearly discriminate beings from landscape in the presence of this "I": it renders everything undecidable, indistinguishable, indeterminate, erasing the background with the imprint of its own determinacy. The point is not that women have no innate "being," but rather that the shape of their being is blurred by the cultural imprint of masculinity.

34. This is not entirely laughable, since it is related to family structures and values. See Alice Miller, *For Your Own Good*, fn. 24 above.

35. Woolf, *Flush: A Biography*, p. 12; *Three Guineas*, p. 50.

36. See Shari Benstock, "On the Margin of Discourse," pp. 204–25, for a discussion of footnotes as defensive network.

37. Woolf quotes from the *Daily Telegraph*, 22 January 1936: "Homes are the real places of the *women who are now compelling men to be idle*. It is time the Government insisted upon employers giving work to more men, thus enabling them to marry the women they cannot now approach" (*TG*, p. 51, emphasis added).

38. The guinea coin was named for the place where the gold was mined. The last minted guinea in Great Britain (1813) carried a profile of George III.

39. DuBois, *Sowing the Body*, p. 139.

Chapter 6

1. Stein, *Three Lives*; p. 108. Derrida, *The Ear of the Other*, p. 140. Further citations as *EO*.

2. H.D., *Helen in Egypt*, p. 1. Further citations as *HE*. I refer to H.D.'s text as a poem, but it includes a prose commentary which was added later. In H.D.'s text, the prose commentary is printed in italics and the poem in roman type. The prose sections often use a collective voice ("we") that functions as a Greek chorus to counter and comment on the action of the poem, summarizing and interpreting, or more often questioning, the meaning of the events it records. Neither joined to nor entirely separate from the poetry, the prose commentaries negotiate the distance between reader and poetic subject ("I"), but they are no more authoritative (or closer to the voice of H.D.) than is the poetry. Grammatical pronoun shifts (I, we, she) within the text demonstrate the positions of referential subjectivity discussed in chaps. 1 and 2.

3. Stesichorus's texts may have inspired Euripedes' versions of Helen, the dramatist also suffering blindness and a later restoration of his sight. Helen blinds her detractors, an appropriate revenge against her function as object of the male gaze. See Graves, *The Greek Myths*, p. 317.

4. See Suzuki, *Metamorphoses of Helen*, for a discussion of Helen's position within binary oppositions.

5. Horace Gregory, "Introduction," in H.D., *Helen in Egypt*, p. vii.

6. In *Modernism Made Manifest*, I discuss the place and function of translation within the development of modernism and provide close readings of translations by H.D., Aldington, and Pound.

7. This is a clinical definition. See Ragland-Sullivan, *Jacques Lacan*, pp. 110, 261: "The symptom is the substitute sign or word—a metaphor—whose "cure" (or translation) would lie in discovering which meanings are repressed in a person's language, and, in consequence, are manipulating their behavior in metonymic, puppeteer style." The cure, as Schneiderman explains, is not to discover the meaning of the symptom but to *subvert* its meaning through "equivocation." See "Art as Symptom," pp. 207–9, and his reference to Freud's belief that "the symptom has a wording" (p. 219). Lacan defined the symptom as a knot, or text; the structure and significance of it was presumably revealed to him by Joyce's *Finnegans Wake*. A Wakean coincidence, perhaps, the symptom is represented by the letter E, Earwicker's siglum. See Lacan, "Joyce le symptôme," an address to the International James Joyce Symposium, 16 June 1975. This paper was first published in *Joyce et Paris*; Lacan dedicated his 1975–76 seminar to Joyce, and a later version of this paper appeared in *L'Ane* under the title, "Joyce le sinthôme."

8. The movement of repression as inscription has its parallels in grammatology's "double writing" (see chap. 4). There are also parallels with archeology which, Wood notes, "destroys the very thing it examines." See Wood, *In Search of the Trojan War*, p. 11.

9. Ibid., pp. 15, 11.

10. See Lacan's resume of Freud, *Seminar II*, p. 105 and fn. 4. H.D.'s writing was powerfully affected by her work with Freud in the 1930s.

11. See Lacan, *Seminar II* and *Séminaire XI*, and Ragland-Sullivan's explanation in *Jacques Lacan*, pp. 110–12.

12. Ragland-Sullivan, *Jacques Lacan*, p. 260. She quotes Sheridan in Lacan, *Ecrits*, p. 137. *Remémoration* works against false (but also necessary) Imaginary unity. Lacan explains in *Seminar II* that the symptom is part of the global economy of the subject, not an isolated phenomenon; he further warns that "the ego isn't identical to the subject, and it is in the nature of the ego to integrate itself in the imaginary circuit" (p. 324). Schneiderman's comments on the function of Poe's "The Purloined Letter" in Lacanian theory reframe the terms of difference between Derrida and Lacan on the structure of the letter ("Art as Symptom," pp. 220–21).

13. H.D.'s text avoids the question of whether Helen eloped with Paris or was abducted by him; as well, she portrays Theseus as a kind and gentle father figure. Abduction-as-translation has been so completely erased from her text that by its absence it becomes a textual symptom.

14. See Graves, *The Greek Myths*, pp. 363–64. Hirsch comments on the analytic setting in *Modernism Revised*. See also Chisholm, *H.D.'s Freudian Poetics*, which discusses psychoanalysis as translation.

15. DuPlessis writes that Helen "remembers in such a way that a tapestry of the mind is rewoven" (*H.D.*, p. 110). This is certainly true, but it cannot result

from memory work. For Helen as weaver see the *Iliad*, Book 3, and Suzuki's helpful analysis in *Metamorphoses of Helen*, chaps. 1, 2.

16. See Spivak's commentary in "Love Me," and my discussion of *fort/da* in chap. 1. As Lacan explains in *Seminar I*, the *fort/da* game is a paradigm for the Symbolic order, and language is central to its function. Ragland-Sullivan comments that "the child is assigned a symbolic value (presence/absence or plus/minus) and a functional one (mastery) to a bobbin reel. As the words *Fort!* and *Da!* came to substitute for the symbol and for its function (to master separation from the mother), sign and symbol became united (*Séminaire I*, pp. 201, 290)" (*Jacques Lacan*, pp. 171–72). It is the *structure* of unification, however, that needs repeated emphasis, readers too quickly reading the bobbin reel (image, icon) as the site of meaning; the child makes a "text" of his mother. In *Seminar II* Lacan examines symbolic dependence on images in relation to Plato's notions of reminiscence and being in/as form. Rather than recollection in memory, he argues for something like structural mechanics that encodes meaning as repetition and movement (p. 87). See also Kloepfer, *Unspeakable Mother*, p. 166 (hereafter referred to as *UM*).

17. See Ragland-Sullivan, p. 113; and Lacan, *Séminaire XI*, p. 198. Weber comments on the necessity of repression for subjectivity in "The Divericator," pp. 1–2; Walsh, "Reading the Real," describes psychosis as a disease in language where the signifier and signified fail to link up.

18. See Ragland-Sullivan, *Jacques Lacan*, p. 115, and Lemaire, *Jacques Lacan*, p. 250. Although *Helen in Egypt* often refers to hieroglyphs as "picture-writing," duplicating scenes of H.D.'s "visions" or halucinations in Egypt and on Corfu, the psychoanalytic process that the poem describes does not confine itself to visual material. It is more than the reading of "picture-memories" that DuPlessis describes (p. 110). See Hirsch, *Modernism Revised*, on hieroglyphics as decoration and "feminine art." Crystal explains that hieroglyphic script is not only visual but a composite of ideographs, phonograms, and determinative symbols that differentiate words that otherwise would appear to be identical in meaning. See *Cambridge Encyclopedia*, p. 199.

19. The child Euphorion, who combines both sexes, is represented as a kind of *jouissance* of the hieroglyph. See Schneiderman, "Art as Symptom," on *jouissance* of the symptom (p. 208).

20. See H.D.'s *Hermione* and my reading of sisterhood as otherness in *Women of the Left Bank*, pp. 344–49.

21. Suzuki, *Metamorphoses of Helen*, comments on Helen's place in the male world of war and within the domestic scene (pp. 40, 63).

22. See Lernout, "Joyce or Lacan," p. 196, and "Joyce le symptôme," p. 17, and *The French Joyce*, chap. 2. Lacan posed the question about why Joyce did not "like" psychoanalysis in private conversation with me, Bernard Benstock, Jacques Aubert and Catherine Millot (1 June 1976); it led to a seven-hour discussion of Joyce's resistance to psychoanalysis and the relation of his writing to his own feared madness. Joyce's fear of madness was based, in part on a history of madness in his family; he misread his daughter's schizophrenia as a sign of her "genius" (linked to his own). See Ellmann, *James Joyce*.

23. Jean-Michel Rabaté suggests Lacan may have attempted to combat his own neuroses by trying to discover in *Finnegans Wake* how Joyce "overcame

his madness by writing the *Wake*" (Lernout, "Joyce or Lacan," p. 202, fn. 4). Macey underestimates Joyce's importance for Lacan (*Lacan in Contexts*, p. 6); beyond Joyce's texts (in which Lacan may have found evidence to support his theories), Lacan identified with Joyce, even to dying a "Joycean" death from stomach cancer (Joyce died of a perforated ulcer).

24. Joyce, *A Portrait of the Artist as a Young Man*, p. 205. Further citations in text as *AP*.

25. Hirsch, *Modernism Revised*, provides an excellent discussion of the form/beauty question in Modernist literature.

26. James Joyce, *Ulysses*, 9:952–54. Further citations by chapter and line number.

27. The message encodes another meaning of translation: "to transmit (a telegraphic message) by means of an automatic repeated" (*O.E.D.*).

28. Senn uses translations as a model for reading Joyce's texts. He comments that "translating . . . means that something changes, becomes 'other' and often—very much—off the topic." See *Joyce's Dislocutions*, p. 24.

29. See Bernard Benstock, "James Joyce: The Olfactory Factor," and Süskind's novel *Perfume*, which examines the dominance of the olfactory in infancy and early childhood.

30. In French, sea/mother (*mer/mère*) and veil/sail (*le voile, la voile*) display homonymic and homophonic characteristics; the veil/sail distinction is apparent only by shifts of gender. These appear as May Dedalus's graveclothes and bridle veil, and the metonymic fluttering sail (referring both to Thetis and Helen) and Helen's rent veil.

31. These words appear only as metonymic "woodshadows" and are not quoted in the text. The allusion is to W. B. Yeats's "Who Goes with Fergus?," included as a song in the first version of Yeats's play, *The Countess Cathleen*. See Gifford with Seidman, *Notes for Joyce*, p. 10. For analysis of this poem as lyric, see Unterecker, *William Butler Yeats*, p. 82.

32. Note that Helen's "failed perfection" is displayed, as a spectacle, in front of her former lovers: Theseus sees her wounded feet and Paris sees her torn veil. In chap. 3 I provide a detailed reading of the relation between reading and rape in *Finnegans Wake*.

33. Se DuPlessis's analysis of Helen in reference to scrim and scrive, *H.D.*, p. 110; on style and stylus, see Derrida's *Spurs*.

34. The informing assumptions of textual editing deserve study, not only because editors are trained to "align" or "regularize" (or even "edit out") the textual features I discuss but because editing is a form of literary critical practice. I am grateful to Barbara Harlow for reminding me that editing is a most "traditional" of literary critical practices (letter of 27 April 1989). The process that engendered the "Critical and Synoptic Edition" of *Ulysses* has raised questions of authorship, censorship, and ownership of texts. For a synopsis of the debates around these issues, see *Ulysses: The Text*, *James Joyce Literary Supplement*, vol. 3, 1989.

35. Richard Ellmann, preface to Joyce, *Ulysses: The Corrected Text*, p. xii.

36. Manuscript versions of *Helen in Egypt* are in the American Literature Collection, Beinecke Library, Yale University. These words follow the line, "breathed differently." *Ulysses* 9.350 alludes to a famous riddle concern-

ing Achilles' name ("What name did Achilles bear when he lived among women?"). The riddle, which has no answer, refers to the time that Thetis dressed Achilles as a girl and sent him to live among women, in order to avoid his destined death in the Trojan War. The "riddling" of names, secret and unspoken, echoes silently in *Helen in Egypt*.

Epilogue

1. Joyce, *Ulysses*, 15.105–07; Kristeva, *Desire in Language*, p. 163.

2. These quotations are from Rose, *Sexuality*, p. 232. For a more detailed discussion of her statements, see chap. 1.

3. A more complex example of alphabet logic is apparent in Joyce's variant spelling of "Dedalus," which differs from the transliteration from the Greek, "Daedalus." The name of the mythic artificer is already a "translation" into English, and the changes from "ae" to "e" in Joyce's texts constructs a kind of *différance*—seen but not heard. Every time we read the printed name, the mythic Daedalus both is and is not invoked. Like Helen, Stephen exists between versions of his name.

4. See Walsh's analysis of Lacan's *Séminaire III, Les Psychoses*, in "Reading the Real," p. 69. Walsh comments that psychosis is "the madness of madness, the otherness of the other" (p. 64).

5. See Lacan, "Le Sinthome," and "Joyce le Symptôme."

6. Suzuki, *Metamorphoses of Helen*, p. 34.

7. Walsh, "Reading the Real," pp. 77–78. See also Kristeva's analysis of psychotic abreactions, *Desire in Language*, p. 240.

8. See Hogan, "Structure and Ambiguity," in Hogan and Pandit, *Lacan and Criticism*, pp. 18–19.

Selected Bibliography

Abraham, Nicolas, and Maria Torok. *L'Ecorce et le noyau*. Paris: Aubier-Montaigne, 1978.

Abrams, M. H. *A Glossary of Literary Terms*. Reprint. New York: Rinehart, 1959.

Allen, Walter. *The English Novel*. New York: Dutton, 1954.

Altman, Janet Gurkin. *Epistolarity: Approaches to a Form*. Columbus: Ohio State University Press, 1982.

André, Serge. *Que veut une femme?* Paris: Navarin, 1986.

Ardener, Edwin. "Belief and the Problem of Women." Pp. 1–17 in *Perceiving Women*, ed. Shirley Ardener. London: Malaby, 1975.

Ardener, Shirley, editor. *Perceiving Women*. London: Malaby, 1975.

Attridge, Derek, and Daniel Ferrer, editors. *Post-Structuralist Joyce: Essays from the French*. Cambridge: Cambridge University Press, 1984.

Aubert, Jacques. "riverrun." Pp. 69–78 in *Post-Structuralist Joyce*, ed. Derek Attridge and Daniel Ferrer. Cambridge: Cambridge University Press, 1984.

Aubert, Jacques, and Maria Jolas, editors. *Joyce et Paris: 1902 . . . 1920– 1940 . . . 1975*. Paris: Éditions du CNRS, 1979.

Barnet, Sylvan, et al., editors. *A Dictionary of Literary, Dramatic, and Cinematic Terms*. 2d ed. Boston: Little, Brown, 1971.

Barr, Marleen S., and Richard Feldstein, editors. *Discontented Discourses: Feminism, Textual Intervention, Psychoanalysis*. Urbana: University of Illinois Press, 1989.

Barreno, Maria Isabelle, Marie Teresa Horta, and Maria Velho da Costa, *The Three Marias: New Portuguese Letters*, trans. Helen R. Lane. New York: Bantam, 1976.

Barthes, Roland. *A Lover's Discourse*, trans. Richard Howard. New York: Hill & Wang, 1978.

Bass, Ellen, and Laura Davis, editors. *The Courage to Heal: A Guide for Women Survivors of Child Sexual Abuse*. New York: Harper & Row, 1988.

Beauvoir, Simone de. *The Second Sex*, trans. H. M. Parshley. New York: Knopf, 1953.

Bell, Quentin. *Virginia Woolf: A Biography*. 2 vols. New York: Harcourt Brace Jovanovich, 1972.

Selected Bibliography

Benstock, Bernard. "James Joyce: The Olfactory Factor." In *Joycean Occasions: Selected Essays from the 1987 James Joyce Milwaukee Conference.* ed. Janet E. Dunleavy et al. Newark, Del.: University of Delaware Press, 1991.

————. *Joyce-again's Wake.* Seattle: University of Washington Press, 1965.

Benstock, Bernard, editor. *James Joyce: The Augmented Ninth.* Syracuse, N.Y.: Syracuse University Press, 1988.

Benstock, Shari. "Beyond the Reaches of Feminist Criticism: A Letter from Paris." Pp. 7–29 in *Feminist Issues in Literary Scholarship*, ed. Shari Benstock. Bloomington: Indiana University Press, 1987.

————. "Expatriate Modernism: Writing on the Cultural Rim." Pp. 19–40 in *Women's Writing in Exile*, ed. Mary Lynn Broe and Angela Ingram. Chapel Hill: University of North Carolina Press, 1989.

————. "On the Margin of Discourse: Footnotes in the Fictional Text." *PMLA* 93 (1983): 204–25.

————. *Women of the Left Bank: Paris, 1900–1940.* Austin: University of Texas Press, 1986.

Benstock, Shari, editor. *Feminist Issues in Literary Scholarship.* Bloomington: Indiana University Press, 1987.

Benstock, Shari, and Bernard Benstock. *Modernism Made Manifest: The Impact of Periodical Publication, 1890–1940.* Austin: University of Texas Press, forthcoming.

Benstock, Shari, and Suzanne Ferriss. *Analyzing Style: Fashion as Textual and Material Construct.* Forthcoming.

Bishop, John. *Joyce's Book of the Dark.* Madison: University of Wisconsin Press, 1986.

Bleier, *Science and Gender: A Critique of Biology and Its Theories of Women.* New York: Pergamon, 1984.

Bridgman, Richard. *Gertrude Stein in Pieces.* New York: Oxford University Press, 1970.

Broe, Mary Lynn, and Angela Ingram, editors. *Women's Writing in Exile.* Chapel Hill: University of North Carolina Press, 1989.

Cantarella, Eva. "Dangling Virgins: Myth, Ritual, and the Place of Women in Ancient Greece." Pp. 57–67 in *The Female Body in Western Culture*, ed. Susan Rubin Suleiman. Cambridge: Harvard University Press, 1986.

Castle, Terry. *Clarissa's Ciphers: Meaning and Disruption in Richardson's Clarissa.* Ithaca, N.Y.: Cornell University Press, 1982.

Chisholm, Dianne. *H.D.'s Freudian Poetics: Psychoanalysis in Translation.* Ithaca, N.Y.: Cornell University Press, 1992.

Cixous, Hélène. "Castration or Decapitation," trans. Annette Kuhn. *Signs* 7 (1981): 36–55.

————. *The Exile of James Joyce*, trans. Sally A. J. Purcell. New York: David Lewis, 1972.

————. "The Laugh of the Medusa," trans. Keith Cohen and Paula Cohen. Pp. 279–97 in *The Signs Reader: Women, Gender and Scholarship*, ed. Elizabeth Abel and Emily K. Abel. Chicago: University of Chicago Press, 1983.

Crystal, David, editor. *The Cambridge Encyclopedia of Language.* Cambridge: Cambridge University Press, 1987.

Selected Bibliography

Culler, Jonathan. *The Pursuit of Signs*. Ithaca, N.Y.: Cornell University Press, 1981.

Culleton, Claire. "Gender-Charged Munitions: The Language of World War I Munitions Reports." *Women's Studies International Forum* 11 (1988): 23–32.

Day, Robert Adams. *Told in Letters*. Ann Arbor: University of Michigan Press, 1966.

Dayan, Joan. "The Analytic of the Dash: Poe's *Eureka*," *Genre* 16 (Winter 1983): 437–66.

DeKoven, Marianne. "Gertrude Stein and the Modernist Canon." Pp. 8–20 in *Gertrude Stein and the Making of Literature*, ed. Shirley Neuman and Ira B. Nadel. Boston: Northeastern University Press, 1988.

De Man, Paul. *Allegories of Reading*. New Haven, Conn.: Yale University Press, 1979.

Derrida, Jacques. *La Carte Postale: De Socrate à Freud et au-delà*. Paris: Flammarion, 1980.

———. "Confrontation, 'Les Fantômes de la psychanalyse'" *Cahiers* 8 (1982).

———. *Dissemination*, trans. Barbara Johnson. Chicago: University of Chicago Press, 1981.

———. "Du Tout." Pp. 497–521 in *The Post Card: From Socrates to Freud and Beyond*, trans. Alan Bass. Chicago: University of Chicago Press, 1987.

———. *The Ear of the Other*, ed. Christie McDonald, and trans. Peggy Kamuf. Lincoln: University of Nebraska Press, 1988.

———. *Feu la cendre*. Paris: Editions des Femmes, 1987.

———. "Fors," trans. Barbara Johnson. *Georgia Review* 31 (Spring 1977): 64–116.

———. "Freud and the Scene of Writing." Pp. 196–231 in *Writing and Difference*, trans. Alan Bass. Chicago: University of Chicago Press, 1978.

———. "Freud's Legacy." Pp. 292–337. *The Post Card: From Socrates to Freud and Beyond*, trans. Alan Bass. Chicago: University of Chicago Press, 1987.

———. "*Geopsychanalyse* 'and the rest of the world.'" Pp. 327–52 in *Psyche: Inventions de l'autre*. Paris: Galilee, 1987.

———. *Glas*, trans. John P. Leavey, Jr., and Richard Rand. Lincoln: University of Nebraska Press, 1986.

———. "The Heritage of the Pharmakon: Family Scene." Pp. 142–55 in *Dissemination*, trans. Barbara Johnson. Chicago: University of Chicago Press, 1981.

———. "The Law of Genre/*La Loi du genre*," trans. Avital Ronnell. *Glyph* 7 (1980): 202–32.

———. "Le facteur de la vérité." Pp. 411–96 in *The Post Card: From Socrates to Freud and Beyond*, trans. Alan Bass. Chicago: University of Chicago Press, 1987.

———. *Of Grammatology*, trans. Gayatri Spivak. Baltimore: Johns Hopkins University Press, 1974.

———. *Positions*, trans. Alan Bass. Chicago: University of Chicago Press, 1981.

Selected Bibliography

————. *The Post Card: From Socrates to Freud and Beyond*, trans. Alan Bass. Chicago: University of Chicago Press, 1987.

————. *Psyche: Inventions de l'autre*. Paris: Galilee: 1987.

————. "The Purveyor of Truth," trans. Alan Bass. Pp. 173–212 in *The Purloined Poe*, ed. John P. Muller and William J. Richardson. Baltimore: Johns Hopkins University Press, 1988.

————. *Speech and Phenomena and Other Essays on Husserl's Theory of Signs*, trans. David B. Allison and Newton Garver. Evanston, Ill.: Northwestern University Press, 1973.

————. *Spurs: Nietzsche's Styles*, trans. Barbara Harlow. Chicago: University of Chicago Press, 1979.

————. "To Speculate—on Freud." Pp. 257–409, in *The Post Card*, trans. Alan Bass. Chicago: University of Chicago Press, 1987.

————. "Two Words for Joyce," trans. Geoff Bennington. Pp. 145–59 in *Post-Structuralist Joyce*, edited by Derek Attridge and Daniel Ferrer. Cambridge: Cambridge University Press, 1984.

————. "*Ulysses* Gramophone: Hear say yes in Joyce," trans. Shari Benstock. Pp. 27–75 in *James Joyce: The Augmented Ninth*, ed. Bernard Benstock. Syracuse, N.Y.: Syracuse University Press, 1988.

————. *Writing and Difference*, trans. Alan Bass. Chicago: University of Chicago Press, 1978.

DeSalvo, Louise. *Virginia Woolf: The Impact of Childhood Sexual Abuse on Her Life and Work*. Boston: Beacon, 1989.

DeSalvo, Louise, and Mitchell A. Leaska, editors. *The Letters of Vita Sackville-West to Virginia Woolf*. New York: Morrow, 1985.

Devlin, Kimberly J. *Wandering and Return in Finnegans Wake: An Integrative Approach to Joyce's Fictions*. Princeton, N.J.: Princeton University Press, 1991.

DuBois, Page. "Antigone and the Feminist Critic." *Genre, Literature as Women's History I*, 19 (Winter 1986): 370–83.

————. *Sowing the Body*. Chicago: University of Chicago Press, 1988.

Dunleavy, Janet E., Melvin J. Friedman, and Michael Patrick Gillespie, editors. *Joycean Occasions: Selected Essays from the 1987 James Joyce Milwaukee Conference*. Newark, Del.: University of Delaware Press, 1991.

DuPlessis, Rachel Blau. *H.D.: The Career of That Struggle*. Bloomington: Indiana University Press, 1986.

Dydo, Ulla. "Gertrude Stein: Composition as Meditation." Pp. 42–60 in *Gertrude Stein and the Making of Literature*, ed. Shirley Neuman and Ira B. Nadel. Boston: Northeastern University Press, 1988.

Eagleton, Terry. *The Rape of Clarissa: Writing, Sexuality and Class Struggle in Samuel Richardson*. Minneapolis: University of Minnesota Press, 1982.

Eliot, T. S. *Collected Poems 1909–1962*. New York: Harcourt Brace, 1963.

Elliot, Patricia. *From Mastery to Analysis: Theories of Gender in Psychoanalytic Feminism*. Ithaca, N.Y.: Cornell University Press, 1991.

Ellmann, Richard. *James Joyce*. Rev. ed. New York: Oxford University Press, 1982.

Elshtain, Jean Bethke. "Feminist Discourse and Its Discontents: Language, Power, and Meaning." *Signs* 7 (1982): 603–21.

Selected Bibliography

Felman, Shoshana. "Turning the Screw of Interpretation." *Yale French Studies* 55/56 (1977): 94–207.

Fifer, Elizabeth. "Is Flesh Advisable? The Interior Theater of Gertrude Stein." *Signs* 4 (Spring 1979): 472–83.

Freud, Sigmund. *Beyond the Pleasure Principle. Standard Edition*, vol. 18.

———. "Note on the Mystic Writing-Pad." *Standard Edition*, vol. 19.

———. "Some Psychical Consequences of the Anatomical Distinction Between the Sexes." *Standard Edition*, vol. 19.

———. *Standard Edition*, ed. and trans. James Strachey. 24 vols. London: Hogarth, 1953–74.

Friedman, Susan Stanford. *Psyche Reborn: The Emergence of H.D.* Bloomington: Indiana University Press, 1981.

———. "Who Buried H.D.? A Poet, Her Critics, and Her Place in the Literary Tradition." *College English* 36 (1975): 801–14.

Garvin, John. *James Joyce's Disunited Kingdom.* Dublin: Gill & Macmillan, 1976.

Gifford, Don, with Robert J. Seidman. *Notes for Joyce.* New York: Dutton, 1974.

Gimbutas, Maria. *The Goddess and Gods of Old Europe, 6500–3500 B.C.: Myths and Cult Images.* Berkeley: University of California Press, 1982.

Graves, Robert. *The Greek Myths.* Mt. Kisco, N.Y.: Moyer Bell, 1988.

Grosz, Elizabeth. *Jacques Lacan: A Feminist Introduction.* London and New York: Routledge, 1990.

Gubar, Susan. " 'The Blank Page' and Issues of Female Creativity," *Critical Inquiry* 8 (Winter 1981): 243–63.

Heath, Stephen. "Ambiviolences: Notes for Reading Joyce." Pp. 31–68 in *Post-Structuralist Joyce*, ed. Derek Attridge and Daniel Ferrer. Cambridge: Cambridge University Press, 1984.

H.D. *Helen in Egypt.* New York: New Directions, 1961.

———. *Hermione.* New York: New Directions, 1981.

Herr, Cheryl. "Fathers, Daughters, Anxiety, and Fiction." Pp. 173–207 in *Discontented Discourses: Feminism, Textual Intervention, Psychoanalysis*, ed. Marleen S. Barr and Richard Feldstein. Urbana: University of Illinois Press, 1989.

Hirsch, Elizabeth. *Modernism Revised: Formalism and the Feminine.* Ithaca, N.Y.: Cornell University Press, 1991.

Hogan, Patrick Colm, and Lalita Pandit, editors. *Lacan and Criticism: Essays and Dialogue on Language, Structure, and the Unconscious.* Athens: University of Georgia Press, 1990.

Irigaray, Luce. *Speculum of the Other Woman*, trans. Gillian C. Gill. Ithaca: Cornell University Press, 1985.

———. *This Sex Which Is Not One*, trans. Catherine Porter. Ithaca, N.Y.: Cornell University Press, 1985.

Jacobus, Mary, editor. *Women Writing and Writing about Women.* New York: Barnes & Noble, 1979.

Jardine, Alice. "Gynesis." *Diacritics* 12 (1982): 54–65.

———. *Gynesis: Configurations of Woman and Modernity.* Ithaca, N.Y.: Cornell University Press, 1985.

Selected Bibliography

Jay, Gregory S., and David Miller, editors. *After Strange Texts: The Role of Theory in the Study of Literature*. University: University of Alabama Press, 1985.

Johnson, Barbara. *The Critical Difference*. Baltimore: Johns Hopkins University Press, 1979.

———. "Fors." *Georgia Review* 31 (Spring 1977): 64–116.

———. "The Frame of Reference: Poe, Lacan, Derrida." Pp. 213–52 in *The Purloined Poe*, ed. John P. Muller and William J. Richardson. Baltimore: Johns Hopkins University Press, 1988.

———. *A World of Difference*. Baltimore: Johns Hopkins University Press, 1987.

Joyce, James. *Finnegans Wake*. New York: Viking, 1947.

———. *A Portrait of the Artist as a Young Man*. New York: Viking, 1964.

———. *Ulysses: The Corrected Text*, ed. Hans Walter Gabler with Wolfhard Steppe and Claus Melchior. New York: Vintage, 1986.

Kamuf, Peggy. *Fictions of Feminine Desire*. Lincoln: University of Nebraska Press, 1982.

———. "Hawthorne's Genres: The Letter of the Law *Appliquée*." Pp. 69–84 in *After Strange Texts: The Role of Theory in the Study of Literature*, ed. Gregory S. Jay and David L. Miller. Tuscaloosa: University of Alabama Press, 1985.

———. *Signature Pieces: On the Institution of Authorship*. Ithaca, N.Y.: Cornell University Press, 1988.

———. "Writing as a Woman." Pp. 284–99 in *Women and Language in Literature and Society*, ed. Sally McConnell-Ginet et al. New York: Praeger, 1980.

Kauffman, Linda S. *Discourses of Desire: Gender, Genre, and Epistolary Fictions*. Ithaca, N.Y.: Cornell University Press, 1986.

Kloepfer, Deborah Kelly. *The Unspeakable Mother: Forbidden Discourse in Jean Rhys and H.D.* Ithaca: Cornell University Press, 1989.

Kristeva, Julia. *Desire in Language*, trans. Leon S. Roudiez et al. New York: Columbia University Press, 1980.

———. "Ellipsis on Dread and the Specular Seduction," trans. Dolores Burdick. *Wide Angle* 3 (1979).

———. "On Melancholy Imaginary." Unpublished paper delivered at Dartmouth School of Criticism and Theory, June 1989.

———. *Revolution and Poetic Language*, trans. Margaret Waller. New York: Columbia University Press, 1984.

———. "Stabat Mater." Pp. 234–63 in *Tales of Love*, trans. Leon S. Roudiez. New York: Columbia University Press, 1987.

———. *Tales of Love*, trans. Leon S. Roudiez. New York: Columbia University Press, 1987.

———. "Woman Can Never Be Defined," trans. Marilyn A. August. Pp. 137–41 in *New French Feminisms*, ed. Elaine Marks and Isabelle de Courtivron. New York: Schocken, 1981.

Krupnick, Mark, editor. *Displacement: Derrida and After*. Bloomington: Indiana University Press, 1987.

Lacan, Jacques. "The Agency of the Letter in the Unconscious." Pp. 146–78 in *Ecrits: A Selection*, ed. and trans. Alan Sheridan. New York: Norton, 1977.

———. "Aggressivity in Psychoanalysis." Pp. 8–29 in *Ecrits: A Selection*, ed. and trans. Alan Sheridan. New York: Norton, 1977.

———. "Desire, Life and Death," trans. Sylvana Tomaselli. Pp. 221–34 in *The Seminar of Jacques Lacan, Book II*, ed. Jacques-Alain Miller. New York: Norton, 1988.

———. *Ecrits*. Paris: Editions du Seuil, 1966.

———. *Ecrits: A Selection*, ed. and trans. Alan Sheridan. New York: Norton, 1977.

———. *The Four Fundamental Concepts*, ed. Jacques-Alain Miller and trans. Alan Sheridan. New York: Norton, 1978.

———. "The Function and Field of Speech and Language in Psychoanalysis." Pp. 30–113 in *Ecrits: A Selection*, ed. and trans. Alan Sheridan. New York: Norton, 1977.

———. "God and the *Jouissance* of The Woman: A Love Letter," trans. Jacqueline Rose. Pp. 137–48 in *Feminine Sexuality: Jacques Lacan and the Ecole Freudienne*, ed. Juliet Mitchell and Jacqueline Rose. New York: Norton, 1985.

———. "Guiding Remarks for a Congress on Feminine Sexuality," trans. Jacqueline Rose. Pp. 86–98 in *Feminine Sexuality: Jacques Lacan and the Ecole Freudienne*, ed. Juliet Mitchell and Jacqueline Rose. New York: Norton, 1985.

———. "Introduction of the Big Other," trans. Sylvana Tomaselli. Pp. 235–47 in *The Seminar of Jacques Lacan*, Book II, ed. Jacques-Alain Miller. New York: Norton, 1988.

———. "Joyce *le symptome*." Pp. 13–17 in *Joyce et Paris*, ed. Jacques Aubert and Maria Jolas. Paris: Editions du CNRS, 1979.

———. "The Mirror Stage as Formative of the Function of the I as Revealed in Psychoanalytic Experience." Pp. 1–7 in *Ecrits: A Selection*, ed. and trans. Alan Sheridan. New York: Norton, 1977.

———. "The Phallic Phase and the Subjective Import of the Castration Complex," trans. Jacqueline Rose. Pp. 99–122 in *Feminine Sexuality: Jacques Lacan and the Ecole Freudienne*, ed. Juliet Mitchell and Jacqueline Rose. New York: Norton, 1985.

———. *Le Séminaire de Jacques Lacan, III: Les Psychoses*. Paris: Editions du Seuil, 1981.

———. *Le Séminaire de Jacques Lacan, XI*. Paris: Editions du Seuil, 1981.

———. *Le Séminaire de Jacques Lacan, XX: Encore*. Paris: Editions du Seuil, 1975.

———. "Le Séminaire de Jacques Lacan: XXI, 'Les Non-Dupes errent,' 1973–1974." Unpublished papers.

———. *The Seminar of Jacques Lacan, Book I: Freud's Papers on Technique, 1953–1955*, ed. Jacques-Alain Miller and trans. John Forrester. New York: Norton, 1988.

———. *The Seminar of Jacques Lacan, Book II: The Ego in Freud's Theory and in the Technique of Psychoanalysis, 1954–1955*, ed. Jacques-Alain Miller and trans. Sylvana Tomaselli. New York: Norton, 1988.

———. "The Seminar on 'The Purloined Letter,'" trans. Jeffrey Mehlman. Pp. 28–54 in *The Purloined Poe*, ed. John P. Muller and William J. Richardson. Baltimore: Johns Hopkins University Press, 1988.

———. "Seminar of 21 January 1975," trans. Jacqueline Rose. Pp. 162–71 in *Feminine Sexuality: Jacques Lacan and the Ecole Freudienne*, ed. Juliet Mitchell and Jacqueline Rose. New York: Norton, 1985.

———. "The Signification of the Phallus." Pp. 281–91 in *Ecrits: A Selection*, ed. and trans. Alan Sheridan. New York: Norton, 1977.

———. "*Le Sinthome*," *Ornicar?* 7 (June-July 1976): 3–18.

———. "The Subversion of the Subject and the Dialectic of Desire." Pp. 292–325 in *Ecrits: A Selection*, ed. and trans. Alan Sheridan. New York: Norton, 1977.

———. "Le Symbolique, l'Imaginaire et le Réel," Paper presented at the Conférence à la Société française de psychanalyse, July 1953.

———. *Télévision*. Paris: Editions du Seuil, 1973.

Langbauer, Laurie. *Women and Romance: The Consolations of Gender in the English Novel*. Ithaca, N.Y.: Cornell University Press, 1990.

Leclaire, Serge. *Psychanalyser: Un essai sur l'ordre de l'inconscient et la pratique de la lettre*. Paris: Editions du Seuil, 1968.

Lemaire, Anika. *Jacques Lacan*, trans. David Macey. New York: Routledge, Chapman and Hall, 1977.

Lernout, Geert. *The French Joyce*. Ann Arbor: University of Michigan Press, 1990.

———. "Joyce or Lacan." Pp. 195–203 in *James Joyce: The Augmented Ninth*, ed. Bernard Benstock. Syracuse, N.Y.: Syracuse University Press, 1988.

Liedloff, Jean. *The Continuum Concept*. New York: Basic Books, 1977.

Macey, David. *Lacan in Contexts*. New York: Verso, 1988.

Marcus, Jane. *Art and Anger: Reading like a Woman*. Columbus: Ohio State University Press, 1988.

———. "Corpus/Corps/Corpse: Writing the Body In/At War." Afterword to Helen Zenna Smith, *Not So Quiet . . . .* 1930. Reprint. New York: Feminist Press, 1989.

———. "Sapphistry: Narration as Lesbian Seduction in *A Room of One's Own*." Pp. 163–87 in *Virginia Woolf and the Languages of Patriarchy*. Bloomington: Indiana University Press, 1987.

———. *Virginia Woolf and the Languages of Patriarchy*. Bloomington: Indiana University Press, 1987.

———, editor. *Virginia Woolf: A Feminist Slant*. Lincoln: University of Nebraska Press, 1983.

Marks, Elaine, and Isabelle de Courtivron, editors. *New French Feminisms*. New York: Schocken, 1981.

McConnell-Ginet, Sally, et al., editors. *Women and Language in Literature and Society*. New York: Praeger, 1980.

McGee, Patrick. "Woolf's Other: The University in Her Eye." *Novel* 23 (Spring 1990): 229–46.

McHugh, Roland. *The Sigla of Finnegans Wake*. London: Edward Arnold, 1976.

Selected Bibliography

Meisel, Perry. *The Absent Father: Virginia Woolf and Walter Pater*. New Haven, Conn.: Yale University Press, 1980.

Miller, Alice. *For Your Own Good: Hidden Cruelty in Child-Rearing and the Roots of Violence*, trans. Hildegarde Hannum and Hunter Hannum. New York: Farrar Straus Giroux, 1983.

———. *Thou Shalt Not Be Aware: Society's Betrayal of the Child*, trans. Hildegarde Hannum and Hunter Hannum. New York: New American Library, 1986.

Miller, Jacques-Alain. "Another Lacan." *Lacan Study Notes* 1 (February 1984): 3.

Miller, Nancy K. "The Exquisite Cadavers: Women in Eighteenth-Century Fiction." *Diacritics* 4 (1975): 37–43.

———. "Female Sexuality and Narrative Structure in *La Nouvelle Hélöise* and *Les Liaisons dangereuses*." *Signs* 1 (1976): 609–38.

———. *The Heroine's Text: Readings in the French and English Novel, 1722–1782*. New York: Columbia University Press, 1980.

———. "'I's' in Drag: The Sex of Recollection." *Eighteenth Century* 22 (1981): 47–57.

Miller, Nancy K., editor. *The Poetics of Gender*. New York: Columbia University Press, 1986.

Mink, Louis O. *A Finnegans Wake Gazeteer*. Bloomington: Indiana University Press, 1978.

Mitchell, Juliet. "Introduction I." In *Feminine Sexuality: Jacques Lacan and the École Freudienne*. New York: Norton, 1985.

Mitchell, Juliet, and Jacqueline Rose, editors. *Feminine Sexuality: Jacques Lacan and the École Freudienne*. New York: Norton, 1985.

Moi, Toril. *The Kristeva Reader*. Oxford: Basil Blackwell, 1986.

———. *Sexual/Textual Politics: Feminist Literary Theory*. New York: Methuen, 1985.

Montrelay, Michèle. "The Story of Louise." Pp. 75–93 in *Returning to Freud: Clinical Psychoanalysis in the School of Lacan*, ed. and trans. Stuart Schneiderman. New Haven, Conn.: Yale University Press, 1980.

Muller, John P., and William J. Richardson, editors. *The Purloined Poe: Lacan, Derrida, and Psychoanalytic Reading*. Baltimore: Johns Hopkins University Press, 1988.

Neuman, Shirley, and Ira B. Nadel, editors. *Gertrude Stein and the Making of Literature*. Boston: Northeastern University Press, 1988.

Period Styles: A History of Punctuation. Exhibition Catalog. New York: Cooper Union for the Advancement of Science and Art, 1988.

Perry, Ruth. *Women, Letters, and the Novel*. New York: AMS Press, 1980.

Prince, Morton. *The Dissociation of a Personality: A Biographical Study in Abnormal Psychology*. 1905. Reprint. New York: Greenwood, 1989.

Rabine, Leslie. "A Woman's Two Bodies: The Ambiguities of Fashion." In *Analyzing Style: Fashion as Textual and Material Construct*, ed. Shari Benstock and Suzanne Ferriss. Forthcoming.

Radice, Betty, trans. *Letters of Heloise and Abelard*. Baltimore: Penguin, 1974.

Ragland-Sullivan, Ellie. *Jacques Lacan and the Philosophy of Psychoanalysis*. Urbana: University of Illinois Press, 1986.

Selected Bibliography

Riviere, Joan. "Womanliness as Mascarade." *International Journal of Psychoanalysis* 10 (1929): 303–13.

Rose, Jacqueline. *Sexuality in the Field of Vision*. New York: Verso, 1986.

Rousseau, Jean-Jacques. *Confessions*, trans. S. B. Glover. New York: Heritage, 1955.

———. *Julie, ou la nouvelle Héloïse*. Paris: Garnier, 1915.

Ruddick, Lisa. *Reading Gertrude Stein: Body, Text, Gnosis*. Ithaca, N.Y.: Cornell University Press, 1990.

Saussure, Ferdinand de. *Cours de la linguistique générale*. 1915. Reprint. Paris: Payot, 1963.

Schneiderman, Stuart. "Art as Symptom: A Psychoanalytic Study of Art." Pp. 207–22 in *Lacan and Criticism*, ed. Patrick Colm Hogan and Lalita Pandit. Athens: University of Georgia Press, 1990.

———, ed. and trans. *Returning to Freud: Clinical Psychoanalysis in the School of Lacan*. New Haven, Conn.: Yale University Press, 1980.

Schor, Naomi. *Breaking the Chain: Women, Theory, and French Realist Fiction*. New York: Columbia University Press, 1985.

Sedgwick, Eve Kosofsky. *Between Men: English Literature and Male Homosocial Desire*. New York: Columbia University Press, 1985.

Senn, Fritz. *Joyce's Dislocutions*. Baltimore: Johns Hopkins University Press, 1984.

Showalter, Elaine. "Feminist Criticism in the Wilderness." *Critical Inquiry* 8 (Winter 1981): 179–206.

———. "Towards a Feminist Poetics." Pp. 22–41 in *Women Writing and Writing about Women*, ed. Mary Jacobus. New York: Barnes & Noble, 1979.

Silver, Brenda R. "*Three Guineas* Before and After: Further Answers to Correspondents." Pp. 254–76 in *Virginia Woolf: A Feminist Slant*, ed. Jane Marcus. Lincoln: University of Nebraska Press, 1983.

Silverman, Kaja. *The Accoustic Mirror: The Female Voice in Psychoanalysis and Cinema*. Bloomington: Indiana University Press, 1988.

Simkins, Scott. "The Agency of the Title: *Finnegans Wake*," *James Joyce Quarterly* 27, 4 (Summer 1990): 735–43.

Simon, Linda. *The Biography of Alice B. Toklas*. Garden City, N.Y.: Doubleday, 1977.

Singer, Godfrey Frank. *The Epistolary Novel*. New York: Russell, 1963.

Sollers, Philippe. "*Comme si le vieil Homère*," *Le Nouvel Observateur*, 6 February 1982.

Sophocles. *Antigone*. *Norton Anthology of World Masterpieces*. Vol. 1, 5th ed. ed. Maynard Mack et al. New York: Norton, 1985.

Spivak, Gayatri Chakravorty. "Displacement and the Discourse of Woman." Pp. 169–95 in *Displacement: Derrida and After*, ed. Mark Krupnick. Bloomington: Indiana University Press, 1987.

———. *In Other Worlds: Essays in Cultural Politics*. New York and London: Methuen, 1987.

———. "Love Me, Love My Ombre, Elle." *Diacritics* 14 (Winter 1984): 19–36.

Spivak, Gayatri Chakravorty, with Ellen Rooney. "In a Word, *Interview*." *Differences* 2 (1989): 124–56.

Selected Bibliography

Stanton, Domna C. "Difference on Trial: A Critique of the Maternal Metaphor in Cixous, Irigaray, and Kristeva." Pp. 157–82 in *The Poetics of Gender*, ed. Nancy K. Miller. New York: Columbia University Press, 1986.

Stein, Gertrude. *How to Write*. Reprint. 1931. New York: Dover, 1975.

———. "Melanctha." In *Three Lives*. New York: Vintage, 1936.

———. "Yet Dish." In *The Yale Gertrude Stein*, cd. Richard Kostelanetz. New Haven, Conn.: Yale University Press, 1980.

Stimpson, Catharine R. "Gertrude Stein and the Transposition of Gender." Pp. 1–18 in *The Poetics of Gender*, ed. Nancy K. Miller. New York: Columbia University Press, 1986.

———. "The Mind, the Body, and Gertrude Stein." *Critical Inquiry* 3 (Spring 1977): 498–506.

———. "The Somagrams of Gertrude Stein." Pp. 30–43 in *The Female Body in Western Literature*, ed. Susan Rubin Suleiman. Cambridge: Harvard University Press, 1986.

Suleiman, Susan Rubin, editor. *The Female Body in Western Culture*. Cambridge: Harvard University Press, 1986.

Süskind, Patrick. *Perfume*, trans. John E. Woods. New York: Pocket Books, 1987.

Suzuki, Mihoko. *Metamorphoses of Helen: Authority and Difference in Homer, Virgil, Spenser, and Shakespeare*. Ithaca, N.Y.: Cornell University Press, 1989.

Todorov, Tzvetan. "Postmodernism, a Primer." *New Republic*, 20 May 1990, pp. 32–35.

Ulmer, Gregory L. *Applied Grammatology*. Baltimore: Johns Hopkins University Press, 1985.

———. "The Post-Age." *Diacritics* 11 (1981): 39–56.

Unterecker, John. *William Butler Yeats*. New York: Noonday, 1959.

Walsh, Michael. "Reading the Real in the Seminar on the Psychoses." Pp. 64–83 in *Lacan and Criticism*, ed. Patrick Colm Hogan and Lalita Pandit. Athens: University of Georgia Press, 1990.

Warner, William Beatty. "Reading Rape." *Diacritics* 13 (1983): 12–32.

Watt, Ian. *The Rise of the Novel*. Berkeley: University of California Press, 1957.

Weber, Samuel. "The Divericator: Remarks on Freud's *Witz*." *Glyph* 1 (1977).

Wilden, Anthony. *Speech and Language in Psychoanalysis*. Baltimore: Johns Hopkins University Press, 1968.

Willis, Sharon. "Feminism's Interrupted Genealogies." *Diacritics* 18 (Spring 1988): 29–41.

Wittig, Monique. "The Mark of Gender." Pp. 63–73 in *The Poetics of Gender*, ed. Nancy K. Miller. New York: Columbia University Press, 1986.

Wood, Michael. *In Search of the Trojan War*. New York: New American Library, 1985.

Woolf, Virginia. *The Diary of Virginia Woolf, 1931–1935*. Vol. 4, ed. Anne Olivier Bell, assisted by Andrew McNeillie. New York: Harcourt Brace Jovanovich, 1982.

———. *The Diary of Virginia Woolf, 1936–1941*. Vol. 5, ed. Anne Olivier

Selected Bibliography

Bell, assisted by Andrew McNeillie. New York: Harcourt Brace Jovanovich, 1984.

————. *The Letters of Virginia Woolf, 1936–1941*. Vol. 6, ed. Nigel Nicolson and Joanne Trautmann. New York: Harcourt Brace Jovanovich, 1980.

————. *Flush: A Biography*. New York: Harcourt Brace, 1933.

————. *A Room of One's Own*. New York: Harcourt Brace, 1929.

————. *Three Guineas*. New York: Harcourt Brace, 1938.

Index

Address: 58, 62, 65, 70, 81, 88, 93–
95, 97–98, 102–103, 108–11,
119–21, 142, 147, 149, 153, 172,
212n., 220n.
Aggressivity: 34; *see also* drives
Antigone: 123–28, 130, 133–36,
160–61
Apostrophe: 45, 49, 51, 52, 54, 60,
62–67, 71–72, 77, 79, 84–85,
108, 116, 136, 143, 172, 189,
210n., 213n., 214n., 219n.
Ardener, Edwin: 134, 222n.
Authority (masculine): 55–58, 61,
68–69, 77, 78, 103–104, 108,
120–21, 131, 142, 149, 152, 154

Babel: 56, 212; babelization, 66, 68
Barthes, Roland: 100, 101, 102, 113
Beauvoir, Simone de: 10
Bellini, Giovanni: 40–41, 43
Body: 24, 27–28, 33—36, 39–40,
42, 89, 112, 126, 143, 202n.,
207n., 210n.; maternal, 36, 38–
40, 43–44; textual, 27, 43; woman's, 23, 54, 78–79, 81, 115,
118–19, 124, 139, 185–86,
215n.; *see also* textuality
Breaching: 20; *see also* trace

Castration: 12, 15, 26–27, 29–31,
38, 129, 192, 202n., 204n., 205n.
Censorship: 58, 102–103, 113, 115–
16, 118, 139, 165, 228n.
Chora: 41 (defined), 206n., 207n.,
208n., 209n., 210n.
Cixous, Hélène: 36, 105, 198n.;
"The Laugh of the Medusa," 36
Cognition: 5
Culler, Jonathan: 51, 213n.

Day, Robert Adams, 120
Death warrant: 94, 104, 106, 109–
10, 133, 218n., 219n.
De-composition: 18
De Man, Paul: 114
Demand: 203n.
Derrida, Jacques: 3–7, 14–20, 46,
71, 163–64, 167, 197n., 198n.;
The Post Card, 45, 86–122
Desire: 10, 11 (defined), 12, 14, 17–
18, 21–22, 29, 38, 54–55, 168,
172, 175–76, 182, 187, 202n.,
203n., 208n., 209n., 215n.; desire
(lower case), 11 (defined), 12, 29,
37, 39, 45, 55, 57–59, 61–62,
64, 75, 77, 82, 88, 90—93, 96–
98, 100, 102–103, 107, 110–15,
118, 121–22, 125, 142, 144, 154,

Index

168, 176, 182–83, 187–88, 195, 203n., 216n., 219n., 220n.

Devlin, Kimberly J.: 212n.

Dictation: 58, 89, 104, 106–107, 109–10, 122

Dissemination: 72, 218n., 219n.

Doubles: 54, 56–59, 61, 66–67, 72–73, 76, 79, 84, 104–105, 108, 112–13, 115, 117–18, 122, 125, 131, 135, 142, 147, 155–56, 165, 174, 176, 178, 186, 218n., 220n.; writing doubles, 88, 116; double message, 97

Dreams: 5, 10, 38, 53–54, 56, 58, 59–60, 72, 116, 167, 169, 176, 182, 184, 186, 203n., 212n.; dream structure, 53

Drives: 24, 27, 28, 33, 42, 207n., 208n.; anal, 29, 34, 37, 208n.; death drive, 31–34, 89; invocatory, 29; oral, 29, 33, 34, 35, 37, 208n.; scopic, 29; urethral, 33, 34

DuBois, Page: 127–36, 162, 221n., 225n.

DuPlessis, Rachel Blau: 186

Economics: 137–38, 143–45, 147–49, 157

Ecriture féminine: 105, 194

Editing: 228n.

Ellipses: 45, 53, 121, 123–62, 140 (defined), 222n., 223n., 224n.

Enceinte: 42, 43

Epic: 178, 179, 180–81, 185; *see also* genre

Epistolarity: 212n., 215n.; amorous epistolary discourse, 89, 90, 92, 94–97, 111, 219n.; epistolary fiction, 86, 88, 93–94, 98, 100–102, 104, 107, 110, 113–15, 118–19, 122, 137–38, 216n., 219n.; law of epistolarity, 86–89, 116

Fantasy: 14–17, 33, 35, 37–38, 41, 43, 101

Fathers, Law of: 124–28, 130–31, 134–35, 161, 221n.

Feminine: 3, 4, 6, 7, 10, 11, 14–15, 23–26, 43–44, 54, 79, 88–91, 95–97, 100–103, 105, 107–109, 114, 117–19, 122, 130, 133, 144, 150, 158, 163, 174, 178, 197n., 199n., 203n., 208n., 209n., 216n., 218n., 220n., 222n., 223n., 225n., 227n.

Femininity: 23, 24, 36, 37, 200n.

Feminism: 6, 7, 129, 137, 200n.

Feminist criticism and theory: 3, 4, 7, 14, 23, 37, 44, 46, 134–36, 152, 190; confessional mode of, 136

Fetish: 4, 96, 119

Footnotes: 44–45, 55, 79, 80–82, 84, 157, 212n., 223n., 225n.

Fort/da: 94–95, 172–74, 200n., 217n., 227n.; *see also* Freud, Sigmund

Freud, Sigmund: 9, 16, 19, 20–21, 25, 26, 27, 33, 44, 46, 105, 125, 127, 128–29, 131, 132, 136, 154, 166, 169, 170, 207n., 208n.; *Beyond the Pleasure Principle,* 94; *see also fort/da*

Gaze: 24, 26, 59, 81, 189, 190, 206n., 207n., 210n., 212n., 225n.

Gender: 6, 8, 14, 15, 17–20, 24–26, 82–83, 85, 88–91, 96–98, 100–102, 106, 108–109, 112, 114–16, 118, 122, 124–25, 127–29, 137, 141, 143–44, 150, 154–55, 163, 196, 200n., 204n., 216n., 228n.; *see also* subjectivity

Genre: biological, 19, 20, 44–46, 84–85, 90–91, 98, 118, 200n., 215n., 216n.; law of, 4, 5, 6, 8,

Index

14, 15, 17, 24, 29, 88, 90, 91, 97, 99, 107, 109, 112, 113, 115, 117–19, 122, 215n., 221n.; literary, 18, 54, 61, 84, 85, 88, 90–91, 100–101, 108, 116, 120, 124, 138, 142, 178, 179, 180, 200n.
Geometric figure: 63, 81, 83, 140
Grammar: 5, 16, 17, 27, 31–32, 49, 51–52, 54, 61–62, 64, 84, 95, 102–103, 108–109, 139–41, 163, 190, 199n., 207n., 213n., 214n., 218n.
Grammatology: 5–9, 18, 21, 42, 167, 208n., 226n.
Guilleragues, Gabriel de Lavergne: *Portuguese letters,* 89, 90, 96, 215n., 217n., 220n.
Guinea coin: 138, 145, 147, 149, 155–56, 159, 161–62, 225n.

Helen: 164, 166, 168, 170, 171–72, 173–78, 188, 191, 193, 225n., 226n., 228n., 229n.; *Helen in Egypt,* 45, 163–78, 183, 186, 188–89
Heloise: 89, 93, 96, 97, 116, 215n.
Herr, Cheryl: 44
Hesitancy: 69, 76
Hieroglyph: 21, 168, 175–77, 191, 227n.
Homosexual phratry: 35 (defined), 41
Hymen: 78, 79, 89, 95, 117–19, 122, 185

Image: 5, 9, 12–13, 24, 27, 30, 33, 38, 41, 61–62, 65, 96, 113–14, 155–56, 162–63, 168, 173, 177, 190, 193, 199n., 206n., 208n., 210n., 218n., 224n., 227
Imaginary: 5, 9, 10, 13, 18, 25, 26, 30, 36, 40, 167–68, 192, 194–95, 197n., 200n., 201n., 203n., 206n., 209n., 221n., 226n.

Imago: 14, 22, 25, 26, 33
Incest: 56, 59, 61, 75, 79, 127, 128, 182, 209n., 212n.
Infantile fixation: 125, 129, 131, 132, 154, 160, 221n.
Invagination: 15, 99
Irigaray, Luce: 105, 106, 206n.

Jardine, Alice: 6, 222n.
Joad, C. F. M.: 152–54, 156
Johnson, Barbara: 7, 49, 51, 100, 107, 219n.
Jouissance: 16, 19, 22, 30–31, 33–34, 37, 39–40, 79, 175–76, 190, 195, 201n., 204n., 205n., 227n.; maternal, 41; phallic, 41; of the woman, 16, 22, 205n.
Jouis-sens: 18, 19, 22, 205n.
Joyce, James: 44, 45, 49, 179, 185; *Finnegans Wake,* 45, 49–85, 179, 197n., 208n., 210n., 211n., 212n., 213n., 227n.; *Portrait of the Artist,* 179–80, 181; *Ulysses,* 163–89, 190

Kamuf, Peggy: 96, 134
Kauffman, Linda S.: 89, 91, 93, 97, 215n., 216n., 217n.
Kingsley, Mary: 143, 144
Kloepfer, Deborah Kelly: 173, 175
Knots: 19, 21, 170–71, 174, 178–79, 205n., 226n.
Kristeva, Julia: 11, 17, 22, 23–46, 119, 167–69, 171, 190, 191, 197n.

Lacan, Jacques: 6–11, 14–17, 26, 27, 33, 44, 46, 99, 107, 166, 176, 184, 185, 194, 195, 197n.
Lack: 18, 115, 121, 129, 201n., 206n.
Lalangue: 17, 18, 21, 22, 42, 207n., 210n., 221n.
Leaks: 156, 158

Index

Letters: alphabetic, 17–21, 25, 30, 35, 40, 45, 62–63, 67, 69, 72, 74–75, 77, 84, 117, 166, 191–92, 203n., 207n., 210n., 213n., 214n., 226n.; genre, 45, 54–58, 69, 73–80, 84, 88–89, 92–95, 98–100, 107–10, 112–14, 116–17, 119–20, 142–43, 145–47, 149–53, 156, 162, 191, 212n., 216n., 217n., 218n., 219n.; see also *senses*

Libido: 204n.

Lisp: 57, 71, 72, 75, 81

Logos: *see* word

Loss: 14, 21, 33–34, 37, 39, 41, 53, 56, 58, 66, 72, 93, 95, 97, 116, 165, 167, 170, 172–73, 175, 178–79, 181, 184–85, 187

Lyric: 64, 178, 179–80, 189, 214n.; *see also* genre

Marcus, Jane: 137, 222n., 223n.

Memory: 20, 24, 28, 59, 62, 72, 93, 111, 138–39, 161, 165, 167–69, 175–76, 182–84, 186, 188, 212n., 227n.; blank memory: 53, 66, 212n.

Metaphor: 42, 127, 128, 130, 135, 139, 165, 168, 171, 175, 221n., 226n.; maternal, 36–38, 40; paternal, 208n.

Metaphysics: 7

Metonymy: 27, 73, 127–28, 130–31, 134–35, 175, 183, 185, 191, 221n., 228n.

Miller, Jacques-Alain: 16, 204n.

Miller, Nancy K.: 90, 96, 216n., 217n., 218n., 219n.

Mirror image: 56, 60, 65, 74, 75, 80, 213n.; opposites, 214n.

Mirror stage: 9, 12 (defined), 13, 14, 24, 26, 28, 30, 33, 34, 38, 59, 94, 202n., 203n., 207n.

Mitchell, Juliet: 8

Modernism: 198n., 226n.; *see also* post-Modernism

Moi, Toril: 23, 38

(M)Other: 11 (defined), 17, 25, 30, 38, 43, 61, 168–70, 172, 174–77, 181–83, 189, 192, 194, 213n.; *see also* other

Mystic writing pad: 19, 20, 205n.

Name of the father: 38, 56, 68, 71, 175, 188, 190–93, 206n.

Narcissism: 61, 74, 96, 107, 110, 136, 221n.; primary, 40, 41, 209n.

Negativity: 17 (defined), 32, 35, 208n.; *see also* death drive

Nonsense: 6, 19, 66, 205n.; *see also* un-signifying

Odors: 156–60, 167, 182–83, 185, 190

Other: 10, 11 (defined), 12, 13, 15, 16, 17, 22, 25, 28–31, 38–41, 43, 59, 61–62, 65, 74, 101, 104, 107, 112, 117, 134, 139, 165–66, 168–69, 171–72, 177, 179, 192–95, 206n., 207n., 209n., 213n., 217n., 219n.; other (lower case), 10, 11 (defined), 12, 17, 30, 65, 107–10, 137–38, 171, 181–82, 192, 228n., 229n.

Oversight: 8

Palimpsest: 165, 186

Patriarchy: *see* Fathers, Law of

Perry, Ruth: 91, 110

Phallic: mother, 24, 37–38, 40, 201n., 206n.; order, 39, 199n., 204n.; signifier, 7, 9, 10, 14, 15, 24, 30, 39, 43

Phallus: 4, 15, 41, 194, 195; law of, 4, 6, 8, 15, 16, 19, 24, 37–38, 43, 99, 102–103, 221n., 223n.

Index

Plato: 102, 103, 111, 121, 218n., 227n.

Pleasure principle: 88, 89, 95, 102, 112, 205n.

Poe, Edgar Allan: *The Purloined Letter,* 98, 99, 226n.

Poetic language: 5, 24, 31, 35, 39, 192, 208n., 209n.

Poetics of absence: 92, 94, 100, 101, 108, 112, 114, 115, 117, 120, 122, 140, 184, 188, 223n.

Postal: principle, 94–95; relay, 89, 199; system, 55, 75–76, 78, 88, 98, 102, 112, 121, 122

Postcards: 56, 88, 102–108, 112–13, 115–18; *see also,* Derrida, Jacques, *The Post Card*

Prince, Morton: 61

Psyche: 8, 15, 20, 27, 29, 36, 126, 128, 130, 139; psyche-as-text, 9; *see also* textuality

Psychic law: 3, 135, 177, 190; failure of, 3, 190

Psychoanalysis: 5, 6, 7, 8, 9, 10, 11, 16, 17, 23, 25, 26, 27, 28, 31, 32, 33, 34, 55, 99, 106, 125, 167, 169, 176, 177, 179, 187, 190, 195, 203n., 220n., 226n., 227n.

Psychosis: 7, 24, 31, 32, 38, 39, 43, 179, 189, 191–94, 227n., 229n.

Punctuation: 52, 103, 108, 137, 139–40, 218n.

Ragland-Sullivan, Ellie: 10–11, 14, 33, 200n., 201n., 213n., 226n.

Real: 9, 11, 17, 18, 25, 26, 36, 40, 42, 129, 174, 177, 180, 184, 186, 191, 193–95, 197n., 200n., 201n., 202n., 209n., 210n.

Remainder: 16, 21, 22, 32, 115, 203n.; *see also* residue

Remémoration: 167, 168 (defined), 169, 172–75, 226n.

Repetition compulsion: 31

Representation: 3, 4, 5, 9, 10, 13, 20–24, 29, 32, 40–43, 57, 94, 106, 114, 119, 124, 134, 139, 168, 184, 189–90, 193, 198n., 216n., 218n.; veil of, 43, 190, 200n., 205n., 214n.; *see also* veil

Repression: 6, 13, 19, 20, 29–32, 34, 45, 51, 53–55, 59–62, 96, 98, 113, 121, 134, 139, 145, 165, 167, 170, 172, 174–77, 193, 200n., 207n., 226n., 227n.; primary, 13, 25, 40–41, 169, 203n., 204n., 209n., 222n.; secondary, 169, 207n., 209n.

Residue: 17, 18, 19, 27, 28, 31, 33, 40, 42, 43, 120, 208n., 209n.; *see also* remainder

Return of the repressed: 31, 209n.

Rhetoric: 5, 16, 27, 45, 49, 51, 53, 54, 61, 132, 133, 136, 139–41, 146–48, 152–54, 156, 161–63, 170, 181, 185, 187, 223n.

Rhythm: 32, 35, 165, 167, 171, 178, 190, 207n., 210n.

Riddle: 60, 78, 80, 81, 217n., 228n., 229n.

Rooney, Ellen: 95, 197n.

Rose, Jacqueline: 3, 8, 14, 15, 22, 24, 31, 37, 190, 191, 203n., 204n.

Rousseau, Jean-Jacques: *Julie, ou la Nouvelle Héloïse,* 96, 111, 114

Sackville-West, Vita: 140–41, 160, 223n., 224n.

Schizophrenia: 31, 34, 57, 61, 208n., 227n.

Schor, Naomi: 40, 209n.

Self: 116; self-difference, 89

Semiotic: 23, 24, 25, 28–33, 35–40, 42–43, 45, 139, 150, 168, 202n., 208n., 209n.

Senses: 12, 13, 43, 183, 185, 199n.,

213n.; chemical, 5, 6; imprinting, 6, 12, 13 (defined), 28, 168, 209n.; mechanical, 5, 6; objective, 5, 6; sensory ordering, 18
Sexual difference: 3, 4, 6, 8, 9, 10, 11, 13, 15, 19, 23, 25, 26, 36, 46, 54, 61, 77, 78, 82, 83, 97–99, 117, 122–25, 127, 133–34, 139, 141–44, 157, 159–60, 162, 171, 177–78, 183–84, 200n., 204n., 206n., 215n.
Sexuality: 3, 9, 10, 11, 15, 16, 18, 19, 22, 63, 64, 74, 79, 83, 95–98, 185, 200n., 203n., 204n., 205n., 208n.
Showalter, Elaine: 134
Sigla: 67–73, 80, 213n., 214n., 226n.
Signature: 58, 76–79, 89–90, 95–96, 108–109, 112, 114, 134, 138, 224n.
Silverman, Kaja: 206n., 209n.
Socrates: 88, 102–107, 109, 111, 121, 218n., 219n.
Sophocles: 123, 135; *Antigone*, 123–37, 159–60
Spanish Civil War: 22n., 227n.
Spatial ordering: 30, 32, 36, 41; textual spacing, 5, 63, 66, 68, 84, 117; *see also* textuality
Spivak, Gayatri Chakravorty: 95, 197n., 220n., 227n.
Stanton, Domna: 209n., 210n.
Stein, Gertrude: 163, 166, 199n.; "Melanctha," 163; "Yet Dish," 72
Stutter: 66, 68, 69
Style: 45, 186, 220n., 228n.
Subjectivity: 8, 10, 14, 15, 17, 19, 21, 23, 24, 28, 29, 38, 39, 41, 42, 51, 54, 56, 59, 62, 65, 94, 102, 112, 115, 116, 117, 142, 163, 165, 168, 174, 176, 178, 179, 180, 186, 189, 200n., 203n.,

204n., 207n., 208n., 210n., 218n., 225n., 227n.; gendered subject, 180, 195
Suffrage: 131, 145, 153, 154, 155
Suzuki, Mihoko: 193
Symbolic: 5, 9, 12, 13, 16–18, 23–40, 42, 43, 46, 59, 98, 99, 128, 129, 139, 146, 150, 170, 174, 175, 178, 181, 189–95, 197n., 200n., 201n., 206n., 209n., 210n., 213n., 216n., 221n., 227n.
Symptom: 137, 140, 165, 166, 167, 168, 171, 174, 176, 177, 191, 193, 197n., 200n., 226n. (defined)
Synesthesia: 13, 33, 43

Text-as-practice: 23, 24, 32 (defined); mastering text, 35, 40
Textuality: 5, 8, 21–23, 34–37, 43, 51, 95, 140, 143, 180, 181, 184, 186, 187, 190, 193, 208n., 209n., 218n.; textual field, 169; textual structures, 171, 198n.; *see also* spatial ordering, unconscious
Thetic: 28–29 (defined), 30, 32, 33, 36, 42, 43, 207n., 208n.
Totalitarianism: 131, 154, 155, 222n.
Trace: 20–21 (defined), 59, 69, 103, 120, 121, 182, 208n.; *see also* breaching
Transference: 11 (defined), 31, 177, 180
Translation: 45, 54, 60, 71, 74, 82, 84, 96, 116, 163, 164, 168, 171, 177, 179, 180–82, 212n., 213n., 226n., 228n., 229n.
Transliteration: 69, 77, 229n.

Unconscious: 6, 8, 9, 10, 11, 13, 14, 17, 18, 19, 21, 25, 26, 30, 31, 32, 38, 40, 51, 54, 56, 59, 60, 130, 134, 165, 166, 168–72, 174–77, 179, 191, 195, 198n., 200n.,

201n., 202n., 203n., 204n.,
205n., 208n., 209n., 213n., 222n.
Un-signifying: 17, 22; *see also*
nonsense

Vagina: 62, 70, 77, 81, 83–84, 118,
214n.
Veil: 7, 118, 119, 124, 130, 133–36,
139, 144, 146, 149, 167–69, 182,
185, 186, 188, 189, 193, 194,
212n., 228n.
Visual order: 3, 4, 5, 13, 26, 33, 35,
157, 183, 210n.; visual field, 59,
190

Walsh, Michael: 192, 193
Wells, H. G.: 152, 154, 155, 156

Woman: 16, 17, 21, 23, 100, 101,
102, 133, 136, 197n., 199n.,
203n., 204n., 216n., 218n.,
222n.; woman as spectacle, 3
Woman-in-the-feminine: 3, 4, 17,
23, 24, 38, 39, 40, 41, 43, 163,
184, 185–86, 194, 195, 201n.,
203n., 204n.; *see also* feminine
Wood, Michael: 165
Woolf, Virginia: 223n., 224n.,
225n.; *Room of One's Own,* 134,
137; *Three Guineas,* 45, 123–26
Word: 8, 39, 40, 43, 177
Writing: 127, 162; scene of, 21, 54,
55, 58, 60, 62, 74, 94, 95, 100,
103–107, 111, 121, 177, 200n.,
214n., 217n.